Love
Devotion
Hell

C.T. ANDERSEN

PAGE PUBLISHING, INC.
New York, NY

First originally published by Page Publishing, Inc. 2018

ISBN 978-1-64214-648-6 (Paperback)
ISBN 978-1-64214-649-3 (Digital)

Printed in the United States of America

This book is in memory of my late husband.
He was taken from our family on Monday, April 16, 2018.
I just wanted us to be friends.

Loved only you
Your Ex-Wife

This book is dedicated to all the people in my life who would always put me down and say I could not make it on my own.

I was told by many different people (that were close to me) to stay with my abuser because I was a woman and I had two children, and life without a man by my side would be too hard as a single woman.

They would also tell me to stay (or go back to him) because he was the breadwinner and I had nothing without him.

I have proven them all wrong. They, to this day, still don't talk to me because I choose to be single. They will not tell me how proud of me they are for being able to buy my own house and take care of my children on my own; they still insist that I find someone to take care of me.

I would like to thank all the ones who understand a woman can take care of herself without a man and be able to stand on her own two feet.

I would also like to thank all the musicians who, with their music, helped me come to see that I can hate my ex for the way he treated me and not feel guilty about it. I found peace once I understood that I could hate his actions and not the man I loved.

The list of music I listened to was as follows:

- Evanescence, "The Open Door"
- Blue October, "Hate Me"
- Ashlee Simpson, "Invisible"
- Nickelback, "How You Remind Me" and "Savin' Me"
- Kelly Clarkson, "Mr. Know It All" and "Because of You"
- Beyoncé, "Best Thing I Never Had" and "Say My Name"
- Carrie Underwood, "Before He Cheats"
- Jazmine Sullivan, "Bust Your Windows"
- Leif Garrett, "Promise Me" and "Sight Unseen"
- Jordan Sparks, "Tattoo"
- Natasha Bedingfield, "Unwritten"
- Britney Spears, "Womanizer"
- Eminem, "Love the Way You Lie"
- Shinedown, "Second Chance"

- Carole King, "It Too Late"
- JoJo, "Leave (Get Out)"
- 3 Doors Down, "Let Me Be Myself"
- Avril Lavigne, "Complicated"
- Keyshia Coli, "I Should Have Cheated"
- Cher, "You Haven't Seen the Last of Me"
- All my gospel albums

As well as so many others, these songs allowed me to heal. These songs helped me understand that it was not something I did; it was just something he could never accept about me. That I am *Love* (we all are).

To my daughters and my close, close friends, thank you for believing in me and pushing me to write down my story, also for standing by my side and helping us out the best that you could, especially when my girls and I were headed for the streets.

To you the readers, I hope you can find peace and *love* within yourselves. Only you can change how you react to someone and take charge of your life; you don't have to stay with anyone who abuses you mentally, physically, and/or emotionally. You can get out and find help. Don't allow them to take your peace.

It is okay to be single.

Contents

PROLOGUE
Love, Devotion, Hell

One Sunday afternoon in New Jersey, as my mother was walking out of the church with her best girlfriend, she spotted a 1958 Plymouth Fury driving out of the church's parking lot. She told her best girlfriend that she was going to marry the man who was driving that car. She was about seventeen or eighteen years old at that time, and my father was either twenty-four or twenty-five.

She found out who the owner was and invited him over to her parents' house one night when they (her parents) had gone out for the night, to have sex with my father. He could not refuse the offer. After she found out she was pregnant, she told my father that she believed it could be his or his best friend. After talking with his friend and his father, he decided he would do the right thing and marry my mother. My father's friend had told my father he was too young and not ready to become a father. So for a short time my mother enjoyed the 1958 Plymouth Fury, for when they decided to move to California in 1968, my father left the Plymouth with his father.

So the one thing that my mother loved the most about my father was left in New Jersey.

My father came to California to become a mechanic; his dream was to become a NASCAR mechanic. At this time, they only had the two children, and my mother was pregnant with her third child. My father knew that he was going to marry a woman who was diagnosed with paranoid schizophrenia.

CHAPTER ONE
The Womb

As David said in Psalm 71:6, "By thee have I been holding up from the womb: thou art he that took me out of my mother's bowels: my praise shall be constantly on thee."

The story of my birth is one that most people can relate to. My mother was breastfeeding my brother and told my father that she could not get pregnant while breastfeeding. Most people back in the sixties believed this to be true.

But as we have learned over the years, this is not true. Women can get pregnant while breastfeeding. So as a backup caution, they had a birth control that came in foam form.

When they found out that she was pregnant, my father was very upset with her. I was a mistake in their eyes.

But God had other plans for me.

I was born on Sunday morning, according to my father, during church hours, which would put it between the hours of 10:00 to 11:00 a.m.

All children love to hear the story of their birth; I am not one of those children. My mother has always explained it to me as the following: She told me that I was born with the umbilical cord wrapped around my neck and that the real me died at birth and the Devil's spawn replaced the real me. She also told that if they had not done what they did by using the foam to try to abort me, I would not be here today and I should thank them for it. She has always called me retarded and backward, and for this reason, I was too slow as a sperm to make it all the way to the egg without the assistance of the foam and that I should really be down on my knees kissing her feet for bringing me into this world.

I've always praised God for allowing me the wisdom of not believing her. I've always listened to this voice within me telling me that I am not what she says I am. I am different and kinder then her.

It is not that I hate my mother, for I don't. She gave birth to me, and for this, I am very grateful. I just know that I am not the Devil's spawn like she says I am.

When I was three-and-a-half years old, my mother and father divorced. I remember moving across the street into the second-floor apartment. My mom was twenty-four years old and had three children now. She was never home much and loved to hang out with the young people downstairs. She would leave us for most, if not all of the day. We would have to get our own food, or one of us would have to go downstairs to get her. That would be me.

I remember standing at the top of the staircase looking down. Next thing I remember, I was walking into the apartment on the right side of the hallway, looking for my mother. There were a bunch of people lying all over the floor, touching and kissing each other; there was smoke in the air. As I looked in and they started to notice me, they all started to reach out and try to touch me. This scared me, for I did not know these people and did not know why they were trying to touch me.

I asked my mother one day about a scar I have above my lip; she said it was because I had fallen down the staircase when I was younger. I remember one time when she was not home, my brother put my baby chair on top of a box crate and he had me climb up into my baby chair to get the peanut butter out of the cupboard so he could have a peanut-butter sandwich. As I was reaching for the peanut butter, the chair started to move, so I sat down in the chair and fell over backward. It took six stitches to stitch up my head, then six more after. I fell over backward again, this time in my baby chair on the floor. I placed my feet on the side of the table and bused the table, and I fell back into the window and split open my head again by hitting the window cell. My mother told me it was because I had gotten angry with her and I did not want to finish my milk.

My mother would leave us at the farmer's market in Los Angeles for hours at a time. She would tell us not to talk to anyone. But as the hours went by, the older people would start to ask us questions about where our mother or parents were. My brother always made me talk to them, and I would tell them she would be back soon. They would then try to give us food.

From what my father has told me, the pastor at our church would tell him if he did not get our mother to put us somewhere safe, he would have to get children's welfare involved and have us removed from her care.

We ended up in the Salvation Army nursery school, all three of us.

As a young girl, I did not like wearing shoes inside the school. I would put them on when I went outside to play but took them off when I came indoors and left them in my cubby.

One day, the teacher was walking by all the cubbies and she noticed my shoes inside. She held them out and asked everyone in the room whose shoes they were. When she found out they were mine, she came over to me after putting them back into the cubby and pulled me by my cheek over to where my shoes were in the cubby. She said I had to put them on, and I told her no, I did not have to, because I was inside the room and not outside playing.

Someone had gone to get the principal because she came in and asked me to come to her office because I would not put on my shoes. I told her that I would wear them when I go out to play but I did not think it was wise to have them on when I was indoors. So she allowed me to go around the classroom without shoes. This made my teacher very upset with me.

The assistant teacher liked me and would always try to get me to participate in class events. I was very shy and stayed away from the other children. I was always the one who had to watch over my brother and sister, so to be separated from them was not easy for me.

I knew how to tie a shoelace; I learned it from watching Mr. Rogers on TV. So when one of my classmates was having a hard time trying to tie the big shoe, I went over and show him how to tie the laces. The assistant teacher caught me doing this and came over and asked me to show her how to tie the shoelace. I told her I didn't know how to do it and walked away.

I remember when I was outside on the playground at the nursery school and some man came out to pick me up and take me home, but I did not know who this man was. The teachers kept telling me he was my father, but I had never seen this man before, so I ran away from him. I climbed up into the tree house that was on the playground. He came over to try and get me down. I moved away from the latter and went over to where the slide was. He then moved to the bottom of the slide to catch me as I came down, but I did not go down the slide. I then moved over to where the pole was, and he followed me over then went to where the rope was hanging, and he followed me once more. This was going on and on until some of the teachers tried to help him. I ended up going down the rope as if it were the pole. I burned my hands, and this person took me home and wrapped up my hands. I still, to this day, do not know who that man was. I have asked my father if it was him, but he has never said yes or no—just that my mother had gotten married to a man after him but before my stepfather Paul.

During nap time, I would lie on the floor, thinking to myself, *I am not the person my mother says I am. I am not retarded, and I am worthy of being here.*

I would pray to God even though at the time I did not know who he was. I just had faith that he was on my side and was taking care of me. I would ask him to keep me on the path he wanted me on and never to stray from it. I would always ask him, "Please don't make me like my mother."

This isn't because I disliked her or even hated her because I didn't. It is because I knew at a very young age that something was not right about her.

I would tell myself that I needed to be strong, and I would repeat in my head over and over to myself, *I know I am better than what she is telling everyone. Stay strong and never forget that I am worthy of being loved*, and then I'd repeat to myself, *I know, I know, I know I am better than what she says I am.*

During the summer, the three of us would play outside all day long. I don't remember if my mother was even home. My sister and I would play in the driveway of the apartment next door to us because it had a little patch of dirt under the trees. We would take our Barbie dolls and pillows and just sit and play with our dolls in the dirt.

One night, our mother called us in for the night and my sister did not pick up her Barbies or her pillow and bring them with her. Our mother asked her where her pillow was, and my sister told her that she had left them in the neighbor's yard. My mother then turned and looked at me and asked me why I did not pick up my sister's things. I told her that I had gotten my stuff and I told Loraine to get her stuff, but she did not listen to me she just ran away. So I just left her stuff lying there.

My mother took me outside at night and walked me over to the neighbors' apartments and told me to walk down the long, dark driveway and retrieve my sister's belongings. I asked if she was going to come with me because it was dark and there were no lights. She told me that I had to do it on my own because I had left my sister's things. I told her that was not fair. Loraine had to pick up her stuff because I had picked mine up, and she should be the one out here retrieving her belongings and not me. My mother told me *no*—it was up to me because I was the older sister and I had to make sure Loraine had all her things, and maybe next time, I would not just walk away, leaving her stuff behind.

So I walked down the long, dark driveway by myself, thinking, *This is not fair*, and thinking how someone could easily come up and just kidnap me and she would never know I was gone. I think I was too upset at my mother to be afraid of the dark, but the funny thing is, as I walked closer to where we had been playing during the day, I found that I could see very clearly in the dark. I learned not to be afraid of the dark, and this is still a very precious gift to me today (being able to see in the dark).

When the three of us would play together, our brother would have us put on shows. The one I remember doing all the time was "Singing in the Rain." We would sing, dance, and twirl our umbrellas in the sunshine. I believe we broke a few of them, so our mother stopped buying umbrellas for us.

CHAPTER TWO
Strength

> God is refuge and strength, a very present help in trouble.
>
> —Psalm 46:1

Our mother was now married, and we had a dad; we were all very happy at that time. We moved from the small apartment into a three-bedroom house in Arleta. Things could not have been better, so you would think.

My second stepfather came into our lives at a time we really needed a father. I remember the very first Father's Day we could now celebrate.

We made him cards, his favorite dinner, gave him bunches of hugs, and told him how much we loved him.

Our mother had us write divorce letters to our father, and we handed them to him when we went to court when our new father adopt us. I don't remember my real father saying anything to us about what was about to happen, as he was a stranger to us. We didn't visit him or he didn't visit us at all; however it was, that worked for the two of them.

My stepfather seemed to be a really nice guy to all of us in the beginning. He loved to bounce us on his knee as if we were riding a pony. As he was bouncing me on his knee, he would put his fingers up inside me with one hand and tickle me with the other to make it look like he was just tickling me in front of my mother, who was sitting in a chair across the room.

I told him to stop tickling, but he would not. He just kept bouncing, and I just kept telling him to stop or I would pee on him.

He did not listen to me, so I peed on him and he threw me across the room. My mother said to him, "She told you to stop or she would pee on you, and that is what she did."

She did not get angry at my stepfather for throwing me across the room; she just simply said, "Next time, you'll listen."

During the warm California summers, we would go over to his parents' house because they had a pool. We did not know how to swim, nor did we have any swim clothes to wear in the pool.

Our step grandfather said we should take off our clothes and just swing in our underpants. I remember him sitting in his chair smoking his cigarette and drinking his beer and just watching as we took off our clothes. This was our first visit to their home and I did not feel comfortable taking off my clothes outside and with a complete stranger watching me. I kept the donut hole (floating device) around my chest at all times whether I was in the pool or walking around and jumping back into the water.

He just kept his eyes on us the entire time. He had dark hair with a beard and mustache. The way he looked at us scared me. Something inside me told me to be very cautious of him for he looked very much like a demon to me. I did everything I could to stay away from him.

After we got done swimming and dressed, he would tell us to give him a kiss for a quarter so we could run over to the corner liquor store and we could get ourselves some candy. My brother would be the first one to give him a kiss on the cheek, and my step grandfather would give him the quarter. Then my sister was next to give him a kiss on the cheek, and she would then be rewarded with a quarter. I would be the last one to kiss him because I didn't feel we should have to kiss someone we didn't know for money.

I told him this was not right and that he should not have us kiss him for money, but he just looked at me with this evil half smile on his face. My brother and sister kept telling me that I needed to kiss him fast so they could go and get their candy. As I moved in to kiss him on the cheek like the other two did, he would move his face so that he could get me to kiss him on the lips, but I was too smart for that, and I would move my head to try and reach his cheek. He would then move his face again, and I backed up and looked at him and told him that the other two had just kissed you on the cheek and that I too would just give you a kiss on the cheek. As I moved in again, he moved his face, so I backed up and looked him in the eyes and told him "No." He laughed an evil laugh at me while my brother and sister were chanting in the background, "Just do it." So I tried grabbing his face and planting a kiss on his cheek, but he moved his head and I moved back, and I told him "No," so eventually, he stopped moving and allowed me to give him a kiss on the cheek. He moved his head slightly so I almost missed his cheek and I almost kissed him on the lips.

He looked at me and smiled then handed me the quarter, and the three of us headed to the corner liquor store to get our candy.

My brother and sister ran and I just walked, thinking to myself that I would not do this again. This was so degrading to anyone, having to kiss someone you don't know for money!

I told my mother, and she said that we were now part of this new family and that kissing my grandfather was no big deal. I told her that he was trying to get me to kiss him on the lips and not just his cheek. She asked my brother and sister, and they told her "No," that I was just being stubborn and that he was just trying to be nice. I believe they were only after the money for their candy. I was thinking about me and how it was making me feel, nothing more. They just tried to make it something it wasn't. I knew the truth.

I always trusted my feelings when it came to people I did not know, and even with my own mother for she was not the kind of mother that most children have! She didn't feed us. She wasn't around; she would leave us in places that were not safe then come back later and pick us up. She always made me watch over my brother and sister and told me that I needed to keep them safe.

Our stepfather traveled a lot when he lived with us, so every time he was home, the two of them would have sex like rabbits. All night long, she would moan and groan and tell him how wonderful he was.

When he was away, she would disappear for days at a time. We had grown accustomed to her not being home or around us all the time, so we did not notice that she would be missing for days at a time. We just went on with our day doing what kids do—play and have fun.

My brother and I attended the elementary school that was on the same block we lived on, just right up the street from our house. My sister was too young to go to school, so she stayed home; she hated being home by herself.

She begged me to stay home with her, so at lunchtime, I would leave the school and come home to be with her.

My mother was at work and would have to come home to drag me back to school; we had to stop in the office to explain why I was leaving school. My mother told the school office that I was retarded and I was making up stories just to leave the school. This would happen on a daily basis.

Sometimes I wouldn't even go to school and my sister and I would be at home alone, but when we heard our mother drive into the driveway, I would hide in a closet. I told my sister not to say anything to her so that I could stay at home with her. But my sister always ratted me out and I ended up back at school and she ended up staying home alone.

I would ask Lorraine why she ratted me out, and she told me that she didn't say anything to our mother—that our mother just knew where I was hiding every time.

When I attended the elementary school on our block, I remember I was very shy. I didn't talk to any of the other children and/or to the teachers; I kept to myself.

One of my teachers kept me after class one day and handed me a present. I opened it and found a hairbrush in the box. I looked at her and she told me it was to brush my hair and that she would show me how to do it. I looked at her, put the hairbrush down, flipped over my head and then started to run my fingers through my hair, and then I threw my head back up and said to her, "Look, my hair is brushed, see?"

She told me to take the hairbrush home and to use it. What she didn't know was that I was being tortured at night by my stepfather when he was home, and I moved around a lot. I also had a cat that loved to knead my hair. I would end up in the morning with big knots in my hair, and no matter how much I brushed it to get them out, I did not manage to get them all out; otherwise, my teacher would not have bought me the brush.

My mother would sometimes brush my hair, and at night, she would just pull at my hair, pulling most of my hair out, and I would tell her she was hurting me, and she just kept pulling and told me I had better learn how to brush my own hair. So I just sat there on the floor holding my head in my hands so she could pull on my hair while she brushed it.

It took her some time to get pregnant, but she eventually did. Our new baby brother was born two days before Christmas. It was 1973 now, and I was six years old.

After the birth of my baby brother (David), the entire family got together at my step grandparents' house.

My mother's parents came out from St. Louis. They were pulling a trailer. This was the first time I was meeting my grandparents and asking them why they had this trailer with them. They told me that they would be staying with us for a couple of weeks. So I went inside the trailer and looked around. It was like a mini house with sink a bedroom, bathroom, and a TV room. I thought it was cool.

My stepfather's family had come over to meet all of us, and this is when we got to meet his baby brother and sister. My stepfather's brother was different. He seemed to have trouble understanding things, and when we played board games with him like Hungry Hungry Hippo, he would get very upset and throw the board and put his hands on the table and started yelling at us, not with words that you could understand, just screaming at us. We did not know what was going on, and his mother, Martha, our step grandmother, came running into the room, telling Joseph to calm down and reaching out to hold him.

We cleaned up the board and put it away. She took Joseph out of the room to calm him down, telling him everything was all right. She then came back to us and set the three of us down to explain what had just happened.

She said, "Joseph did not like to lose at any game, and he did not understand nor had the mind-set to understand that sometimes you lose."

So she told us that anytime we played with him, we would have to let him win.

Any time we played with Joseph, we allowed him to win every game. I believe Joseph was in his mid twenties.

Later, Laura, our step aunt, explained to my mother that her father had beaten Joseph so severely that it caused him to have brain damage. This is why Joseph is the way he is today and she stays away from her father.

We, later that day, drove Joseph back home to where he stayed. He lived in an institution where the retarded and Down syndrome people lived. This is when I discovered I was not retarded like my mother had always said to everyone about me. For when I walked into this big ballroom they had on the campus where he stayed, I was greeted by about fifteen people who had Down syndrome, and they were walking very fast toward me and trying to hug and squeeze me. I was trying very hard to get away from them because they were scaring me. I did not understand why they needed to touch me.

When I looked at their faces, I noticed that their face structure was all similar to each other, and I did not look that way. So I did not understand why my mother was always saying I was retarded for I didn't even look like they did.

I didn't even have the temper that they had when they didn't get what they wanted.

I thought when she called me retarded, it was something like being stubborn or doing and saying what I wanted to do with no regards to anyone else. I did not know that it meant some sort of brain damage. So when we left Joseph at the home in Camarillo, I was thinking to myself on the long drive home that this woman that said she had given birth to me may not really be my mom. For I was nothing like she said I was.

I asked her one day if she had adopted me because I do not believe she gave birth to me; I was nothing like her, nor did I act like her. I didn't think like her and didn't want to be anything like her.

But she looked at me, and she reminded me of my birth story and how I, the real Catherine, had died at birth and the devil's spawn had gone into my body.

We did have some fun times with our stepfather. Our mother decided to go on a family trip, driving from California to St. Louis to visit our grandparents. We had a station wagon so the three of us could put the back of the seat down and use the back of the car as a big bed. We drove through what is known as the four corners that would be where Arizona, Utah, Colorado, and New Mexico all meet. My mom would stand on one of the corners. I would stand in another. My brother and my sister would stand on the last two remaining states; that way, each of us was standing in a different state.

We then continued on to St. Louis. We were very excited, for this was our first family outing together, and we had never visited our grandparents before.

My mother and father do not have any brothers and sisters, so we do not have any cousins, aunts, or even uncles, just the two of them.

So when my mother married Paul and he had a family, she had us do a lot of family activities together. When it was just the four of us, we did not go out, go on family outings, or even visit with family members. So this was a very exciting and new thing for all of us to experience.

We spent most of our time driving and a short amount of time, only about a day or two with our grandparents. While in St. Louis, we went to the Gateway Arch next to the Mississippi River, we rode in the elevator to the top so we could overlook St. Louis. On the way home, we had gotten a big round ball that was filled with air and had a string on it so you could hit it and it would come right back at you.

We were playing with them in the back of the station wagon. I was holding onto my rubber ball. My sister had just gotten done, bouncing hers back and forth off her hand when she grabbed it and it blew up in her face. She did not get hurt. It was just a loud noise, as if the tire on the car had just popped. My mother screamed, and Paul asked her what was wrong. My mother always reacted to the smallest of noises with a very loud scream.

My sister was crying because now she no longer had her toy. I quickly gave her mine because I was afraid it too was going to blow up in my face. She was very happy to have it and played with it (it did not blow up in her face).

Some would think by looking at us we would be the perfect little family. This was something my mother had always wanted—to have seven children and a loving husband.

My grandmother decided to take the three of us on a camping trip with the trailer. We headed off to the campsite with her while my mother and her husband stayed home; they were going to join us later that week. While at the campsite after getting the trailer all hooked up with electricity and the sewer line, we went outside to explore the campground.

My sister was not wearing shoes, and she accidentally stepped on a bee, and it stung her between her toes. Our grandmother sat her down on the steps, got some water and earth and made a mud pact for the area where the bee had stung my sister. I asked my grandmother why she was putting a mud pack on the bee sting, and she said to me that the mud would help draw out the poison from the bee.

My grandmother had a cat, and we had it with us on this trip. As my grandmother was cooking, the cat decided it would go over and try to eat the bacon she was cooking. The cat stuck its face down near to where the bacon was cooking, and he accidentally burned off his whiskers. All you could smell was the burnt hair, and the cat looked very funny walking around with only whiskers on one side of its face.

The campground had a swimming pool that the three of us along with my grandmother went to the pool for a late-afternoon swim.

There were a lot of dragonflies around the pool, so I watched the dragonflies swooping in above the water and then flying away. I'd never seen a dragonfly before, and it was very pretty. In the bathrooms, they had daddy longlegs, and this was the first time I had ever seen a spider with very long legs. So this was a very fun and educating time for the three of us, and we got to spend some time with our grandmother, whom we did not really know too well.

About a day or two later, my mother, stepfather, and her friends we called Uncle Danny and Uncle Fred showed up. We, all except for my grandmother and sister, decided to go for a walk along the river creek. We brought the cat with us, and my brother was holding him.

As we were walking along the river creek, we heard two gunshots, and the bullets landed close to us. We stopped looked around and heard someone yelling from up above on the hillside that this was private property and we needed to turn around right now and leave. So that is what we did.

My mother, stepfather, and her friends decided to go to the sulfur bath. The sulfur bath smelled like rotten eggs. So we kids were not allowed to play in it because it contained a lot of minerals that would not be beneficial to us young kids.

We did have a lot of fun those two weeks camping out with our grandmother.

On another outing with the trailer, we stopped at my grandmother's cousin's house. We knew her as Aunt Marge. Aunt Marge and I were in the kitchen making breakfast. She had asked me what I wanted to drink with breakfast, and I told her Kool-Aid because that was my favorite drink as a child. She said that she did not have any in the house so I would have to pick something else. I told her we had some in the trailer and I would go and get it.

So I ran out to the trailer to get the Kool-Aid. I did not stop to put on shoes, so I was barefoot running through the damp morning grass. Once I got to the trailer, I reached out with my right hand to grab the door handle to open the door. As I did, I felt electricity running through my body and I could not remove my hand from the door. So I put my left hand on top of my right hand and pulled off my right hand, and now my left hand was stuck to the trailer door. All I remember was the dog (that lived with Aunt Marge) was barking its head off.

I don't remember the electricity hurting at all. All I remember is that I could not figure out how to take both hands off the door at the same time.

Someone must've heard the commotion because my mother came running out barefoot as well and grabbed my shoulder, and now she two had electricity running through her body, only she was yelling and screaming at the top of her lungs.

I heard Aunt Marge yell, "Just unplug the trailer!" Someone must've gone around back to unplug the trailer from the electrical hookup.

Then my mother started screaming we needed to get her to the doctors now. Aunt Marge said, "No, we need to see what kind of damage she has done to herself." So they took me inside the house and laid me on the floor in front of the TV. I lay there for a while watching TV as everybody else was setting up for breakfast.

My mother asked about her husband and where he was. So she told my sister to run out to the trailer to see if he was inside, and my sister said, "I'm not going, so someone volunteered to go out there. They found him asleep inside the trailer."

As everyone was gathering around the table that they had set up out back on the porch that was screened in, my mother started yelling at me to get up and get out there to eat. I remember lying on the floor trying to move. My head kept saying, "Arms, move," but my arms did not want to move. So I thought, *Okay, I will take this in baby steps*. I tried to pick up my head and move it from the left side to my right side of my face. I eventually got my head to move to the opposite side and said, "Okay, I can do this." Meanwhile, my mother was still yelling at me about every three minutes to get up and move or she would come in and get me.

Someone told her to leave me alone, that we would need to see if I was paralyzed but not to rush me. But she didn't listen; she just kept on yelling at me. So as I was lying on the floor looking toward the couch, I thought if I could just get over there, I could use the couch to help get me up.

So again I started thinking about moving arm and it did not move, so then I thought, *Okay, let's see if I can move my shoulder*, so I started to move my left shoulder around in a circle and eventually worked it down to my elbow and finally from my elbow to my hand so now I could move the left arm. I was like, *Okay, I can do this*, so I started on the right side moving the shoulder down to the elbow and eventually to my hand, and now I had two arms and I could pull the upper half of my body toward the couch. As I inched my way over to the couch, I realized the bottom half of me was not going to be as easy. I got to the couch and I put my left hand on the arm of the couch and propped myself up with my right arm still on the floor, and then pulled with the left arm and got my body halfway onto the couch. Then I slowly started to move my legs under me. Eventually, I did make it all the way up to a standing position, and now I had to go the bathroom. I was thinking, *How I am going to make it to the bathroom before I pee in my pants? I have not taught myself to walk yet.* So I grabbed the right leg with the right arm, pulled it forward, and then grabbed my left leg with my left arm and pulled it forward. Now I was slowly walking and trying to make it to the bathroom before I peed all over myself.

I was standing in the bathroom, trying very hard to get my fingers now to work because I forgot to move them as I was pulling myself up from the floor, so now, trying to unbutton my shorts with fingers that did not work was not going to be easy. So, yes, I ended up peeing on myself, but I thought, At least no one could see me because I was in the bathroom by myself and I could easily clean this up. When I was done, I made my way out to the patio where everyone was eating, I sat down to eat, and my mother said to me, "So I guess you didn't do much damage to yourself after all." I just sat there, not eating. Things worked out okay for me after I started to move everything.

We finished off that trip with stopping by my great-grandparents' farm (my grandfather's parents). My mother had told me all about her grandmother's apple sauce and how it was the best you would ever taste. I loved apple sauce, so I was really looking forward to meeting her and having some of her homemade apple sauce. As we sat down for lunch (now I was very hungry because I did not eat breakfast), I helped myself to a lot of apple sauce. One big mouthful into my mouth, then I spit it out back onto the plate. It went faster than I put it into my mouth. My mother looked at me with horror and anger both at the same time. She asked me what I was doing. I told her that the apple sauce tasted funny; she told me to eat it, and I told her no. I was sent down into the basement for disobeying my mother. Then my brother and sister followed, not much longer after me. I was thinking to myself, *Next time eat something you do not like*, only because I was extremely hungry now.

My grandmother told her daughter to taste the apple sauce. They found out that it was a bad patch and that maybe my great-grandmother had not sealed the jar properly when she canned it.

My mother had to come and get all three of us. Yes, she did let us finish eating and they got a new jar of apple sauce and it was the best I had ever had (I make it myself now).

When school had started up again, we found ourselves going to the private school that was about five miles away from our house; it was kindergarten through sixth grade.

On the first day, my mother took us into the office to enroll us in this new school. As she was leaving, she looked at me and said, "Try getting out of here."

This was a private school, so it had a gate around the parking lot; the parking lot was also used as the playground at recess time.

I remember looking at her and thinking to myself, there was no need to leave the school now that my sister was here. I also thought, *This woman does not understand me at all*, and that she was crazy. She had always told me that I had to look after my brother and sister, and now with all three of us together at the same school, there was no need for me to have to watch over her.

At Calvary Lutheran School/Church, I really enjoyed going to school because this is where my relationship with God blossomed and became something much more than just a voice within me.

So we started off the new school year at a new school, and my brother had to repeat the second grade and I had to repeat first grade. For me, it was because I kept ditching school to stay home and watch over my sister, and also for the mere fact that we were now in a private school and the public school did not teach us at the level we needed to be at.

On Wednesdays, we attended church, and they had each grade sing on Sunday each week. So every six weeks, I got to sing in church. I loved singing—that was my favorite part of going to church. The lessons were good too.

The pastors would come into the classroom and teach us a Bible lesson each week. Sometimes they would ask me questions, and they did not like my answers because I believed like Moses, you could talk directly to God and he would answer you. I would tell them that yes, Jesus did die for us on the cross, but God is our heavenly Father and we should go to him directly with our questions. They pretty much told me that we needed to pray to Jesus and asked for forgiveness for all our sins. I told them I understood that, but why not go directly to God and ask him for he answers all your prayers and questions and will help guide you through life?

The one pastor walked over to me and patted me on the head and said, "Okay." So to say I was a handful would be an understatement when it came to the pastors at my new school.

I did not understand why they did not understand, for God is always there for us and you can talk to him directly at any time. Because when I first heard about Moses and how God spoke to him directly, my little head lit up like a light bulb, thinking, *That is the person in my head.* So Moses became my first hero, and I learned everything about him so that I could understand more about this voice within me and guiding me.

I loved how Moses would argue and tell God no. It allowed me to be completely open and trustworthy of God because that is how I knew him. I can turn to him and ask him anything and he would always be there for me. So I would just sit there quietly and listen to the lesson and think in my head, *They just don't fully understand what God can do for us.*

At night, as I slept, I would have nightmares, I was walking in a very dark, cold maze where all you could hear was the crying of people and feel pain and sorrow everywhere. I would just stand there and just listen to the people crying in pain and tell them, "Everything is going to be okay." All they had to do was follow the light and they would be set free. But these people did not want to go into the light because they could not forgive themselves for the pain they had caused others in their lifetime. I told them that it was okay for them to go into the light because God forgives all of us. Some of them left. I did not see it with my eyes, but I could feel the energy in the darkness change. Some of them wanted to leave but could not because something much darker was holding them there.

I knew I didn't belong there because I was a bright light, and the brighter I shined, the more the darkness tried to put me out. So I could only see a very small number of what looked to be like rocks everywhere, but I was able to walk around them without running into them. Even though I couldn't see them all of the time, I could feel the entities around me moving away as I got closer to where they were hiding with in the darkness. I felt love when I was in that place. Even though it was cold, dark and lonely, I knew I was never alone in the darkness. I could feel the darkness trying to consume me. I can understand why some people allow that kind of darkness to consume them, you feel lost and alone in that place, and it swallows you up fast if you give up to this kind of darkness, and the moaning becomes too strong and you can lose your way easily. As a young child, I would visit there almost nightly, and I would tell the people it was all right; they could step out into the light, not knowing that I was that light for them and not understanding why they were coming at me. I knew God was the true light and not me. I would tell the people to trust and believe in God for he was the only way.

Our father came back into our lives, and he was now dating a very nice, pretty woman named Brenda. I really liked Brenda a lot because she was really nice to us. She talked to us, and she asked us questions; she did seem to care about us. Brenda was young and wanted children of her own.

My mother met Brenda for the first time when she and my father came down to our house to pick the three of us up. My mother told Brenda that she would never have children with our father because he had gotten an operation after which he could never have children again.

We got to spend about two weeks with my father and Brenda (now they are married) during the summer one year. Something must've upset Brenda because now she just left us outside in the sun all day to play with each other. She used to take us to the pool, but she stopped doing that.

We baked under the California summer sun with no sunblock on us; we were getting second- and third-degree sunburns. The neighbor would see us sitting outside, so she decided to take us into her house just to get us out of the sun.

When our mother came up to get us after the two weeks, I asked her if I could stay with my father and his new wife because I really liked her and thought she was pretty.

My mother was a little upset over this, and she had noticed all three of us had sunburns. She started yelling at Brenda about how she had neglected us by leaving us out in the sun and allowing us to get burned in the sun.

That was the last time we visited with our dad, and shortly after that, Brenda divorced him. That was really hard on me because I had asked my mother to go and live with her because I liked her better. I would never tell my mother how I felt about anything ever again. She didn't believe half the things I said to her as it was; she always told me I was jealous of her husband and that I was trying to take him away from her.

I was in the car with my stepfather and one of my mother's friends, and they were talking about her. She was driving the vehicle in front of us, and it was sagging on the left-hand side because of her weight. They were saying that it was because of her weight that the car sagged on that side and watch when she gets out, it will pop back up.

I was thinking to myself as they were laughing and joking about her, *Is this what true love is— when you talk about the one you love behind their back and make fun of them?* I was very angry and upset with Paul. So when we got to the house, I got out of the car, ran into tell my mother what he was saying about her, and I told her that he really didn't love her.

She, for some reason, had always thought of me as her biggest rival when all I was, was her child and I would never ever want to sleep with or take away her man. She promised her friend (Fred) that when I was older, he could marry me because he thought I was pretty. I did not like him because I was only seven years old at that time. I did not want to be married to him, but that was an ongoing joke for my entire childhood. Even my brother and sister joke about it to this day. If you were to ask my mother, she would tell you that that was just a joke and she meant nothing by it. But that man stayed in our lives and made me gifts that he had handmade for just me.

For Halloween, Uncle Fred made us full head masks and we were the three little pigs. The school had a parade with all the classes coming out and parading around the yard. The teachers would pick which one of us had the cutesiest Halloween costume.

My sister, who was the smallest of us, took first place for being the cutest pig even though we were the three little pigs. She took a ribbon and shoved it in my face, saying, "See, I'm the cute one. You may be the pretty one, but I have a ribbon saying that I am the cute one." No big deal to me because I was tired of being labeled the pretty one and having men trying to touch me.

We were out shopping for groceries one day with my step grandfather, who loves to smoke, and in those days, you could smoke inside the grocery store—or at least he did.

He thought it was cute to sink the cigarette into my arm. I did not find that to be cute, so I ran over to my mother and told her that he had just put his cigarette out in my arm. He looked at her and told her that he would never intentionally try to hurt me and that I had run into him and that is how I got burnt. She told me to pay attention to what I was doing and to not run into him.

So I kept as far away from him as I could, running around the fruit stand as he chased me to burn me again with another cigarette. If he went right, I would go left, then he would move to the left and I would move back to the right. I did not want to get burned again.

He would pretend that he was not paying attention to me as my mother called for me to catch up with her, so I would move slowly on the opposite side of the fruit stand, watching him the entire time to see what he would do if I caught up to my mother, and at the last minute, as I was almost to her, he would come around from behind me and burn me again—sometimes in the same arm, sometimes the opposite arm, whichever one he could reach as I was running away.

I remember lying in my bed, looking at my burns and scratching at them and thinking as I was making a bigger hole in my arm that I needed to make myself numb to the pain and not allow anyone to get close to me to hurt me like this again. No matter how much they tried to hurt me, no one would be able to hurt me more than I could hurt me.

My stepfather would come in at night and would touch me, so I would pee on him to get him to stop. My sister would always make fun of me because I would pee in my bed. But she did not know that he was touching me at night when I was sleeping.

One night, while I was in the second grade, he tried to get on top of me to force himself on me, and the voice in my head said, *Kick and don't stop kicking*, so I started kicking as hard as I could, and eventually he got off me.

In the morning, my legs were so sore that I could barely move. My mother still made me go to school, and she took me into the office and told them that I had been attacked by a ghost and I had been kicking at it all night long. I told my mother that morning that her husband was trying to sleep with me; she did not believe me and told me it was a ghost attacking me.

I was shocked when she told the office this because she knew the truth—it was not a ghost—and I had told her that I could feel his body and if it had been a ghost I would go right through it.

My teacher had to assign another student to me to help me walk. I couldn't even stand up to go to the bathroom because my legs were hurting just sitting at my desk. I ended up peeing on myself in class. The other students started laughing at me, so the teacher sent them outside to play and got me some dry clothes and asked me why I did not raise my hand and ask to go to the bathroom. I told her I wouldn't have made it to the restroom.

So when the class came back in, she told them that it was not right to make fun of somebody who is handicapped and cannot fend for themselves. The class just looked at me, and she told them that my legs were hurting me and that is why I did not get up and go to the restroom—because my legs would not have carried me that far. So it became a Bible lesson that day on how to be kind to people who are handicapped, even if it was for just one day.

I did not like all that attention and would not play with any of them on the playground. I stayed away from all the kids. The teachers made me play with the other students. I was really good at handball. The kids already disliked me, so for me to be good at something just made them dislike me more. When we played dodge ball I would always be the one left inside the circle. The only reason I was good at dodge ball was because I didn't want the ball to hit me, it hurt too much. I learned that if you catch the ball than the person who threw it at you would have to take your place in the circle. So I tried to catch as many as those balls as I could. I did not like being in the circle.

In the sandbox, they had monkey bars, and I would hang upside down from them. I loved looking at everybody upside down; it was kind of cool. The teachers did not like for us to just hang upside down, so they were always telling me to get down.

Our mother allowed us to spend the night over at our step grandparents' house. The one time we did this, my step grandfather came into the bedroom, where my sister and I were getting ready for the night my mother had given me one of her old sleeping gowns. I like the way it flowed when I turned in it; it made me feel like a little princess. When my step grandfather came in, he told me that I looked very grown-up and very pretty in this nightgown. He started walking toward me, and I slowly backed out of the room. He came at me again, and I moved down the hallway, keeping my eyes on him and not on where I was going. At the end of the hallway was a wall mirror, and I turned to run, not knowing that I was at the end of the hallway (this was our first time sleeping over and I did not know the layout of the house), so as I turned, I smashed the right side of my body into the mirror, and as it came crumbling down around me, he was saying that I would have seven years of bad luck. I kept my head in my hands with my eyes closed, listening to the voice within me saying, *You are going to have seven years of good luck.* Every time he would tell me "seven years of bad luck," I was repeating in my head, *Seven years of good luck, seven years of good luck.* Then I heard his wife come out and tell him to leave me alone and go back to bed. She came over to me, asked me if I was all right, looked at me closely, pulled whatever parts of the mirror that may have been on me off, and told me to go back to bed, that she would clean up this mess and not to worry about it. We never spent the night over there again.

One night, when my stepfather tried to molest me again, I peed on him, and he would then leave me alone. I got up to take a bath to clean myself up. I started doing this every time he would try to molest me. I would pee in my bed, take a bath, change my sheets, and place the towel on the wet part of the bed.

One time, as I was getting out of the bathtub he walked in and I was just covering myself up with a towel and he asked me what the mark was on my leg. I have a birthmark that is high on my inner thigh, and he wanted to get a closer look at it. That would mean I would have to spread open my legs so he could see it. I sat down on the toilet, wrapped myself in the towel, tightly looked him in the eyes, and told him no. He put his hands on my knees, and I yelled out for my mother while keeping my eyes on him, yelling to her, "Tell your husband to leave me alone."

She yelled from the bedroom, "Paul, leave her alone." He sat there, looking at me for about a minute or two before he got up and walked out.

I believe it was that next day he decided to leave our mother. He had tried leaving her many times before, but she would run into the bathroom screaming and yelling saying how she was going to kill herself and she would start swallowing pills and cutting her arm. This time, he just looked at me and walked out the front door. My sister, who was behind him and telling him not to go, looked at me and yelled at me that this was all my fault that he was leaving, I remember telling myself, *Finally he is gone*, and patting myself on the back and smiling on the inside. I was extremely happy that he left.

Now with my stepfather no longer living with us, I had to wake everyone up for school. My mother would wake me up at 5:00 a.m. and tell me what the chores were for that day. I do not remember answering her in my sleep, but I must have because she would get angry at me when I did not do whatever it was she had asked me to do. So she started to ask me to repeat what she had just said to me because that was the only way to wake me up. If I could repeat everything she had told me, then I was fully awake.

Not only could I talk in my sleep but I was also a sleepwalker.

We would turn on the TV and watch cartoons as we were getting ready for school. We did not know how to tell time, but I did know after a certain cartoon was over, we would have to start heading out to school. When they changed the lineup of the cartoons, we would be late for school.

We now rode our bicycles to school. My mother told me to stay with my brother and sister and to make sure they made it to school and home safely and to never leave them behind. So when my sister's bike had a flat tire, I told my brother to walk home with us. He just took off on his bike and left my sister and I to push the bikes home together alone.

When my brother's bike was broken, he would walk with us. I remember him and I walking to school one morning. My sister must have been homesick because it was just him and I. When some boys started teasing him about walking with his girlfriend, he and I did not look alike, so I guess these young boys thought I was his girlfriend, but when it was the three of us walking together, no one teased him because my sister looked a lot like him and my sister and I looked a lot alike.

Then after school, when it was time to walk home, he told me to walk by myself and not even think about walking with him. I told him that Mom had told me never to leave him or Lorraine behind and that I needed to stay with him. He told me no and ran off and left me standing there. So I walked home alone. This didn't bother me because I could see him in front of me walking and I knew he was safe.

My mother no longer cooked for us, so we had a lot of frozen food, and when we did cook, she made me do all the cooking. She would tell me how to do it and then walk away. I would have to use a chair by the stove in order to stir the spaghetti and/or whatever we were cooking on the stove top.

On the weekends, I remember the four of us being home alone. My sister and I would be in our room playing with our Barbies, and my brothers would be in their room playing with their cars. When I got tired of playing with the Barbies, I would turn on the TV, and *The Mickey Mouse Club*, would be coming on, and I would hear my little brother running down the hallway toward the living room to watch the opening of *The Mickey Mouse club*, and then he would leave, only to return when he heard the ending song come on.

My mother taught me how to change his diaper. With boys, it's a lot different from changing diapers of a girl. Because once you remove the diaper, boys have a tendency to pee when the cold air hits them. So I learned to throw the diaper back on top of him when I saw that he was about to pee.

During the divorce battle, one morning, my stepfather and step grandfather came over to pick up my little brother for the weekend. My mother made my sister and I wait with him outside on the porch with his diaper bag, waiting for them to come and pick him up. David was just wearing a diaper and nothing more because it was a warm sunny day. All his clothes were inside the diaper bag. As they pulled up in front of our house, my little brother was very excited and started to run toward the car. They had stopped on the opposite side of the street, so I picked up my little brother, my sister picked up his diaper bag, and we headed across the street to hand him over to his father. My step grandfather had gotten out of the car and was standing on the sidewalk behind the car videotaping us as we were walking over to the car to hand off our brother to his father. He (Paul) was sitting in the backseat of the car with the window rolled down. My brother was in my arms, squirming around, trying to get out of my arms so he could get to his father. He was very happy and wanted to go with his father. I was holding onto him tight and trying to get him to hold still because I was watching my step grandfather videotaping us and I didn't want my little brother to look so eager at wanting to spend time with them. So as I slid my brother through the open back window of the vehicle, my step grandfather stepped off the curb to get a better shot of what we were doing after my sister handed Paul the diaper bag. I grabbed my sister's hand and turned my back to my step grandfather, and we headed back toward the house. We never once turned around to see them leave; we just went right into the house.

The next day, when they did not return with my brother, my mother started to get nervous. She kept calling my step grandfather's house to see what was going on; we heard nothing from them. My mother called her mother (in Saint Louis) and asked her what to do. So then my grandmother had to come out from St. Louis to help my mother (her daughter). My mother (that same night) eventually called the police (after talking to her mother on the phone) to make a report of a missing child last seen with his father. I don't think much came from it at the time because they were still married, so they told her to give it some more time. Eventually, we got a phone call, and he was found at the Children's Hospital in Los Angeles about two days after the exchange. I remember all of us piling into the car and headed off to Children's Hospital to see what had happened. When we get to the hospital, we all walked up to the nurses' station and asked them about David my brother. I remember them looking at us funny. I didn't understand why at the time they were pulling our mother off to the side to talk to her. A police officer showed up and started to explain things to her.

After some time, they allowed us to go into the room where he was. I got to go in with my mother and grandmother to see him. I stood there by the incubator and looked at this baby and didn't recognize him. He was purplish in color and swollen everywhere. His eyes were black and blue, and he had to have breathing tubes in his mouth and his nose just so he could breathe. I did not understand what was going on and what had happened to him, or even if that was him because again, it didn't look like him.

We went back out to the nurses' station, and my mother asked the nurse again what had happened to him, and this time, I heard the nurse tell her that the father of the child had reported that the mother had molested the victim and beaten him. I remember looking at my mom and my grandmother, thinking, *We did not do this to him*, and I didn't understand why they were blaming us; we were the ones who had reported him missing.

We spent a lot of days and money in the Van Nuys courthouse fighting the charges that Paul her husband was claiming against us. My mother had never believed me when I told her that my step grandfather was putting cigarettes out in me, but now when she found out that Larry, my step grandfather, had put cigarettes out in her son's private area and how he tried to force himself on me, this was her opportunity to believe me because now it came in handy for her. She wanted to take this as an opportunity to win custody of her son.

Now I would have to take the stand and tell the story of how I handed off my brother in perfect condition to his father while being videotaped by my step grandfather.

Only when I told them my step grandfather had it all on video, I then I became a hostile witness, and everything I had said was to be deleted from the records, and then they dismissed me from the witness stand. They did their very best to try and blame my grandmother, who wasn't even there the time, because they could not get the charges to stick to my mother, for it was not her who had handed off David to his father—it was me—and I was only eight years old.

So my mother got partial custody of her son. We would see him one year during the summer and the next year during Christmas break.

I remember going home that night after court and praying to God that he needed to send my guardian angel to watch over my baby brother because he needed my guardian angel more than I did; I knew I would be all right on my own.

My brother and his dad moved to Colorado, and now my mother would have to pay for a one-way ticket if she wanted to see her son.

We had heard that my brother and his dad had gotten into a car accident. As the story goes, my stepfather was driving along a winding mountain road when he said he saw a deer and swerved to miss it, and over the side of the mountain they went. My stepfather had fallen out of the car at the top of the mountain and watched the car rolled down over one hundred yards with his son in the backseat in his baby chair. According to the witnesses who helped him get back to up to the road, they claimed, there was no deer and that he had just headed straight off the side of the road.

According to the police report, my brother's baby seat had come loose from the seatbelt and had gotten stuck on the floor behind the passenger's sheet with him still in it, and the passenger's seat moved back over the top of him, and so as the car rolled down the hill, he was stuck underneath the passenger's seat inside his baby chair, and that is how he survived the crash. The responders to the crash said it was a small miracle that he survived and that he must have some very powerful angels watching over him.

When I was told this story, all I could think about is how glad I was that God had answered my prayers, and I remember telling God, "Please keep the angels with David because he still needs them more than I do."

After the divorce, things got a little crazy with the three of us in our mother's house. We spent a lot of the time by ourselves and playing in the street with the neighbors. We knew that when the streetlights came on, it was time to go in.

One of our friends, who lived up the street from us, had a pool, and when her mother had a man in her life, the pool would be full of fresh, clean water so we could swim during the hot summer days. We would pretend we were the Kool-Aid man and then fall backward into the pool.

I remember swimming in the deep end, going all the way down to the bottom and touching the floor then turning to head back up toward the shallow end and thinking in my head that I was not going to make it. I then heard this voice tell me that I could breathe under-water and so I took in a small breath, just enough so I could make it back up to the surface of the water. I was shocked and told my friend and my sister what I just did. They did not believe me and told me to do it again. It had scared me so I just played it off as a joke, but I did know that I had taken a breath underwater; I just knew enough not to try it again.

While we were playing in the pool, my friend Nicole's mom's boyfriend came out to swim with us. He came up with this game where we sat on his lap and then he would lift us up to the top of the water, and he would tell us to make our arms and legs straight, and then he would push us out toward the deep end of the pool like a rocket. When I was sitting on his lap on the steps of the pool, waiting for my sister to swim out of the way, he would touch me in my private area. I only allowed him to do it twice because the first time, I wasn't sure that he was really touching me; I was in shock. Then it happened again, and I then stopped playing the game with him. I grabbed my sister and got out of the pool to go home.

I talked to my friend about it, and we all told her mother, and her mother was very upset and told us to go home, and that was the last time we went swimming at their house.

I found out later that Nicole had gotten molested by the boyfriend and now he was no longer dating Nicole's mother.

When she saw my sister and me, Nicole's mother apologized to us for not believing us.

We would play out in the streets and in the wash around our house. We used to go into abandoned buildings just for the fun of it. I remember it was very dark in the one building we went into. We had our friend David with the three of us. David and my brother and sister were all saying how they couldn't see anything and how they kept running into chairs and the walls and then started to say that there were ghosts in the room just so that they could scare each other. I looked around, telling them, "No, that's a chair near you and you're about to run into it," because remember, I had the gift of being able to see in the dark. So then they would put me out in front, and they would follow me so that they wouldn't run into anything; it was fun.

Gemco was about two blocks away from our house, and my mom would always send me to the store to pick her up a box of pads. My brother and his friend would follow me to the store just to see what I was getting because my mom had made it a big secret and told me not to tell anyone what I was buying. So every time before I left the store, I would pick up a piece of mint candy. They were only a penny at that time for one. I thought there was no harm and rewarding myself with a piece of candy. My brother would tell my mom that I was spending her money on candy; I would tell her it only cost her one penny and I showed her the receipt. Charles took a Hot Wheels car from the store without paying for it, and my mom found out about it and told him to take it back and apologize to the store manager, so he did. Gemco was a lot like Costco today, where you needed a card to get in; we kids would just walk in with a family and then spend our days walk around the store.

School started up again, and now I was in the third grade. My teacher was Mrs. Peachy. My mother put my sister and I in the Girl Scouts. My sister and I would go camping with the Girl Scouts. We learned how to ride a horse with the Girl Scouts, how to survive in the wild and be kind to people. We went camping with them. I loved being in the Girl Scouts. My brother and I started learning how play the accordion. She also volunteered the three of us to sing when they had concerts after church on Sundays. I loved singing up on the stage with my brother and sister; the only thing was, my sister couldn't carry a tune, so I had to sing louder than her so that she would sound good. My mother would always tell me that I was never good enough to sing by myself, that I always needed to have my brother and sister by my side and never thought about singing without them. I know she wanted us to be like Donnie and Marie, or the Brady Bunch. My favorite song to sing in church was "This Little Light of Mine" and "Go Tell It on the Mountain." We listened to the eight-track tapes of John Denver, Barbra Streisand, Neil Diamond, and then mostly soundtracks from the movies like *007* and the *Jesus Christ Superstar* soundtracks. We weren't allowed to listen to the radio.

One day, Nicole's brother was walking down the street and was upset about something his girlfriend had done. My sister, brother, and David were outside on the porch when he was walking by them and my sister started teasing him about his girlfriend; that was when he came up onto the porch and hit her. I heard the commotion because I was inside the house. As I headed out to the porch, my sister came running in because Nicole's brother had hit her in the mouth and knocked out her front tooth. Nicole's mother had to take my sister into her dentist's office, where she had to pretend that Lorraine was her daughter (Nicole) so she could have her front tooth fixed.

I don't know why my brother didn't stop him, but he didn't. My brother and sister didn't always get along, and he would fight with her and I would have to break them up.

At night now, I would dream about a big white mansion. It was whiter than any white I had ever seen before. This whiteness had shown so brilliant that it almost had color in it. I would walk around this mansion and hear voices as if they were coming to this house to see me. I remember saying, "No, I don't want anyone here but me." I could hear the voices stopped where they were, and then they just disappeared, so I walked around looking at all the rooms and thinking to myself, *This must be mine. This is where I'm coming when I die.* I told God that I didn't mind having people here in my house; I just didn't want to see them ever. I told God when I was younger that he could send people my way who were lost and couldn't find their way in life, thinking maybe I could help them. When I was walking around my mansion one day, I decided to put a little piece of me into a jar, and I sealed it up and placed it on a high a shelf on the very top where no one could find me. This way, no matter what happened to me on earth, I would always have a piece of me that was safe and tucked away where no one could find me and hurt me.

In this place, what you feel around you is love, a love that is not known down here on earth, and you have this constant feeling of being loved and hugged all at the same time. You know you are in a place that is safe and where people would never hurt you. You would never even think something like that when you are there. Yes, I did ask to keep the people away only because I wanted to be alone. I did want people around; I just had too much hurt from the people on earth. I wanted to know what it would be like to just feel love and respect and have no one around me except me because by this time in my life, I was tired of being hurt all the time. Anytime I needed a hug and to feel love, I would go there at night. I still do to this day.

We did visit our dad again. This time, he was dating a woman named Carol; she had two sons. She was really nice, and she gave my sister and me Sonny and Cher dolls. We again played outside, roaming the completes where he lived. We saw this young boy sitting in the window of the house he lived in. Bobby, my dad's girlfriend's son, asked him to come out and play, but he always told us no, he couldn't. It was a short visit with our dad and his girlfriend and her one son.

We took a trip to Bakersfield to visit with Uncle Fred (the man my mother had been saving me for). As we were driving up the steep mountain through Gorman, our car broke down and we stopped at the gas station to get it fixed. The young man told my mother that he could fix it and then told her how much it would be. He kept looking at me. I was standing by the back end of the car on the driver's side, and he was under the hood of the car but on the passenger's side of the car. So when he stood up to talk to her, he would look at me.

She told this young man that she did not have the money to get her car fixed, but he could use me as payment. I remember looking at him. He smiled as almost to say yes, but I said what I thought was in my head only but really it was out loud, that I was only thirteen years old. He then stepped back away from the car and said, "No, I cannot do that, Mama." We then had to leave the car at the station and try to catch a ride into Bakersfield. My brother was very upset with me because I did not sleep with this stranger so we could get our car fixed; I told him if he wanted the car fixed that badly, he should have had sex with him. A truck driver took us into Bakersfield and dropped us off at a Foster Freeze. Our mother called Uncle Fred to come and pick us up. He took us to his house dropped us (the kids) off, and then helped my mother with getting her car fixed.

Uncle Fred had decided to throw a party that night; he invited his friends and their children over. One of the young men tried to get me to have sex with him. I kept fighting him off. I would go into the kitchen where the adults were hoping someone would help me, but when Fred tried to help me, my mother pulled him back and said, "She will be just fine." This young man did not take "No" for an answer. He pushed me up against the refrigerator, and that is when my Uncle Fred came over to help.

He asked me if I was okay. I told the young man to leave me alone again. I then went to the restroom to try and get away from him, but as I came out, he was standing in the hallway waiting for me. He pinned me against the wall and started to kiss me, then he tried to unzip my pants. I kept trying to get him off me. The harder I pushed him, the more he would try to get into my pants. The bedroom door next to us opened, and he pushed me in the room. Thank goodness my sister was in the room because if she had not been there, he would have raped me. I told him to leave me alone because that was my sister on the bed and I needed to see if she was all right. I picked up my sister and walked her out to my mother and told her that Larraine was not feeling well and we needed to go home now. My mother, for the first time, listened to me, and she grabbed my brother and we left instantly. That young boy even came running out of my uncle's house looking for me. Thank goodness we were all in the car and driving away.

The new school year went as any normal school year goes, although I did get an award at school for the most attendance for the past three years. I have not missed any school days except for the one when they were giving me the award. I happened to be out sick that day, and my sister got it for me and brought it home. I got a certificate to a Christian bookstore where I could go and pick out a gift for myself. My mother and grandmother took me, and I found this beautiful cross necklace that had the Lord's Prayer in the middle of it, and when you looked through the little magnifying glass in the middle of the cross, you could see and read the Lord's Prayer. I loved it so much that I wore it every day. I only took it off to take showers and go to bed.

Nicole had come over to our house, and she asked me if she could see it, so I showed it to her. She thought it was cool, and then one day, it ended up missing. I went over to Nicole's house to ask her if she had it; she never answered the door. As I walked down the driveway back up toward the street to leave, she opened her front door real quick and dropped my necklace on her porch. I turned around and went back to get it. I picked it up and looked at it and noticed that she had taken the Lord's Prayer out of the middle of it by breaking the little magnifying glass on the front. I dropped it and told her she could keep it now. As I walked home, I told myself, *Never, ever fall in love with materialistic things again.*

I did get in trouble once at school. One of my friends had borrowed some things from me and the other girls in class. Now when you borrow something from someone, you are to give it back to them at the end of the day. But not Lisa—she wanted to keep everything she had borrowed. One day, when we were out for recess, I followed her into the girls' bathroom and asked her for the items she had borrowed from all of us. She told me she was not going to give them back. So when we walked back out to the play yard, I looked up to where the principal's office was. The principal was sitting in the window watching us all.

I looked him in the eyes then back at Lisa, asking her again to return the items she took. She said no, and as she said no, I kicked her.

The principal called us both up to his office; Lisa got to him first and started to mouth off to him. I came in and sat down at his desk. I know what I did was wrong, but what she had done was much worse. I explained my side of the story after Lisa got done cursing at him about what I did and how she should not be trouble. He told me that what I did was wrong and that I would have to run on the school track team (it was made up of boys only). I said no, I was not going to do that. He looked at me and said to me that I had legs like a horse; I was going to run track for them. I thought, *How cool, I have legs like a horse, so now I am running on the track team for the school.* Lisa had her mouth washed out with soap, and she was made to retune all the items she had borrowed from everyone and apologize for keeping them as long as she did. The boys did not like having a girl on their team, and when I ran at the meets, the other teams did not like having to run against a girl. One of the boys' dads on the other team even told his son to trip me because I was running past him.

Another hero of mine from the Bible was Job and how he had lost everything that was dear to him. What I did learn from Job was that no matter what people around you said you can argue and fight with God and tell him how you feel about things that are going wrong in your life, you never ask him, "Why me?" Just accept it for what it is and always know God has your back. "He never gives you anything you can't handle" was a phrase thrown around a lot when I was younger. So I never felt sorry for myself.

That summer, the three of us would walk over to Mrs. Peachy's house and she would tutor us. She did not have kids of her own, but she was married, so she took us in and treated us as if we were her children during the summer and she would feed us when we were with her. She moved closer to where we lived, so it was a shorter walk now to her house. She taught me how to bake and decorate cakes. We helped her with grading papers. We only listened to records at her house—the really old stuff like jazz, the ones that didn't have words to them, but it did make me appreciate all types of music.

I remember watching an episode of *Chips* on TV, and they were talking about latchkey kids. I thought to myself, *That's us*. We came home from school, we did our homework, and we cooked dinner without a parent at home. So I asked my mother, "Are we latchkey kids?"

She said no because she was home at night. I told her that the TV program said that if you have a key and you're going home and no parent is at the house when you walk in, you are a latchkey kid. I think she just walked away from me without answering. So I never brought it up to her.

We had a plum tree, a grapefruit tree, a lemon tree, and a strawberry bush in the backyard; we did have a lot of fruit to eat and we made a lot of lemonade because we never seemed to have food in the house. Our mom would take us out to eat when she got paid instead of buying groceries. We did not have a lot of food in the house when our mother did go grocery shopping; the food would go quickly with the three of us eating. She would always tell us we were eating her out of house, but isn't that what kids do?

Our mother got into witchcraft and started to burn candles for money and men. She made my sister and I help her with this. She would write on a piece of paper what it was that she wanted, and then she would place it under the appropriate candle. She told us a story about how we came from royalty in England. The woman, who was a chambermaid, had gotten pregnant by the king, and once she had the baby boy, they were both shipped here to the States because this boy was the first son if this king, but he was not of pure blood. They landed in Salem. Our mother also told us that we came from a long line of witches and one warlock. She told us that this woman had cursed (or was cursed) with a spell that would not allow any of her bloodline to be happy with the person they truly loved.

When our mother said whatever the spell was, we were to stand there and just listen and think about the words she was saying. Not me—what I did was think in my head, *God, please protect my sister and me with your white light. Please do not allow any of what our mother is doing to rub off on us.* I would keep my eyes closed and I could see a white barrier around my sister and me. She eventually bought an Ouija board, and she taught us how to play with it. Anytime we would sit down to use it, I would again ask God to protect us.

One afternoon, the police officers blocked off our street because they had been catching a robber and he had just hopped over the fences into backyard of the neighbor who lived across the street, so my sister and I ran to our brother's room because it had a big window in it and it faced the neighbor's house across the street so we could see everything. Anytime the police officers would look our way, my sister and I would duck. We were afraid they would see us and then knock on our door and ask us questions. Our mom was not home to answer the door, and without her being home, we thought we would get in trouble. They must've caught him because they eventually left.

One evening, when my mom was home, we were sitting in the living room watching TV and waiting for the chicken pot pies to get done in the oven. When they were done, I went into the kitchen with my mom, and we took them out of the oven and put them on top of the stove, and she told the other two to come in and get their dinner. We went back out into the living room to watch TV and eat. My sister got up and got her dinner, but my brother had not gotten up to get his pot pie, so my mother told me to go get his pot pie and give it to him. I told her no—he was a big boy and he could get his own dinner himself. So as he walked into the kitchen, a car came crashing through the dining room area. So of course, my mother flipped out because her son had almost gotten killed (the car was nowhere near him) and this was my fault for not going into the kitchen to getting him his dinner. I don't know how it was my fault this old man who was driving his car came crashing through our dining room area. After all, I wasn't the one driving the car.

We were home one evening with our mom when she discovered that one of the cats had gotten out. She asked all three of us which one of us had let the cat out. Of course, none of us did, so she spanked us all and then told us to go and take a bath together. The three of us were in the bathtub. Our mother scolded me for not watching the other two and then hit me with a belt. I was the one who got in trouble the most because I should've been watching them. How that worked I didn't know, so we all got spanked. We ended up in the bathtub when our brother decided to confess to my sister and I that he had let the cat out, so now we're trying to drowned him in the bathtub for lying and getting us both in trouble and allowing our mom to spank us for no reason when we heard a commotion in the living room. We stopped trying to shove his head underwater and sat there looking at each other. The next thing we knew was that a police officer had come into the bathroom and told the three of us to get out and to get dressed. As we walked by the living room area, we saw our mom pinned behind the front door, yelling at us to tell the officers that she was with Uncle Joseph. The officer that had gotten us out of the bathtub told us to go into our rooms and to put on some clothes. The officer followed my sister and me into our room and stood there watching us while we were putting on our clothes. We kept our backs to him of course. Then by the time we were done dressing, our mom was no longer in the house and we found ourselves in the backseat of a police car and heading toward the Van Nuys police station.

They put us in a room that had a lot of drugs, money, and guns in it (the evidence room). We sat at the table not knowing what was going on when finally the two officers came in and asked us if we knew why we were there. We told him no, we had no idea why we were there. They said something about our mom walking down the street with a bunch of different guys on her arm and how they had been watching her. We told them that wasn't true—our mom would not do that—but we really had no idea what they were talking about.

We ended up in foster care. Our brother went to one, and my sister and I went to another. The one my sister and I went to had this nice couple that allowed us to stay with them. She had a VW bus. I remember it because I thought it was cool because it looked like a little minibus and it had a lot of seats in it, and I wanted one when I grew up. She took us to see her mother in an old-timer's house, and she would wash her hair in the sink. That was strange, but she was nice, and her husband was very quiet, didn't talk to us much. I remember the first night there, going to bed and praying to God and asking him to watch over our mother and help her get out of the trouble she was in so that we could get back home and watch over my cat because I really missed her. I also asked God to watch over my brother because he wasn't with us and I knew my sister would be fine because she was with me. We may have been with this woman for only about three days and the two nights when our mother came to get us.

This was the start of us being put into foster care and then eventually coming home to our mother after she fixed what she needed to fix. The other foster care I remember was going to the lady who had a daughter about my age, and she looked similar to me so her friends would tease her and tell her that I was prettier than her and that maybe next time she should take in foster boys and not foster girls. I remember they were working on a dance at the school we were now attending and they partnered me up with someone's boyfriend, so of course, the girl threatened me because she was afraid her boyfriend would leave her. So I pretended to be sick and went back to my foster care mother and finished up the day at home with her. I would help her with the two babies that she had. I would go outside and play on the monkey bars she had in the yard and I would just sing to myself and to God and just did what I wanted to do. This went on for about a week—me going to the school pretending to be sick and then going back to my foster care mother. My foster care sister, Connie, didn't like me much because again I looked like her, so she would take my sister with her to her friend's house and leave me alone. I guess she thought I would be jealous because she was spending more time with my sister than with me. I didn't mind; I liked being alone, and I knew when this was done and we went back home, I would have my sister and she wouldn't. So what did I care that she would go off and play with my sister? I found things for me to do on my own.

The day our mother was coming to get us, I told my sister not to run off and play with Connie, but she didn't listen to me. So when our mother came to get us, of course, my sister Lorraine was not at the house. My mother asked me where she was and why I wasn't watching over her, and I told her she wanted to run off and play. I had told her not to, but she did, so we had to wait for her to come back to the foster home. When we got home to her mother's house, my sister was covered head to toe with poison oak. I looked at her and told her she should've listened to me. My mother had to go and pick up some Caladryl lotion from the store to help soothe the itching, and yes, she even had it between her toes.

Going in and out of foster care went on for some years. Our grandmother had come to stay with us and her daughter to help out because we kept getting taken away from our mother. She stayed in her trailer that was now parked in our driveway. I had hoped that would be the end of it, but it wasn't.

Our mother started to date an old friend of hers and my father. His name was Fred; he was a probations officer. One day while visiting him at his house in Silverlake, my brother, sister, and I, along with three neighborhood kids were out playing on the hillside. Someone yelled, "Last one to the bottom is a rotten egg." I took the dirt hill slow because I am afraid of heights, but the moment I got down on the sidewalk, I took off as fast as I could down toward the street. I did not see the stick that was lying on the sidewalk, and I tripped over it and slid down the sidewalk on my left knee and right hand. I put a big hole in my knee, and blood ran down my leg. My brother and sister just kept on running, leaving me alone to go face our mother on my own.

When she saw it, she just looked at me and told me to clean it up. I had to wear her short skirts to school because my knee was a mess, and I could not put pants over my knee because the pants would stick to my skin and pull off any scab that had formed.

I was afraid of men, and I had a male teacher (this was the first year I had a male teacher). When he would come near me, I would get up and move away from him. Now I had to wear a short skirt; I was not happy. He had stopped my mother and asked her if everything was all right at home. He told her that he had noticed that I would always get up and move away from him every time he got close to me and that he was concerned. My mother told him that I had a crush on him. I almost died, and I think he knew that was not true because of the look of fear on my face and I must have turned white as a ghost.

The next time we got pulled away to foster care, my sister and I ended up in juvenile hall because they could not find a home for us, and once again, my brother ended up in foster home without us.

I was thirteen-and-a-half years old. My sister was twelve, and my brother was fifteen now.

As we entered juvenile hall, we were met by a jailer. The guard took us to the showers and told us to get undressed. I looked at her and said, "You have us mistaken for someone else. We are only here because there were no foster homes to place us in. We are not criminals, we have not broken the law, and we do not have to take off our clothes and shower—we are already clean."

She looked at me and told me either I take off my clothes or she would do it for me. I smiled at her and said, "No, I got this." As I was taking my clothes off, with her watching us, I was thinking to myself about the *Charlie's Angels* episode where they ended up in jail and had to do what my sister and I were about to do. That's all that kept running through my head as I stood there under the shower head, showering in front of the strange woman.

They sprayed us down with something; I guess they thought we had bugs, whatever. They gave us old clothes to wear; we could not put ours back on. Then we headed over to the nurse. She gave us a TB shoot. I looked at her and told her that we had already had our TB shots and we were current with all our shots, so there was no need for this and that my sister and I would not be here long enough for her to read it. I told her we would be gone in three days; I did not really know if this was true or not. She stuck me in the arm anyway.

They then took us to the bungalow where we would be sleeping. When we walked in, both sides of the building had doors. There were about six doors on each side, then we walk through double doors to the eating area with the kitchen on the right side. As we kept walking forward, the showers were off to the right with the bathroom. Then you had another set of double doors. We walked through the double doors and more sets of doors on the right side and left side. They opened the one door, and they had three single beds inside this room. They woke up one of the girls and asked her to go to another room for the night. This was going to be my bed for the night. My sister was still with me and holding onto me as tight as she could. They told her she would have to sleep in another room on the opposite side of the building because it is where the younger girls were sleeping. I sat down on the bed with my sister, and we just held on to each other. I told the lady that this was a mistake and we did not belong here because we had done nothing wrong. She kept trying to pull my sister off me; there was no way we were going to separate that night. One of the other guards went out to get the head guard. When the head guard came into the room where my sister and I were sitting on the bed, she told the other two girls in the room to leave. I explained to her that this was a mistake and we had not done anything wrong to be here. They (the police) didn't have a foster home for my sister and I to go to and we would not be here for very long time. She told the other guards that my sister and I could stay together for this one night only, that my sister would have to go and sleep with the other girls her age for the duration of time we were going to be in their care. So my sister and I curled up on the single bed for the night.

In the morning, the three girls who lived in that room came in to get their belongings and headed over to the showers. The one girl told me and my sister and I we would have to shower every morning with them.

My sister and I did not move. The guard came in with two shoe-boxes, one for my sister and one for me. She told us to guard these with our lives because the other girls here would take them from us. Everybody had the same supplies in the shoebox—they were just different colors or a different flavor of Chapstick.

I looked at this stuff in the box and thought to myself, No big deal, because these are things you have in your ordinary life such as a toothbrush, a hairbrush, lotion, Chapstick, paper, pencils, and a little stuffed animal. The stuffed animals were all different, so I could see how if somebody liked it, they would just take it or maybe try and hurt you and then take it from you. Now I was very afraid and did not like the situation we were now in. The guard told us (my sister and I) that we didn't have to shower this morning but tomorrow we would be joining the girls in the shower. She then turned around and walked out of the room.

Then another guard came in and took my sister down to the opposite side of the building, where she would be staying with the younger girls. The girl who had to leave her bed first came in and asked me after her shower how old I was. I looked at her closely now and discovered she was pregnant. She told me that all the girls at this end of the building were going to be mothers, and she said I would be next. She walked out of the room and started talking to one of the other girls in the hallway. I heard her tell this girl to stop doing cartwheels because she would lose the baby. I sat there on the bed looking into this box and thinking to myself, *This is all they have in this place?* It made me feel sad for them.

We met in the dining room area for breakfast, and my sister did not sit with me. She sat with the younger girls who were talking to her and asking her a bunch of questions. My sister asked for a fork to eat with because all they had were plastic spoons. My sister asked the lady why they did not have plastic forks and only the plastic spoons. The lady told her it was because someone could hurt somebody with the plastic fork, so my sister broke off the head of the spoon and held it out toward the lady and said, "I can hurt you with this."

We did attend class in juvenile, and during the afternoon hours, they allowed the kids to play and intermingle with each other. Juvenile hall has both young girls and boys, so they would run off behind the building, and this was why so many of the young girls were pregnant. My sister told one of the guards that she saw some kids making out and the guards did nothing.

At night, we would all gather in a big hall to watch a movie. The one girl (the one that I had taken the bed from) seemed to be the leader, and she introduced me to a boy and that he would be my boy-friend. I remember looking at her and telling her no. She was not too happy about that. She told me that she had promised him that the next girl who came in would be his girlfriend. I told her that we were not going to be staying here for much longer and to find someone else. Then I moved away from her and him. As I looked around the room, all you saw were the young kids paired off into groups of two. I thought to myself, *This is not the place for us to be*. The next day, we got up and showered with the girls; this was my very first time having to take a group shower. I tried as hard as I could to keep my back to everyone, but they were all just running around playing, throwing their soap at each other, and acting really goofy. I remember using the hand towel to cover up as much of my body as I could and just standing under the one shower head, not looking at anyone, keeping my eyes on the drain in the floor.

This was our second day in juvenile hall, and the girls were asking us questions on how we got there, and so I told them that we didn't have a foster home to go to so they put us here. That same girl I took the bed from looked at me and told me that she too had a younger sister in this building and that they had beaten up a police officer and that is how they ended up in juvenile hall. Then she called her little sister over and said, "Nobody touches her, for I will kill you if you do." I don't know if it was her real sister, but this one girl watched over the younger one like I did with my sister. Same routine as the day before—off to school, then after lunch, free time. I would help clean up after lunch and just talk to the guards and try to stay away from all the other kids.

On the morning of the third day, my sister and I did not have to shower. They took us to the dining area and had us eat breakfast, then they walked us to a bus. As I passed the nurse in the main building, I looked at her, pulled the sleeve of the shirt I was wearing up so the nurse could see my arm, and said, "See, I told you we did not need to have the TB shoot, and you will not have the change to read it for we are going home today." I did not know that to be true at that moment, but something in me said we were not coming back. I do not know what happened to the clothes my sister and I were wearing when we arrived because we did not change back into them before we left on the bus. This bus was waiting to take us to our court hearing. We got to ride on the bus that had bars on the windows and read "Los Angeles Sheriff's Bus." I still, to this day, think how cool it was to be able to ride on that bus because not many people got to ride on this bus that was for criminals when you yourself were not a criminal.

We were taken to the LA courthouse on Temple Street. We arrived at the courtroom, and we saw our brother our mother and grandmother along with our natural father and his wife.

As I walked in, I looked around at everyone, not really knowing what to think. I was just happy to see the three of us together and hoped that the judge will send us home with our grandmother and mom.

The judge took the three of us into his chamber and sat us down and started asking us questions about our father. I told him we did not know our father and we had only spent a short time with him; he was like a stranger to us. He then asked where we would like to go: should we go home with our mother or should we go home with our father? I told him again we did not know our father and that I would like to go home and be with my mother, and my brother and sister agreed.

He sent us back out into the courtroom, and then he went up to his chair and sat down. He then said that he was going to have the three of us spend one year with our father to get to know him better because he felt we should know our father as a father and not a stranger.

My mother started to rant and rave, and he had her removed from his courtroom. Now it was just us three kids, my dad, his new wife, the judge, and a few other people in the room. He told us that we needed to go with our father. I remember holding onto the bench with my hands and saying, "No, I do not know this man. I'm not going with him." My brother and sister jumped to their feet and stood by a door that led out of the courtroom through a passage that everyday people were not allowed to go through. I sat there for what must have been a very long time because the police officer in the room came over and started talking to me and telling me everything would be all right and that I needed to be with my father. I just sat there shaking my head, saying no. They tried to pull me off the bench but couldn't because I was holding onto it tightly. I even wrapped my legs underneath the bench so they could not pick me up and carry me out. My dad came over to talk to me and tell me everything was going to be okay. I then heard the judge say, "She's just a young girl.

Get her out of my courtroom now." I could hear my mother yelling at the door, but I was not sure what she was saying, but I could hear her yelling. They eventually got me up, and we walked out through a door that did not lead to the same area where our mother was. It took us to a private elevator, and we went down to the first floor and off to the car with our father to live with him and our new stepmother for one year.

My father lived in Santa Paula. Santa Paula is a small town with not much to do. Now I would finish off the last half of sixth grade in a new school in a new town with our father I did not know.

My stepmother Carol had told me that the only reason she married our father was that he had daughters and she had always wanted a little girl. Carol had two sons with two different men. I had asked her about our Sonny and Cher dolls. She had made us leave without them the last time we visited our father. She told me that she had given them away because we did not want them. I told her she had told us to leave them with our dad so that we would always have something to play with when we visited him. She basically called me a liar, and so I dropped the subject and walked away.

Carol would always make me wear a dress that had spaghetti straps for sleeves. I did not like having my shoulders exposed to the sun after getting sunburned at a younger age. My shoulders would burn almost instantly out in the California sun even with some block on. So I would wear a T-shirt under the dress, and then when she saw me no matter where we were, outside on a baseball diamond or in the house, she would tell me to take off the T-shirt, and when I said no, she would start pulling at the T-shirt to get it off for me. So I learned not to wear the T-shirt under the dresses, and then I would avoid the sun and sit in the shade as much as I could. That way, she got her way and I got mine.

When it came time for sixth-grade graduation, she picked out a dress for me, and this time it did not have spaghetti straps; it was a sleeveless dress. I was thirteen-and-a-half, and I had bigger breasts than she did. So to wear the tube-top dress without a bra was very uncomfortable for me. But given my stepmother's track record, I knew if I had put on my bra, she would have taken it off me in front of everybody because that's the kind of stepmom she was.

In the year that we stayed with them, my father had made a room out of the dining room for my sister and me; it was right off of the kitchen. Our dad's house was a two-bedroom house—it wasn't made to hold five children—and since her oldest son, Robert, lived with them and her youngest son, Michael, came over to visit them, my brother got the boys' room and my sister and I got the dining area. Our dad covered the entryway to the kitchen off with some plywood, and he had bought twin beds with a table that had a radio in it. So my sister and I had a radio in our room; this was the first time I had listened to music on the radio. I remember this one song that came on; it was about how this young boy and how he would move around a lot and he would never settle down with a girl. The song was called "The Wanderer," and the singer's name was Leif Garrett. I thought to myself every time I heard the song, this song was about me because I had moved around a lot as a young girl, but it was never because of some boy. A counselor I had to talk to (court-ordered) would tell me that I needed to get a boyfriend because she felt I was lonely and needed one. I told her I was only thirteen years old—why would I need a boyfriend? That was the last time I saw her. The song "The Wanderer" meant everything to me as a young girl. I still, to this day, listen to that song and dance around in circles.

I was lying in my bed one day during the summer listening to Casey Kasem's countdown, and every once in a while, he would give you a story behind one of the songs on the countdown. He started talking about the young singer who sang the song "The Wanderer" and how he and his friend had gotten into a car accident. At that time, I did not know who Leif Garrett was, but I do remember reading an article in one of those teen magazines. My stepmother insisted on me having this one magazine called *Teen Beat*. So I ran over to where I kept it, picked it up, sat down on my bed, and read the article again, and now I knew who this person was, and then I started praying for him and his friend and asking God to watch over them. All because of how much that one song meant to me.

Now with my dad, I started listening to artists such as Diana Ross, Pat Benatar, Billy Joel, Willie Nelson, Billy Idol, and Kiss. These were people and songs I had never heard of before. The radio opened my eyes to a whole bunch of different music. This is the type of music that our mother did not want us to listening to.

My stepmother would always tell me to be home by three. It was hard to be home by three when school was just letting out at three. So every day, she was upset with me because I could not walk fast enough to make it home at three. One day, as I was walking home with my two girlfriends, this young man on a motorbike stopped us. As we were all standing there talking to him, my friend Dee introduced him as her stepbrother Wayne. That is when my stepmother appeared out of thin air and said, "I told you to come straight home," grabbed me by my long blond hair, and pulled me like a dog on a leash (only the leash was my hair) the half block home (that is how far or close I was to getting all the way home). As she was pulling me by my hair, all I could think about was how stupid she must look right now to my friends.

My brother did not make it the full year with our father. He had gotten into a fight with Carol's older son, Robert, and so now my brother was living with a foster care family—only the system did not know he was there. My father knew this man named Fern because at the time, my father was showing dogs, and Fern had a big dog kennel and showed world champion cocker spaniels for a living. He and his wife did not have children, so they were foster parents and they would put the foster kids to work in the kennel. My father, sister, and I would drive over to Fern's house to visit with our brother and help out in the kennel. They taught us how to shave the dogs and get them ready for shows, so yes, I did know how to cut the cocker spaniel to make them look like they did on TV. It was called *the show cut*. We would also bathe the puppies and help out when one of the female dogs were giving birth. When one of the puppies were still born, we would wrap it in the towel and rub them, and most of the time, the puppy would come back to life. Some of them did die, so we would bury them in the yard. Every once in a while, my dad, my sister, and I would drive over to Fern's house for the day. At the time, my sister and I would visit; they had three to four foster kids with them. One of the boys, Fern, and his wife were taken care of; we had met them before, one summer when we were visiting our dad. He remembered us, but I did not remember him. I do remember talking to a kid who always stayed in his house and did not come out to play with us because he was not allowed outside when his mother was not home. He would just watch us from the window, playing outside. I thought to myself, *This is a small world after all.*

With my dad, I finally found that missing piece within me. I'd always thought to myself that I was different from my mother and even my brother and sister, and now with meeting my grandmother, I knew where I came from because I was more like her than everybody else in my family. I was standing in the doorway between the kitchen and living room watching her clean; she was singing and dancing while she was cleaning the house. She and my grandfather had just come over to visit and get to know us when she decided that the house needed to be cleaned, so off she went, singing in Danish to herself while she was cleaning. My father walked up behind me and said something to her in Danish, and it seemed to startle her, so she turned around and said something back to him in Danish and waved the piece of cloth in her hand and then went back to doing what she was doing. My father looked at me and said, "She does that all the time," and I remember being very upset with him. I looked at him and said to him, "At least she's happy." I then walked away from him.

Our stepmother, Carol, had taken us over to her sister's house to visit with her sister and family one weekend. Her sister had two daughters. One of her daughters (Jackie) was about thirteen, and the other one was a one-year-old baby. Jackie, the older daughter, was very shy, so we hung out in her room and we listened to her collection of records. She had a little 35 record player machine. So we would put on a record and just dance around the room and have fun. Her mother (my stepmother's sister) came into the room and told us that we needed to go outside and play. I think the only reason my stepmother, Carol, took us over to her sister's was because they wanted Jackie to get out of the house and mingle with other girls and not just hang out in her room all the time.

My stepmother, Carol, took us clothes shopping while we were visiting her sister. We ran across some T-shirts that had pictures of famous people on such as Sean Cassidy and Leif Garrett, and some even had rainbows and unicorns on them. I remember being drawn to this one T-shirt that I preferred over the one she wanted me to have, but I was too afraid to say I wanted it because it had a boy's (Leif Garret's) face on it, and I did not really want a guy's face on my chest, so I moved it to the side and picked up one that had a unicorn on it. She looked at me and said no. She picked up the one that had Sean Cassidy's face on it and said she was going to buy me this one.

So she made me put it on when we were all still at her sister's house, and I remember standing in the room, scratching away at the sticker and hoping to scratch off the face. Whatever sticker they used to put this on the T-shirt held up. No matter how hard I tried to scratch it off, it did not even crack or fade and/or peel off. The little voice in my head said, *You should have just gone with the one with the other boy's face on it because it would have made both of us happy*, but remember, I did not know who Leif Garrett was—it was just a face that looked kind.

We attended church with our dad and stepmother in Oxnard. My dad belonged to the Baptist Church. They have a children's program before church, and our dad, of course, put us in it. I sat there listening to the lesson. I can never forget what they were teaching us. The man was saying how when things go wrong in your life, you need to stop and pray to God and ask to forgive you for your sins and to tell the devil to back off. This is when I got introduced to this devil creature. He was saying how we should blame the devil and not God for the evil that happens to us. I thought it was the funniest thing in the world to blame someone for the things that were evil. For up until now, I knew that the evil came from the men in my mother's life and not from this thing called the devil. So every time we attended church with our dad, I was not fully listening to what they were preaching about because it was always about blaming the devil for something. I knew not to give any of that energy to something I did not believe in; the evil was something that man did and not the devil.

This is where I discovered John the Baptist. He became my third hero in the Bible.

I like John the Baptist because he was upfront and never talked to you in riddles. Not a lot of people liked John the Baptist—I'm not sure why, but he is not one of the most sought-after prophets. John the Baptist I fully understood and admired.

We would go on social events and hang out with all the other kids at church. My brother befriended this young girl with very tomboyish looks. I remember my stepmother telling my dad, "You can't tell which one is the boy and which one is the girl." She was talking about my brother and his new friend. My dad laughed and said, "Yeah, you're right," and I remember sitting there looking at him, thinking, *Wow, even you too.*

My brother wore glasses and had crooked teeth at the time because my mother could not afford to get him braces, so a lot of people picked on him. I would be the one who would stand up and protect him because that was my job. So anytime someone said something about my brother or sister, I would ask them a simple question: how would it feel if someone talked about you like that? Then I got up and walked away. We had been sitting at a table at some church event.

My sister and I had gotten sick that winter at our father's house; we had a fever of one hundred degrees. He decided to put my sister into a bath of cold water to help bring down her fever. I believe she started to go into convulsions in the bathtub because I could hear them asking each other what they should do now as she was hitting the side of the tub. After they brought her back into the room and left, I asked her what happened, and she told me they put her in the water and her whole body started to shake.

I had gotten a really bad ear infection; my left ear started to bleed. I felt sorry for my dad because this was his first time ever having to take care of sick children, and with how sick my sister and I were, it would not have been easy on any first-time parent. He even got or had a medical book to help him.

It was the weekend, so he could do very little for the two of us until Monday, when the doctor would be in his office. My sister's fever did break, and she was feeling better by Monday, but he still had to take me in to see the doctor. The doctor said that the infection had spread down into my jaw and he would have to give me ear drops to help clear this up. Normally they would not use ear drops because it could damage my eardrum, but with how bad it had gotten, this was the fastest way to cure me.

I do remember not eating much of anything because my jaw hurt, and I could only lie on my left side to help drain out all the pus and blood coming out of my ear.

When I turned fourteen that summer with my dad, my stepmother and my dad bought me a makeup kit. My stepmother said that all young girls should wear makeup. I was not the type of girl to run around with makeup on; my mom wore a lot of makeup and I didn't like it. The one time I put on nail polish, my dad said to me that I needed to put more on or clean underneath my nails because he could see all the dirt and that I looked like a streetwalker with it on. I took off the nail polish and never wore it again. As far as the makeup kit went, I did not know how to apply it, and I left it in my room.

One morning, when everyone got up, Carol came out of the bathroom upset because someone had taken her mascara and rubbed it in the toilet. Of course, she blamed me and said I needed to return the makeup kit they had given me. I told her I would never take her mascara and rub it all over the toilet, but she could have the makeup kit back as I didn't need it.

My friend Connie lived on the same block as us. She lived about four houses down from us, and she invited me over to spend the night. Turned out Connie really wanted to cross the street and hang out with the boys, so she told her dad something about being at my dad's house so that we could hang out with the young boys across the street.

We were in the backyard of the boys' house with another boy and us two girls when one of the boys decided to light up a cigarette. I did not like cigarettes. I didn't want to be anywhere around them, but Connie said that she needed me to stay so that she had some sort of excuse for her dad. So I stayed with her. They handed me the cigarette. I pretended to smoke it; all I did was put it in my mouth and then turn my head away so they could not see me pretending to blow out the smoke, then we all heard a knocking at the gate.

Turns out Connie's dad called or walked over to my dad's house and asked where we were. Connie's dad must've known she had a crush on one of these boys, and both her dad and mine were knocking at the gate.

Connie went home with her dad. I was walking home with mine. I was thinking to myself, *I am in big, big trouble*. I was so scared that my dad could smell the cigarettes on me and he knew that I was smoking, so I promised myself right there and then never to do it again.

All my dad said to me was that Connie tends to lie to sneak out and have fun. Connie did not attend the same school as me. Her dad had her in private school, and from what she told me, she was engaged to get married to someone she did not like, and I believe he was older than her. So of course, with us being young, both of us the same age, she just wanted to have some fun. I was never banned from going over to her house; she was grounded and could not leave her parents' house. So we stayed in her room, and we listen to records and danced. Blondie was her favorite artist, so we listened to Blondie a lot.

When she was no longer grounded, the first thing we did was cross over the Main Street to DD's house to hang out with her. Now DD had a stepbrother whom Connie liked. He would ride her around on the back of his motorbike. This same boy had cut us off on the day my stepmother decided to embarrass me in front of all of them, so of course, he asked me about that, and I told him that she was my stepmother, and he said, "No need to explain anything more." He understood. So after he got done giving Connie a ride around on his motorbike, he asked me to jump on. So I did, and unlike her, I held onto the back end of the seat. I did not wrap my arms tightly around him. So he would drive very fast and then stop for no reason to try and get me to slam into his back, but that didn't work, so now he tried popping a wheelie to see if I would let go of the seat and grab him; that did not work. When he finally stopped and

I jumped off, all he could say to me was that I had excellent balance, and I said "Thank you" and walked away.

Later that evening, he and Connie started making out, and she asked me not to say anything to anyone because she wasn't supposed to be doing that, and I told her, "If you're engaged, you shouldn't be doing it at all." I don't remember visiting her after that incident, so I don't know what happened to her.

Carol's oldest son, Bobby, was always getting high and ditching school. He had asked me to write a note to the school nurse, excusing his absence. I told him I did not want to do it, but he told me I had to and that I was the only one who could because I wrote nicely and neatly, just like his mom. I told him I would do it only if he would leave my sister and me alone or least be nice to us. It was because of him my brother was now in foster care. Bobby and my brother had gotten into a fight, and Carol stepped in to break them up, and my brother hit Carol in the face, so Carol told my dad that my brother would have to go. I was on the verge of leaving soon only because Carol didn't like me, and now she was starting to make up lies about things I had not done like her mascara in the toilet. So he agreed to be nicer to us as long as we did not rat him out to his mom about the drugs and the notes. So I became his note writer.

One day, DD had asked me if I could spend the night. It was a Saturday, and so I asked my dad if it was all right if I went over to DD's house. He went to ask Carol if it was all right that I spent the night with my friend. She said no because we needed to go to church tomorrow morning and she did not feel a young girl should be spending a night at a friend's house. So my dad came back to me and told me, "Carol says no."

I looked at him and asked him, "Why? You are my blood, she is not. You have to decide whether your daughter can spend the night at a friend's house. You don't tell her when her son can or cannot spend the night at his friend's house, so I don't understand why you have to go and ask her for permission for me to spend the night at a friend's house."

My dad looked at me and said, "Make sure you're home by eight o'clock in the morning."

I smiled and said "Thank you" and gave Carol a devilish smile as I left the house.

I went over to my friend's house. Her stepbrothers were home, and my stepbrother just happened to be there as well. They were in the room doing drugs—I believe it was called hash and I was not 100 percent sure, but this is what they were doing: they took a spoon and placed this little brown square onto the spoon and they lit up a lighter and they waved the lighter underneath the spoon to melt this brown square. What they did with it I do not know because I walked out of the room at that point. What I do know is that they got very hungry and started munching on some chips, and eventually, my stepbrother went home. Now remember, we only lived across the Main Street from DD's house, so he made it home safely, walking across the main street. I stretched on the floor in the living room to go to sleep. Everyone else was in their rooms, and DD's mom and stepfather had come home and retired to their rooms.

As I lay there on the floor sleeping, I heard a door open, and I heard someone walking out toward the living room. I whispered, "DD, is that you?" I did not hear anything, so again I whispered, "DD, is that you?" That is when her stepbrother lay down next to me and tried to kiss me.

I pushed him back and said, "I thought you were dating Connie." He told me that he wanted to use her to get to me, and if he had to kiss her again he was going to suck on her tongue because she always held it still when he French-kissed her, and anyway, she had gone back to her school. Then he French-kissed me.

I remember hearing a knocking at the door, and when someone answered it, it was my sister reminding me I needed to go home now because I would get in trouble if I didn't make it home by eight o'clock (in five minutes), so I grabbed my stuff and I said goodbye to my friend—no breakfast, nothing, just ran out. Her step-brother asked me to stay. I told him no, I needed to leave. So my sister and I made it home just in the nick of time. Turned out that my father sent my sister to get me so no one would be in trouble and we would not have to listen to Carol scolding us on how I was a disobedient child.

If only she knew the truth about her son.

For some reason, Carol made us kids eat at home while she and my dad would go out and eat. They would take us kids with them even though we had eaten at home, and we would sit in the restaurant watching the two of them eat. So I told my dad, "Instead of dragging us out here on your date, you should just leave us at home." The next time they were going out, they decided to leave me at home. Bobby was out at a friend's house, and they took my sister with them. I was watching *The Love Connection* when Bobby decided to come home. He was higher than a kite and kept asking me if I could smell the marijuana on him. I said yes. He then went to change his clothes, brush his teeth, and use mouthwash then came back out to the living room and sat down and asked me if I could still smell it on him now. I told him that he smelled better, and he asked not to say anything to his mother, and if she asked me, he had been sitting here with me all night, and I said okay. So we were watching *The Love Connection* together (a really good program to be watching with two young kids alone in the house). Bobby asked me if he could change the channel. I said, "Not a problem," and we started watching a TV show called *Roots*. That is when he decided to call our top show dog Toby: Kinta Kinte, and he started to wrestle with the dog. I told him that he needed to be nicer to the dog or he would turn him into a mean dog. Bobby did his own thing and didn't listen to anyone.

Michael would come over every once in a while to visit us. Michael lived with his dad, and from what I can remember, Bobby didn't know who his real dad was. So every once in a while, we would go over to Michael's dad's house and play with all of Michael's toys. Michael had everything from the movie *Star Wars*—you name it, he had it, and sometimes he had more than one of the same item. You could not just walk into Michael's room and not see something from *Star Wars*; it was everywhere.

Michael's dad had a cute little Porsche. I told him that I would be back for it one day and that he needed to hold on to it for me. I did not care what it looked like by the time I was old enough to drive it; I just wanted it. He laughed at me. I also thought it was kind of weird to see my stepmother and him together when she was married to my dad, but it was none of my business what this lady did behind my dad's back—we must have been her cover-up, I don't know—but we did visit with Michael's dad quite a lot, and we even met his mother Michael's grandmother.

DD and her family moved to the opposite side of Santa Paula into a house because they had been living in an apartment across the street from us. So her stepbrother would walk me home after I was over visiting with DD because remember, he wanted to be my boyfriend, and I kept telling him no. He would then kiss me, and he would ask me to have sex with him. I would tell him no, and he asked me why. I told him I was too young to get pregnant and I was going back to my mother's to live with her. He told me that I could stay with him and we could get married and that I did not have to leave him. I told him no; I wanted to go home and live with my mother. I did not want to be married at fourteen. I told him we could not be boyfriend and girlfriend anymore and that maybe he should start dating my friend Terry because she really liked him.

I do remember there was this one young boy I thought was cute; he delivered the newspaper. There was a mudslide on the hills by my dad's house, and there was mud coming into my dad's house. Luckily for him, it was only in the garage and not the house itself, so we were cleaning it up when this boy who delivered the newspaper happened to ride by, and I shouted out, "Hey, cutie!" He turned around and came back and said hi. I was shocked to find out he wasn't as cute up close as he was from a distance. I told myself, *Make sure you see them up close before you yell out to them "Hey, cutie."* I remember my sister laughing at me, but she too had thought he was cute from a distance but also agreed that up close, he was not so cute. I talked to him for a short time before my dad walked back into the garage, and that was when he (the newspaper boy) left. My dad just gave me a look.

When it was about four months before my sister and I moved back to our mom's house, I had started packing up everything. My stepmother came into the room and asked me what I was doing. I told her that I was just packing up some things to get ready to leave. She told me that I could not take anything home because she and my dad had bought it. I looked at her and said, "So you want us to leave everything here and take nothing home?"

She said yes, because we might need something when we returned to visit them.

I was shocked by this because I knew she did not want me back but she did want my sister to leave; she even told me she wanted her to live with them. So I said to Carol that was not going to happen and we were not coming back. "If we left everything here, you would end up having to throw it all away because our dad would never see us again—he doesn't want to." So she allowed me to pack up my stuff, and she walked out of the room.

My dad came home with a man we all knew as Uncle Helgi. I remember asking my dad, "Why is our Uncle Helgi here, and how do you know him?" My dad looked at me and he said, "This man is not your uncle. He is my uncle."

I remember getting into a fight with my dad, saying, "No, Mom has always said he was our uncle and we would visit him and the two women he lived with, Aunt Lorries and Aunt Ann." Now remember, my mother had us call every man in her life *Uncle*; turns out, this man whom we would spend a lot of our childhood with was really our great-uncle. So I told my dad how we would go over and visit the three of them and Uncle Helgi would always invite us into his room to give us hard candy; he was really nice to us. My mother would tell us to stay away from him because he was grumpy and a mean old man, but behind her back, he would wave us over and give us candy and a two-dollar bill. He was never grumpy with us, and he was always really nice to the three of us. When Uncle Helgi passed away, our father did not allow us to attend his funeral. I asked my father why we could not go to Uncle Helgi's funeral. He said it was because Carol did not want any of us kids going. Again, we were closer to our Uncle Helgi than we were to our own father, so when he did not allow us to attend the funeral because Carol did not want us to go, it hurt me. None of us would be going because Bobby did not want to go. I was really hurt by my father's decision because I remember my Uncle Helgi as always being really nice to the three of us and to find out that he was a family member made it even harder for me not being able to attend his funeral. He was the only family member we had.

Since my brother was not in "real" foster care, he would come over and visit us. It was Christmas time, and the church was having all the kids get together and go caroling in the neighborhood on the back of a truck filled with hay. The three of us (my brother, sister, and I) arrived at the school early; we were playing tag and running around just having fun. When a young boy showed up, he decided to play with us. We played hide-and-seek. When we got tired, we all sat down to rest. The young boy looked at me and said, "Come sit here on my lap and let's talk about the first thing that pops up."

I told him, "No thanks."

He said, "Then just come over here and sit on my lap."

"No, I am fine where I am, thank you."

When the rest of the kids and grown-ups arrived and it was time to go on the hay ride, I made sure I was sitting at the far end, nowhere near this young boy, and all I kept thinking how lucky I was to have my brother and sister by my side.

When New Year's came around, we spent the day with our brother over at Fern's house. I went upstairs to visit my friend Lisa, who was one of the foster girls living there. She was sitting on the bed watching TV when that young boy who we met that one summer came into the room and lay down on the bed with us. He kept poking at Lisa. She kept telling him to stop; he then tried to poke me and I told him no leave me alone. I put a pillow in front of me to try to keep him from poking me again. He would just hit the pillow and not me. He just kept poking at Lisa, and I decided to get up and walk out of the room. He asked me where was going. I told him, "Out of the room."

Someone had suggested that we stay up all night to bring in the New Year together, and we made a bet as to who could stay up the last. I'm not much for staying up late, but what the heck, why not? So he got up and left the room. Lisa and I decided to take a nap so that we could win the bet; the boys did not know that we girls were upstairs resting. I told Lisa that I was a restless sleeper and that she should not roll up next to me. So we put pillows in between us, and we each had one leg hanging over the side of the bed. I closed my eyes and fell asleep. When I woke up, Lisa said that I was a very mean, nasty sleeper because she had gotten a little too close to me and I had started hitting her (according to her). I told her that I was a restless sleeper and not to get near me but she didn't listen to me. I think she did it to see what would happen because she didn't believe that I would hurt her.

So now as the night wore on, we were all downstairs in the TV room watching scary movies to try and scare each other and waiting to see which one of us would fall asleep first. My sister and the other foster girl that lived there fell asleep first, but they were the youngest of us so we knew they would go first. Now it was only the teenagers up. Which one of us would be falling asleep next? Lisa and I just looked at each other and smiled because we had taken a nap earlier.

We stayed at past eleven o'clock, and I think that was when boys finally gave in, so we girls won the bet. I think it was something like cleaning out the kennels while the winning team sat back and had lemonade watching the losing team clean.

We had less than three months before we would be heading back to our mother. My stepmother asked my sister if she wanted to stay with them. My sister was the only one my stepmother liked.

When the time came for us to leave, all three of us went back to our mother. The pickup point was back in the same courtroom with the same judge asking us if we wanted to stay with our father or go home with our mother. We all chose our mother because of the look she had on her face when the judge asked us whom we wanted to stay with. You see, our mother could control us by just a look or the snap of her fingers. We knew when she snapped her fingers at us we had better move quickly and do whatever it was she wanted us to do. She called us by our full names when she was angry with us, so we knew not to upset her and do as she told us. She was now living with her boyfriend, Fred, the probation officer in Silverlake. If you know the Silverlake area, the houses were on the hillside and some of the homes were anchored to the hilltop on stilts. Luckily, Fred lived about four houses at from the street, so you didn't have to climb several flights of stairs to get to his house.

We finished off the school year and one full year in the LA school district. The girl (Stacy) who lived across the staircase and just off the street below Fred's house became a close friend of mine. Stacy told the kids at the middle school that we were her cousins and that they needed to leave us alone or she would beat them up. Now Stacy was half Hispanic and half white. The three of us had blond hair and blue eyes and were very much white. So it was very nice of her to tell these kids to leave us alone. I remember Stacy asking me to go with her during the lunch hour to visit a friend's house. They did not live too far away from the school. She told me to put on her bandanna to help cover up my blond hair. So when we got to his house, she asked me to stay outside as she went in. I believe she was there to pick up some weed. This friend of hers was too old to attend school and he was in a gang and the bandanna she asked me to wear was their gang colors. He came outside, took one look at me, and asked me if I wanted some weed. I told him no, I did not do that, and he looked at me funny. She came out of the house and told him not to worry about who I was and that she wanted me to be there with her but now it was time for us to head back to the school. He said something to her about staying; she said no, we had to get back to school. We were lucky he let us go, and Stacy never took me back to his house.

One weekend, I was sitting outside on the steps doing nothing when this young girl Sunny sent down and we started talking to me. She lived further up the hill in the house that Fred owned, and her parents were renting it from Fred.

There were two other children that lived on this hill where we had befriended Scott and Samantha. When Sunny and I were sitting outside on the steps talking in front of Fred's house, one of Scott's friends came by. We were talking about something when he asked me to go off and have sex with him. I told him no, and I stood up to walk away, when he got upset and pushed me so I fell and twisted my right arm. I just lay on the steps holding my arm when Sunny, the young girl, who was about eight years old, spread open her legs to reveal a hole in her crotch area and said, "I have a nice warm hole for you to put that in and I'm not wearing any underwear." The two of them left together. I got up and went into Fred's house and told my mom what had happened. She said that I would have to wait twenty-four hours before she could take me to the hospital. She wanted the swelling to go down before they looked at it.

So the next day, my mom took me to the hospital, and they put a half cast on my arm from my wrist to my elbow then the wrapped it with medical cloth. My sister and I slept on the floor and my brother slept on the couch because Fred's house was just a small shack with one bedroom, and that's where our mother and Fred slept. I slept with my arm up on a pillow to elevate it when my brother walked by me and kicked my arm. I got up and I hit him over the top of his head with my half cast; luckily for him, it wasn't a full cast because when I hit him on the head, the cast broke at the wrist area and we had to go back to the hospital to get a new one. He learned to be more careful when he walked by me and my arm.

I bought a Pat Benatar record called *Crimes of Passion* because of the one song on it called "Hell Is for Children." I would play that back to back to back and sing it to my mom every day.

Lisa asked me to babysit her niece while her sister, mom, and she went out for the night. I asked her where her dad was, and she said he was out. I told her I would watch her niece for her. It got really late, and the little girl was sleeping, so I lay down on the couch waiting for them to come home. Now remember I don't like staying up late and I am a very light sleeper, so as I lay on the couch, I heard Stacy's dad come in and he was drunk. I remember not moving, hoping he did not see me, but he did and he came over to me, knelt down by my side, and landed a big, fat kiss on my lips, and I pushed him off me, and I got up and ran out of the house.

The next day, I went over to Stacy's house to tell her what had happened (I don't think they paid me for the night). I don't remember seeing much of Stacy after that night because it really upset her mom to see me when she found out that her husband was making advances toward me. I never went back in her house or babysat ever again.

Fred had two children of his own—a boy and a girl. The boy would come over and visit with his dad and the girl never came over.

Fred and my mom liked to party, and they had alcohol everywhere. They would invite their friends over to drink. Now as for us kids, we had nowhere to go, so we sat on the floor while the adults sat on the couch drinking and having fun. After they left, my brother then could sleep on the couch, and we girls made up the floor to sleep. My mom and Fred went into the kitchen. I remember going to sleep and dreaming that I was walking through the French doors into the kitchen. The next thing I remember was waking up on the toilet peeing; I don't know how I got there. So after I washed my hands, I walked through the bedroom area and back out to the living room to lie down and go back to sleep.

In the morning, my mom asked me if I remembered what I had done that night. I told her yes, I had gotten up and went to the bathroom, no big deal. She said no, that I had gone into the kitchen, pulled out a bowl from the cupboard, sat down at the table, and demanded breakfast; that was when she told me to go to the bathroom and that's how I ended up in there. "You don't remember getting up and sleepwalking?"

I told her no.

After some time living with Fred, he decided he was tired of playing house with our mom and us and he was going to break up with her. He had told her he and his wife were going to try and work things out because after being with us for some time, he missed his children. My mom did not take that very well; she decided to take the drugs Fred had in his bathroom. She took as many as she could while following it with whatever alcohol he had handy. Normally, my mom would run into the bathroom screaming, "You don't love me, you don't love me!" and cutting her wrist from left to right. This time, she did it right with taking the pills and drinking the alcohol.

Fred called for an ambulance; they put her on a stretcher and drove her to the hospital because she was unconscious. He drove the three of us to the hospital, and we waited in the hallway for her. I remember there were these two women in the same hallway with us when the paramedics brought in someone on a gurney. I did not see who it was, but one of these two women started crying, "My baby, my baby!"

The paramedic looked at her and said, "No, this is their mother." She looked straight at me. Fred asked us to get up to follow our mother into the room. The woman stepped to the side and looked at me straight in the eyes as I walked by her. I remembered feeling embarrassed.

They decided to pump out her stomach, and Fred told the three of us to stand there and watch as they did this. He told us that he never wanted to see us like this and told us how harmful drugs could really be. I was thinking to myself as I was watching the floor and not them pumping out my mother's stomach and watching her going into convulsions while they were trying to save her life by shoving a tube down her throat and into her stomach that this man had all the drugs in his house and he did not want us to be like our mother? How can someone say that and believe it when they themselves did not live that life, the kind of life he was now trying so hard to preach to us?

For the next three days, she stayed in the hospital, and Fred took care of us. I felt sorry for him because I don't think he had ever had to fully take care of children the way he had to take care of us for those three days. He had to make sure we had breakfast, lunch, and dinner. He had to make sure we got to the bus stop on time, take care of us after school, make sure we did our homework, and then have us get ready for bed. When my mom was released from the hospital, Fred asked her to move out, but she told him we had nowhere to go. For some reason, we could not go back to our house in Arleta. So what they decided to do was to have the family that was renting his house up the hill move into our house in Arleta, and we moved into Fred's rental house. He did not charge her any rent.

CHAPTER THREE
Faith

Then the king commanded, and they brought
Daniel, and cast them into the den of lions. Now the
King spake and said unto Daniel, Thy God whom
thou servant continually, he will deliver thee.
—Daniel 6:16

We moved into Fred's rental house higher up that same hill. We now
had to climb three sets of staircases (about thirty to thirty-five steps
each) and then walk up a steep pathway to the house.

The house was partly on stilts and the other half was on the
mountain side. The part that was on stilts had a room under it that
we kids played in. When my brother, sister and I were at school, some
of the neighborhood kids that did not go to school would hide out in
that area and smoke weed and do what kids do while ditching school.

My mom lay around in this sheer nightgown. She would just lie
on top of the bed, not drawing the curtains so people who were walking by could see her lying on her bed and in her sheer nightgown.

When the three of us came home from school, we would often
find the young kids standing in front of the glass door looking in
at her, this made me very upset with her because, how could she
lay there showing off her body to these young kids and not caring
enough about herself to cover up? I had to take care of our mom and
to make sure she was covered up so that the people who were passing
by would not see her lying there in almost nothing.

My sister and I did the grocery shopping almost every week and
by ourselves. Once our mother showed how to get to the grocery
store from where we were living, she stopped going with us.

It was a long walk to the top of the steep hill we lived on, and then we had to walk down the other side to the bottom of the hill. It was a long trek down to the grocery store. On our way home, we would bring the shopping cart with us. Once we reached the street we lived, we could no longer use the shopping cart because it was a staircase from here on up. My sister and I had discovered that if we took one of the streets before the one we lived on, we would end up about halfway up the side of the hill to where we lived. We would be skipping a lot of stairs. It was easier for us to then carry the bags the rest of the way home. It did save us some time using this shortcut, and it made it a lot easier on us. We would carry the bags two by two up to a landing then go back and get more, and then once we had all the bags out of the shopping cart (about seven in all), we would then start moving them two by two up the steep steps to the next landing then go back down and get more. This would continue all the way home by picking up two bags, putting them down, and going back to get more.

On one of our weekend trips down to the grocery store, we decided to buy our mother a yellow rose because yellow was my sister's favorite color. So I learned how to shop on a very tight budget. I wanted to make sure I could get this rose for her because I loved her and I wanted her to understand how much we cared for her. When we got home, and after we put the groceries away, I handed our mother the yellow rose and told her it was from the three of us even though my brother was not with us. I felt he would've wanted to give it to her as well. My sister had no problem with us buying the rose to give it to our mother.

Instead of our mother saying "Thank you" and saying how much she loved us, I got a lecture on how I had wasted her money on buying her this dead flower. It would've meant more to her if we had just picked the wildflowers that were growing on the hillside. My sister then told her that this was all my idea and that she had told me not to do it.

I just remember standing there holding the flower and thinking I would never try to show or tell our mother how much I loved her ever again. I never stopped loving her; I just would never showed it in a way that she could understand it. I just kept it inside my heart. Even to this day, I don't tell her I love her. I do tell her, "I understand you did the best you could with the three of us."

My mother got a new job delivering phone books, and she would bring us with her during the weekend; we would help our mother deliver the phone books. We would have to go to a building that had all the phone books, and we would put them in the back seat of a car. We loaded up the back seat from floor to ceiling (along with the trunk) with as many phone books as the car could carry. The three of us would have to squeeze into whatever little space there was because the phone books were more important than us kids; the more area you covered, the more money you could make. As we were delivering the phone books, the car became lighter and began to have more room for us to sit in the back seat. Our mother decided that she would pick up this hitchhiker she saw on the side of the road. I remember begging her not to, and even my brother and sister begged her not to because we had just heard about this hillside strangler person and how they had found one of his victims not far from where we lived and they had not caught him, and this man she was about to pick up could be the hillside strangler. She ignored all three of us and picked him up. As he was getting into the car, he looked in the back seat and saw the three of us, and he looked a little nervous and I was sitting there praying, "Please God, do not let this be the hillside strangler or anyone who would try to harm us." We drove him a couple of blocks when he decided he wanted to get out of the car, so my mother pulled over and let him out.

I think that was when I started breathing again because I was in such fear and praying so hard that this person would not hurt us I think I forgot to breathe. On the day she got paid, we would go out and eat. I remember telling her, "Why don't we save this money and go to the grocery store and buy food?" That way, we could use the car to take the groceries home, and my sister and I would not have to carry them home. I don't remember what my mother said to me, but I do remember my brother and sister looking at me and saying something like "Can't we just have fun every once in a while? Do you have to ruin everything?" So I sat there in the restaurant eating quietly.

One night, police officers showed up at the house. My brother, sister, and I were all sleeping in the bedroom (because the house had only the one bedroom and it was located toward the back of the house). We heard our mother talking rather loudly to the officers, and that is what woke the three of us up. When the three of us came out of the room, it startled the police officers because they did not know we were there. They were saying something about how she was using drugs and allowing youngsters to smoke marijuana in the house. Some of the officers had gone down under the house in the basement where the neighborhood kids would like to hang out during the day and smoke weed. The one officer came up into the house with a human skull in his hand and accused our mother of witchcraft, and they pulled out the Ouija board and said, "This is how she was casting her spells."

I remember looking at the officer and thinking, *We are not witches and we are not casting spells, at least not in this house.*

The officer asked our mother if there was someone she could leave the three of us with while they took her down to the station to straighten things out. She left us with the neighbors Scott and Samantha's parents. I believe we stayed there with them for about three days. Now Scott and Samantha's parents were nature lovers and they grew marijuana on their lot and their shower was outside in the back of their house—no walls around it, no shower curtain—all out in the open for everyone to see you standing there in your birthday suit taking a shower. I would make sure that I always had something on when I took a shower. I did not want people looking at me in the nude while I was showering. My sister did not care; she would just shower in the nude outside in the open air.

Anytime Samantha and Scott's parents got wind that the police were on their way up the hill, they would have the three of us come over to help with moving the marijuana plants. This was like a game with us and the police. The police never knew what we were doing, and their parents never got trouble as long as the five of us would hide the plants while Scott and Samantha's parents were talking to the police. They would keep them occupied on one side the house, and then as they slowly moved to where the five of us were, we would move the plants to where they had just been standing.

Samantha liked to come over to our place and play with the Ouija board, so the three of us would sit on the floor and play this game. We would all blame the other one for moving the plastic piece over the letters on this board. According to the rules of the board, you were to put two fingers from each hand on to this little triangular piece that had a big hole in the middle of it, and each person that was touching the plastic piece would take turns asking silly questions like, "What is the name of my husband?", "How many children will we have?", "What will he look like?" etc. I remember not thinking much about the game and just playing along with it, then for some reason, Samantha started asking about some little girl who lived in the house and who had died either in the house or within the area. I remember looking over to one side the room and almost seeing this little girl standing in the room with us. That was when I took my hands off the board. Samantha asked me why I did that. I told her that I thought I had seen a little girl standing in the room. I didn't want to play the game anymore. From that moment on, while we lived there, I would always see this little girl in the living room. She didn't do anything, she just stood there, and so one day, I told her it was okay—she could go. I didn't see her anymore.

When my mom got a better job with PacBell in Burbank, she decided we were going to move back to the house in Arleta. I don't really know why we moved again, but we did, and now, we were starting in a new school and a new town. Now we had to take a bus from Arleta into Burbank every morning.

On our first day in the Burbank school district, our mother was with us to enroll us in the schools (my sister and I attended the middle school and my brother attended the high school). I believe we dropped off my brother first, then we headed over to the middle school.

We sat down in the principal's office, my sister and I, after our mother got done enrolling us into this new school, she then went off to work. The principal wanted to get to know his new students before sending us off to class, I don't remember what we were all talking about but we had just been attending school in LA where it was rough because you needed to know all the right gang signs to throw as you were walking down the street so you don't get beaten up.

I remember these one girl flipped me off (with her middle finger) as she and her friends were driving by my sister and me from the car she was in. I flipped her off with my middle finger because she had just done that to me. They stopped the car, and this girl got out. She walked over to me and got up in my face. She was yelling and screaming at me for flipping her off. I remember just standing there, calmly looking her in the eyes and saying to her, "I'm sorry—I thought you were just saying hi to us. I was just returning the gesture you just threw at me." That is when she slapped me across my face, and then she told her friends to get back into the car and they sped away.

So to be sitting in the principal's office and having this man talk to us about whatever was he was talking to us about didn't really mean much to me. He must've said something that upset my sister because she started threatening him, and he told her that her attitude was not permitted here and she needed to change her ways.

As the day wore on, the rumor about what had happened in the principal's office grew into me being the one who attacked the principal and started hitting him and cursing at him. That to me was rather funny, but I didn't stop that rumor because I was thinking I'd rather the kids in this school think it was me being a bully and not my sister.

My sister and I would walk to our mother's work after school. My brother joined the chorus at the high school, so most nights he would stay late at school.

Our mom would get off of work at 5:00 p.m., so my sister and I would wait for her in the break room till she got off. We would do our homework, and if she gave us some change, we could get some snacks out of the vending machines.

When she came into the break room during her breaks, she would sit with us and her female friends. The man that worked there would go and sit on the couches closer to the TV after they got their snacks.

Most of these men were gay, and our mother's favorite phrase before she left the room was that she could turn any gay man straight after sleeping with them. I remember sitting there watching her leave the room as she said this. I could see the expressions on the men's faces; they would sit there and joke about what she had just said.

One of them took her up on her challenge; his name was William.

My sister and I started taking the bus home after school and not waiting for her anymore when she started dating this William person.

One evening, my sister and I were walking home from the bus stop when we saw this man in the street outside in front of our house with his pants down around the middle part. You could see his butt crack from half a block away; it was out for everyone to see. His head was inside the trunk of his VW bug. He had most of his car's engine in our front yard. As my sister and I were walking close to our house, I kept thinking, *Please don't let this one be someone our mother is interested in.*

When we got to our house, he turned around and said hello to us. We looked at him and we ran inside the house. I remember leaning on the front door, telling our mom, "Please, Mom, don't get hooked up with this one."

Her favorite saying to me was, "You never want to see me happy. You always want to see me measurable and alone."

I told her, "No, but you can do better than that."

He came in, took a shower, and then the two of them went out for the night. It must have been a Friday night because they did not come home until the next day.

Saturday sometime in the afternoon, when they finally came back, our mother looked at us and said we needed to be nice to William for he was moving in with us because they had just gotten married.

I remember standing up and telling her, "No, you didn't. I told you not to marry him."

Now we had a new stepfather, and our mother was pregnant, as if four children weren't enough for her, but she has always wanted to have seven children because seven is God's number.

With our stepfather moved in, things changed, and not for the better. We had to give up certain everyday things. At first, it was little things like a shower curtain when I would take a shower. I would have to now hang a towel over the shower curtain rod. My stepfather would come in and sit down on the toilet and try to catch a glimpse of me naked while taking a shower. He'd always get angry at me because I would have a towel hanging from the rod to block his view. When I got out of the shower, my mom would be yelling at me because I had gotten more than one towel wet. Besides the one that I would use to block his view, I would have one on the floor so that the floor wasn't getting wet and I wouldn't slip on the wet floor when I got out of the shower.

I told my mother that if she allowed us to have the shower curtain back, I wouldn't have to put one on the floor and hang one from the rod, and I didn't appreciate her husband trying to sneak a peek at me while I was taking a shower and could she please get him to stop.

Now remember this house in Arleta is the same house that my stepfather Paul had tried to molest me in. Now to have this man trying to see me naked was like having all this repeating itself again. A new stepfather in the same house was like déjà vu, but this time, I was older and wiser and a lot harder to catch.

They moved their bed out into the living room area and turned what was the bedroom into now the living room. I told my mother at the time that that was a stupid move because now we did not have access to the bathroom or the kitchen. We would have to walk into where they were sleeping to go the restroom, take a shower, and to enter the kitchen to eat. It did give them more privacy because the girl's room was right off her room and the boy's room was down the hallway, further away from her and William.

Eventually, the telephone disappeared because our stepfather said we were using it too much and we could talk to our friends from school. Also, he didn't believe that teenagers should be spending their time on the phone.

Next to go was the water, and we now had to walk down the street to Mrs. Peach's house to shower. Then eventually, the electricity was gone, and we had to do everything by canteen light.

Our mother and he both made good money at the phone company, so I did not understand why we would have to go without electricity, phone, and water.

All my mother would say was that William didn't believe we should have all these kinds of comfort, that we should learn how to without it. It would make us stronger and tougher.

After the birth of his first daughter, she got pregnant again a few months later.

Our mother had always made our clothes for us (by hand), but now she didn't have the time anymore, so for the first time, she took us out clothes shopping, only we weren't allowed to bring the clothes home. She put them on layaway, and we would pick them up before school began; she told us it was because she didn't want us to ruin them before school started.

For my ninth-grade promotion, she made my dress for me, one that I picked out. It was a dress that resembled something from the TV show *The Little House on the Prairie* dresses. It had puffy sleeves, it was form-fitting around the breast, and then it had a full skirt that fell below my knees. The under layer was a silk blue, and it was covered with a white fabric that had flowers cut out of it so you could see the silky blue fabric underneath where flowers were missing, like a big doily. I loved it because it was a nice old-fashioned dress and it covered my shoulders—no spaghetti straps and no tube top.

Our mother would talk about her son Charles (the firstborn) and her youngest daughter, Lorraine, all the time to her friends. One day after school, my sister and I stopped by the office to wait for her to get off. She was standing in the hallway with about four of her friends talking about how good her children were and how proud she was of the two of them, when one of the women looked at me and asked me if I was her sister. My mom quickly answered her before I could even open my mouth and said, "Oh no, that's just Catherine." The lady looked at me, and I smiled at her and told her that I was her firstborn daughter and Lorraine was her second daughter, then I just walked away. That is when I learned my mother didn't talk much about me at all to anyone, but she did brag about my brother and sister all the time.

I also was dragged out with her and William to the movies. We went to go see *The Rocky Horror Picture Show* with some of William's gay friends. I really don't know why she took me with her, but she did.

We had one of Nancy's birthday parties at a pizza place; the same gay men had come with us to celebrate her birthday. He told my mother while looking at me, "If I ever wanted to try to be straight, I would like to use your daughter here."

I looked at him funny, and in my head, I heard myself say to him, "I would never sleep with you," then I got up and walked away from them all.

Now gay men want to sleep with me too?

My baby brother David was out visiting us during the summer this year when we decided to go to the movies. We were making it a family affair. Everyone had to go; even our grandmother was out visiting us at that time. As we were about to get in the car and leave, my brother Charles asked our mother if he really had to go (he wanted to stay home). She told him no, he did not have to go with us, so I then asked her (because I was standing next to her when he asked) if I too could stay home. She said no.

I said that was not fair. "You are letting Charles stay home, and I am only one year younger than him. I should be able to stay home too."

William came up behind her and heard most of our conversation when she repeated herself (saying no to me). That is when William grabbed me by the arm and started dragging me toward the car.

The car was an old station wagon, green with wooden panels on the side, the one we use to take vacations in with Paul. We left it here at the old house when we all lived with Fred. Our mother and William made sure the water and electricity were on again before David's visit. Our mother did not want David to go back to his father's house and report that he had to take a shower at someone else's house and that we had to use lanterns to see with at night.

I tried to pull away from William as he dragged me toward the car. There was a big grease spot right behind the car. He flung me toward the back end of the car. I slipped on the grease spot and slid across it as if it was ice under my feet and right for the back end of the car, the minute I knew I could not stop myself, I put both hands up to try and stop myself from slamming into the back window. I had both hands up and I prayed as I was sliding toward the window that it would not break as I ran into it. It would have worked if the back window was up. So lucky me, I hit the back end of the car with only my face. I hit the car hard and right across the bridge of my nose. I thought for sure this time I was going to die, or I hoped I would if I didn't.

I got into the back seat next to my grandmother. Lorraine was next to her when Lorraine said to me that I had hit the car hard enough to move it with them sitting inside.

They loaded up everyone else that was going (David and Nancy), then William and our mom got into the car, and off we went. We were on our way to see the movie *Tron*. I did not want to see it—that is why I had asked if I could stay home.

On our way to the UA Theater in Van Nuys, my grandmother looked at me and said to her daughter, "I think we need to take Catherine to see a doctor."

My mother asked me without even looking at me, "Do you think you need to see a doctor and spoil the whole day for the rest of us?"

I told her no, I was fine and that we could just go ahead, straight to the theater to see the movie.

I did notice as I was talking to her that it sounded as if I had a cold, and lucky for me, my face was still numb from everything. So it did not hurt at that moment in time.

As we sat there in the dark watching the movie, my face began to hurt, so I got up and went to the bathroom; I walked in to the restroom to use the toilet, and then after I got done, I slowly went over to the sink area to look at my face. I was alone in the bathroom (thank goodness) because when I raised my head to look at myself after washing my hands, I almost started to cry. I could not cry because it hurt too much. Both eyes were swollen and black and blue; my nose was red, black, and blue. I looked like I had just gotten out of a fist fight with someone and I lost.

I walked back into the theater with my head down so no one could see my face and sat down next to my grandmother, trying very hard not to cry, I did not want my nose to run because I could not blow it.

My grandmother asked me if I was all right, and I told her yes, but I really wasn't, but she could do nothing about it.

After the movie, we stopped for ice cream at an ice cream shop across the parking lot from the UA. I said nothing this time when our mother asked who wanted ice cream.

We went inside and my face was still looking down at the floor, when I almost bumped into someone. I had to look up for a minute. The man looked at me to say sorry, but the moment he saw my face, he stopped, and this look of fear came over his face. I remember just looking at him holding back tears and smiling a half smile at him as if to say, "I know I look bad, but it's okay."

One Saturday morning, my baby brother and I decided to go outside to play. Only my mom and her husband were having sex and we did not know how to get out of the house. Now we could have gone out the back door, but Charles did not want to us to go into his room to exit the house. In my room, we had a big sliding window, so we could go that, way but because of my sister, I had gotten in trouble the last time I tried doing that, so I wasn't going to try that again. I looked at David and said, "Okay, here's the plan. We walk through the bedroom as fast as we can, looking down at the floor. I will open the front door, and they will never know we walked through the room."

As I opened the door that led into their (now) bedroom, David was following me. The two of them were going at it like rabbits. I closed the door behind David. I turned back around and started heading for the front door. As I got to the front door, someone on the outside rang the bell, so I opened the door just a little bit to stick my head out, and he had asked me if my mom and dad were home. I smiled, and I could feel myself lighting up like a little lightbulb and looking at him and saying "Yes." I then opened the door completely, and he was standing on my left side so I scooted out around him on my right side, and now he had the full view of my stepfather on top of my mother having wild sex. I remember seeing his face as I passed him—he kind of turned a little pale, his mouth fell open, and I just kept going. By the time I got to the end of the porch to the first step, I remembered David, so I stopped and turned around to see where he was. He must've slowed down during our walk to the front door, because by the time my mother noticed the door was open and someone was standing there watching her, David was in the doorway and I could hear her yell "David!" He came running out, and the two of us ran down the street. I, to this day, don't believe our mother knows that I was the one who opened the door because she never saw me; I was already outside.

One day, while we were out at the mall in Glendale, a woman walked by me. She had ear piercings that ran all along the outer side of her ear. My stepfather turned around and looked at me because I was watching her and I think I said to my sister a little too loudly, "That's cute."

So my stepfather said, "Do you want to get your ear pierced again?"

I told him, "No, I just thought it was cute. That doesn't mean I want to pierce my ears again for the third time." We were walking by a store that had a big sign out front saying, "Get your ears pierced here and you get a free pair of earrings." So my stepfather, who was wearing his terry cloth shorts and no shirt started pushing his fat hairy body on me and pushed me toward the store. I kept telling him to leave me alone. I didn't want to get my ears pierced again. My mother and the rest of the gang just kept walking while he pushed me inside the store. The lady came over and asked if I wanted to get my ears pierced, and as I was opening my mouth to say no, my stepfather beat me to it and told her yes.

I looked at him and I said, "No, I do not want to get my ears pierced." I looked at the lady and I said, "No, thank you," and tried to walk out of the store. As I moved to go around him, he moved, and now he was in front of me, and he pushed me into the chair.

He said, "Sit down so that the lady can pierce your ears." I took one look at her. She looked very confused and scared. I looked at him because he was still standing in front of me, so I sat down in the chair. She came over to me, and asked if I was all right and if I really wanted to get my ears pierced.

Now as she was talking to me, he was walking up next to her and he said, "Yes, she would like to get her ears pierced."

I was holding back tears now because I really didn't want to do this. I looked at her and I said, "It's fine, let's just do this." So now I had three holes in each earlobe, and this one really hurt. So the lesson I learned that day was to never comment on someone and the way they looked and/or what they were wearing or even how many piercings they had, at least not while my stepfather was around me.

When we finally caught up to my mother, she asked what had happened to us, and of course, my stepfather blamed me by saying I begged him to get my ears pierced. Of course, when I told her no, she didn't believe me; she only believed him. She still believed everything the man in her life was telling her to be true, and everything I said would always be a lie.

We moved out to Sylmar into a smaller house; this house had two bedrooms. My brothers shared one with David, and our mother and William were in the other one. My sister and I slept in the living room. We still had our bunk beds from our old house. I slept on the bottom; my sister slept on top. We still do not have a phone in our house, but we did have running water and electricity.

When my sister and I would get into fights, our stepfather would come out of his room (most of the time with no clothes on) and throw a dildo at my sister and me, and he said to us, "I want to watch."

Of course, my sister and I would then stop fighting, and I told him he was gross.

My stepfather did most of the cooking, and I remember not eating much anymore at home because I did not like his cooking. I preferred to cook, and he would complain, so I would just leave the kitchen and not eat.

One day, we were all sitting in front of the TV in the living room (where my sister and I had our beds) watching a program when our stepfather handed our mom her plate and then he decided to go down on her in front of my sisters and me. My mom looked over her shoulder at us with her dinner plate in hand and said, "This is the kind of guy you need, someone who will cook for you and go down on you without ever having to ask him to do it, someone who could fulfill all your needs."

Of course, my sister and I were grossed out by it and told her to take it into her room because we did not have anywhere else to go and they did. They got up and left the room; of course, they had sex.

She would watch her porn movies when we were at home trying to do our homework; she would say to William that she could write a book about sex and make a better porn movie than the ones they were watching.

She gave birth to his second daughter; this child had brown eyes the very first one in the family to have brown eyes. The first five of us had blue or bluish green eyes, so our mom was very happy to finally get one that had brown eyes. I used to tease my mother and Betty about their brown eyes. I would hold my baby sister and tell her that because of her brown eyes, she would always be full of shit. Our mother did not find this to be funny, but I was tired of her putting me down all the time and having her husband trying to peep in on me every time I took a shower—yes, even in this new house, he would still try.

I joined the choir with my brother. I remember our mother came to the audition, and before I went in, she took me aside and reminded me that I was not good enough to even try out and to always remember that my brother was better than I was. So when I was called in to audition for the school choir, my mother went in and sat down to listen to me and to make sure I did not perform at my best.

I don't remember anybody else's parents being there. I think she was there to intimidate me, but it didn't work completely. I did sing, and I made it into the school choir. I just didn't want to be on the same one with my brother because I knew it was not my place to compete with him, so I joined the girls' choir; they did not spend as much time competing against other schools. The girls' choir did join up with the show choir to compete in the big competitions and to perform at school.

I was also in photography class, and one day, as I was walking to class, I saw this young man walking down the corridor in front of me. The voice in my head said this was the man I was going to marry and I was to take him as he was and not try to change him in any way. I remembered as I was looking at him walking in front of me, I looked up out toward the sky. It was a cloudy day, but some sunbeams were shooting down from the heavens and hitting him as if the light were shining on him like a spotlight. I yelled out to him, "Hey, you with the cute ass!" He turned around, and I quickly jumped into my classroom. I remember being so excited because this was the first time I had found someone I thought I would be interested in. Know I hadn't seen his face, but I knew in my heart he was the right one for me because I heard the voice in my head tell me he would be the one I would marry. I was not even thinking of getting married to anyone before I meant him.

After class, he was waiting for me outside my classroom door, so he walked me to my locker. I told him my name, and I got his, and then we went off in different directions for next class.

I found out he was a football player, and so I would hang out on the football field every chance I got, but because I was in choir, I would spend a lot of time after school in the choir room practicing for concerts and waiting for my brother to get done with his rehearsal. When we would wrap up with our (the girls' choir) part and before my brother was done, I would run out to the football field to see if I could catch Leonard and to talk to him.

One night after I got done with rehearsal and my brother was running late with his rehearsals, I went over to the football field and asked Leonard after his football practice was done if he would like to go for a run. He said yes and asked me to wait for him by the basketball gym locker room, and so I did.

As we were running down the street, he asked me if I had a crush on anybody at the school. I said yes, and I told him that there were five guys that I thought were cute but there was only one I really liked and wanted to get to know better. Now as far as these five guys were concerned, I was just lying to him about that because I did not want him to think I was easy.

So he asked me who this one guy was. I said, "It is you." He stopped running, and I just kept going.

McKinley Park was about seven blocks away from the school, and that was where we were running to. It turned out that he worked there, and he asked me to stay outside while he went inside to get his work schedule.

The truth was he had gone inside to talk to his friends and ask them what they thought about me because every once in a while, I would see someone peeking their head out of the gym door and looking at me. Eventually, he came back out and I asked him, "So what do your friends think about me?"

He looked at me then said he was inside getting his schedule and not asking his friends to check me out. Then one of the older men opened the gym door and called him and me over. He looked at me and said, "It is nice to meet you," and that Leonard was a good kid.

As we ran back to the school, I asked him again, "You weren't inside telling your friends to check me out?" I had this weird connection with him already; I could almost feel what he was feeling and know what he was thinking—not all the time of course. As for this incident, I did know what he was feeling. As we ran back to the school, I wasn't sure that I had done the right thing by telling him I thought he was cute and wanted to get to know him better. I was also thinking after we said goodbye, *Thank goodness I told him there were four other guys I thought were interesting.*

I started writing his name on my book covers, and in one of my classes, the young girl who sat behind me tapped me on the shoulder, and she started asking me questions about him, and I told her what he looked like, and she then told me she was his cousin, and she and I became good friends.

Now they weren't blood cousins; her family and his family were both immigrants and their families came over together on the bout, and the two families decided to become close and the kids then would just call each other cousins because they were in a new country. She told me that he had just lost his mother last year to cancer.

The next time we met up again (it was after school hours and on the school property), I got done with rehearsal early. I was waiting for my brother when I saw Leonard, and I asked if I could talk to him.

I told him I was really sorry to hear about his mother passing just last year and that if he ever needed to talk to someone, he could always turn to me. He was surprised that I even knew about his mother and it was really hard for him to talk about it with anyone, but he did thank me and gave me a big hug, and he even cried a little.

When Leonard and I officially became boyfriend and girlfriend, he started telling me who I could hang out with, and I would tell him I like all my friends and he couldn't tell me who I could and could not hang out with. But he told me if I wanted to be his girlfriend, I could not hang out with a certain group of people. So I told some of my friends that I couldn't hang out with them during the lunch hour but after school, we would get together, and on the weekends, Leonard never needed to know that I still hung out with my friends just because he didn't like how they looked. They were not the popular kids in school.

When he had an away game, he would tell me that I would need to be there for him. I told him no, I could not be at the away games and that I could only attend the ones here at the school. He said, "If you loved me, you would be at the away games to watch me play."

I told him, "No, I have other commitments and I cannot attend any of the away games. This does not mean that I do not love you, simply that I cannot get there and I have other things to do," but he was not one to take no for an answer to anything.

So when I saw him the next time at school, he was a little upset with me. I asked him what his problem was, and he told me it was because I did not make it to the away game. I reminded him that I could not attend any of the away games because I had choir and I had to get home to help my mom with the babies. He did not talk to me for a while, and I just went on my way.

I joined the ROP class, so on Wednesdays, I had to wear a dress to school because after school, I would be modeling. At first, we were bussed over to the Beverly Hills high school, where we learned how to do runway modeling and how to model in front of the camera. I also did some modeling at the mall and learned about colors and what looked good on me and what colors did not look as good on me at JC Penney in the Glendale Galleria.

At the end of the class, we had a big modeling show, and we invited our family and friends, and the teacher had some top modeling agents to the show.

I even Leonard if he would come, and of course, my mother and sisters had to be there. Leonard was sitting with my sister, and he had told her that if I came out on stage with a guy, he would break up with me.

Now I was backstage getting ready for the show, and the teacher had paired me up with one of the boys and another girl, so there were three of us hitting the runway at the same time. So when I stepped out onto the stage, the other two were already on stage. Leonard got upset because one of them was a male. I did my catwalk; they each did theirs. We met in the middle at the top of the stage, I leaned in on his left shoulder, the other girl leaned in on his right shoulder, and we just posed.

Then we left the stage. I thought I did a good job, but when my sister (Lorraine) came running up to me after the show, my sister said Leonard was very upset because I had walked out onto the stage with that boy. My happiness inside me melted away. Leonard asked me if we could go to dinner after the show. I told my mother I would be going to dinner with Leonard and not to wait for me. When we were in the car, he was complaining the entire time that I had touched the guy's shoulder, and I looked at him and I said I wasn't the only one on stage and I had all my clothes on, so I didn't understand why he was so upset. I did not kiss this boy. He told me he just didn't like seeing me with other guys and that maybe I should give up this modeling thing. I told him no, that I wanted to see how far I could go with this modeling thing. He took me home without stopping to get something to eat.

My mother took me to see an agent, and she told me that I would need to have a breast reduction because my breasts were too large. I looked at the lady and said, "Sorry, I'm not changing who I am to fit into some image the industry wants, and I will not become a stick figure to fit in ether." I was only 118 pounds and 5'6" at the time. I got up and left the room. She was a little shocked and stunned by my reaction. I guess most people would do anything to become a model, a movie star, a singer, but that was not who I was. If they didn't like me the way I was, then I was not interested in becoming something they wanted me to be. I love who I am and how I look.

When the baby (Betty) started to call the neighbor *Mommy*, my mother decided that she would take the night shift at work and William would work during the day so that way, someone was always home to watch Betty. It upset my mother to no end that Betty was calling the neighbor *Mommy*.

Leonard had asked me to go out on a date with him, and of course, I said yes, so I gave him my grandmother's numbers to call me. Instead of going home with my mom, I went over to my grandmother's place to wait for him. It was my first time ever going out on a real date with a boy. He was running late, and I was beyond nervous; I was pacing back and forth thinking he wasn't coming. I was hungry, and I was deciding whether or not I should just eat and give up on him or continue to wait when he finally called an hour and a half after the time he told me he was going to pick me up. I gave him the address to my grandmother's place again. We ended up going out on a double date with one of his friends and a girl that his friend liked. We went to an Italian food restaurant. I remember sitting there trying to eat some of the bread, but because I was hungry and nervous, I could not eat anything. By the time dinner came out, I was too sick to my stomach to eat. I excused myself and went to the bathroom. The girl who was with us followed me in and asked me if I was all right. I told her this was my first time ever going out on a date and I was really nervous. She looked at me kind of shocked and said, "This is the first time you've been out on a date?"

I said, "Yes."

She then said that she had something that I could take to help calm me down, some sort of pills.

I told her, "No, it's okay, I will be fine."

We went back out to the table, and we decided to pay the bill and go out for a drive. We ended up at the pier in Santa Monica. Leonard and I were just walking around, talking, trying to get to know each other better, and his friend and his date went off in another direction to make out. Leonard and I sat down where we were on the sand and talked. Some time had gone by, and we noticed the other two were missing. We got up and started walking around. We found them behind the lifeguard stand making out. I looked at Leonard and I gave him the ground rules: there would be no kissing in public. Holding hands was fine, touching each other on the shoulder and tapping of each other's butts was fine, but absolutely no kissing in public. Kissing in public meant to me that the people who were doing it were looking for attention and not looking at the one they were with as someone they wanted to spend a lifetime with. To see couples in public making out, rubbing up on each other hands everywhere, I felt, was disrespectful.

When he drove me back to my grandmother's place, he did give me a quick little kiss on the lips, and off he went. The next time we went out together, we grabbed something at a fast food place and headed up to the mountains to make love for the first time. When I saw him Monday at school, he totally avoided me and would have nothing to do with me. I was a little shocked, confused, and hurt. Now I thought to myself, *The one time I wanted to have sex with someone that I liked, this is what I get in return—him totally rejecting me.* I didn't understand it, but after a couple of days of him avoiding me, I decided to ignore him and not even look for him during school hours. I didn't even call him.

Almost a month later, he came running up to me in the hallway, pulled me aside, and asked me if I was pregnant.

I looked at him funny. "What?" I asked him.

He said, "Are you pregnant?" He then told me that he had been on his knees praying for the past weeks that I would not be pregnant. He said to me that he was too young to have a baby. Later that day, we got together to talk about girls' menstrual cycle and how a girl can only get pregnant about three days out of the month. I was thinking to myself, *I've had sex education class twice now and did he not listen during his class? Or maybe they just don't teach the boys about the female menstrual cycle.* I also had health class, and it taught us the effects of drugs. They even brought in three people that had been addicted to drugs to tell us what the side effects were and what it would to our bodies. The one guy who snorted cocaine was missing his nose. The one who smoked cigarettes had a hole in his throat, and he had to cover it up in order to talk to us I don't remember what the third one was talking about because by this time, I was not paying attention to them anymore. I knew what drugs could do to you. I did watch my mother get her stomach pumped, and having to watching her lie in a coma because she was high on something to make sure she did not kill herself—well, that wasn't fun either.

Anytime I would need to call Leonard, I would have to walk down the hill to the pay phone at the local liquor store. I usually took Nancy with me but not always, so that way, Lorraine only had Betty to watch.

One of Leonard's friends liked me, and so Leonard asked me to go out with his friend. I told him no, I would not do that. He then said to me, "If you love me and really care about me, you would do this for me."

I looked at my friend Georgia and asked her what she thought.

She said, "You're not married to him, so why not? You might like the friend better." So I told Leonard I was only doing this for him and no other reason.

I went out with his friend that Friday night. It was around Christmas time, because we went to his boss's house for a Christmas party.

I spent almost all night in the bedroom with the boss's daughters playing games with them. We came out to eat, and then we sat around the table talking. I was getting bored, and it was getting late, so I asked if we could leave. Pinto (the boy's nickname because of the kind of car he drove) told his boss we had to leave.

As we were getting into the car, he asked me if I wanted to go see a movie. I said sure, as long as we did not go to the UA Theater because Leonard had a part-time job there. Turned out that he only worked during the summer for the park, so he really did just take me over to the park to show me off to his friends. My gut feelings were right.

So where does Pinto take me? To the UA Theater because he knew Leonard would be there. I was by the door waiting while Pinto got the tickets. We went in and the movie had already started and the room was full of people. The movie he had chosen to watch was called *Purple Rain*. We found two seats on the end of the aisle. Every once in a while, I would look behind me to see if Leonard would be popping in to check up on us. One time, when I turned around, I caught him standing there; he moved behind someone, hoping I did not see him, but I did.

After the movie ended, I told Pinto I would like for him to take me over to where my mother worked so I could get a ride home.

He said he would, but he wanted to show me something first. He then drove us over to Westwood Village. I do not know why we had to walk around Westwood; I think it was because he was not ready to go home. We talked mostly about Leonard and how I liked him and no one else at school and that he did not have a chance with me because I was not interested in him. That did not stop him from trying to get me to hold his hand; he even tried to get me to hug him. I would just move away from him and remind him that I liked Leonard.

He told me that he knew of a move that would crack my back without hurting me. I did not hear exactly what he had said to me, so I said "What?" to him. He walked up to me, and now we were face to face. Then he grabbed me to hug me. I put my arms across my chest before he put his around me and then he lifted me off the ground. Then he asked if he had cracked my back. I said "No," so he moved in to try again. I put my hand up and said, "Take me to my mother's work now," and he did.

One night after choir, I went down to the football field to see if Leonard was still at school. Turns out they had just gotten done with practice, and Leonard asked me if I could wait for him to change. He wanted to talk to me. I said, "I will be here when you get done." I waited for a long time. I think everyone on his team had gotten done and had passed me on the staircase before he finally came out.

We went for a walk to talk about things; of course, he brought up Pinto, and he asked me what we had done that night. I told him about the party and how I stayed in the daughters' room and played with them. He did not believe me. He heard we were at the movies that night. He said he did not see us and that he did not even know we were there until Pinto told him. I told him I saw him duck behind someone when I looked at him. Of course he denied that. Then he said that I gave Pinto a big hug. I told him, "No, I didn't, but Pinto would not take no for an answer, so he did grab me." I had put my arms across my chest so that my breasts did not touch him at all, and if that is what he was calling a hug, then yes, but it was a one-way hug only.

Leonard then said that Pinto had told him I had rubbed my boobs all over his chest.

I looked at Leonard and laughed. "I did not, and remember, I only went out with him because you asked me to."

Leonard then moved in as if to give me a hug, but instead, he unbuckled my bra strap with both hands, and in my head, I got this impression of tissue paper falling out of my bra. I looked at him and said, "Are you happy now?" I turned around and refastened my bra.

When I had my back to him, he said, "What do you mean?"

After I readjusted my breasts back into my bra, I turned back around to face him and said, "You thought paper would fall out of my bra. You think I stuff my bra with tissue paper?"

He did not say anything more to me, and we walked back to the school. As we were walking back, I reminded him again that he was the one who had asked me to go out with his friend and how I only did it for him. If he wanted to be upset with someone, he would have to look in the mirror and not at me.

We were not talking to each other at this point.

As the school year came to a close and prom was in the air, Pinto came up to me in the basket ball gym and told me that Leonard was going to ask me to the prom. I told Pinto that if Leonard wanted me to go with him, he would have to ask me himself.

I told my mom that I might be going to prom and if she could make me a dress.

Leonard never asked, and he ended up taking another girl to prom.

That summer, Leonard did call me. He would have to leave a message with my grandmother and then my grandmother would tell my mom, then my mom would tell me.

As I was leaving to go down to the corner and call Leonard one night, Lorraine decided to pick up the rifle that William kept behind the front door and point it at my head.

I started to yell at her, "What are you doing? Put the gun down!" It was the summertime. My sister and I were home watching the babies. Both our mom and William would work the same schedule so the two of them would have more time with each other. I did not see any emotions in Lorraine's eyes. He just stared at me with this faraway look in her eyes. After asking her to put the gun down a few more times and trying to hide behind one of the babies (I did not think Lorraine would shoot one of the babies, but hiding behind one of them would not help with stopping the bullet from hitting me as well), I decided to just sit on the floor and wait to see what she would do. The two babies were tiring to get into my lap, and I just kept pushing them back. I told my sister, "Do you really want Mom to walk into the house to find me and the babies dead and blood all over the place? What would you say to Mom? Why are you doing this?"

She did not answer me. Finally, after some time with her pointing the gun at my head, she came around and said that she did not want to be left here in the house alone with the two babies, she did not want me to go out.

I looked at her and said, "Okay, then put the gun down and I will stay here with you." So she did, and I did not go down to the liquor store to call Leonard that night.

Leonard and I did go out on dates, and then after eating and/or sometimes seeing a movie, we would have sex in the back seat of the car. I would come home from my date, and my sister would always ask me what movie we saw, and once I started to tell her about the movie, she would stop me and tell me I was doing the dating thing wrong. I knew what she meant (I should not have been watching the movie— I should have spent the entire time having sex). Little did she know we did both. Our mother would always tell my sister and I that we should get knocked up by a rich boy and have him take care of us for the rest of our lives. I did not believe in that theory. I did not think we women were only good enough to stay at home pregnant, barefoot, and in the kitchen cooking. I had enough of the cooking thing and I wanted more for myself. I did not want to have children and force a man to marry me. I wanted the man I marry to love me and want to spend time with me. Someone who cared about me and would protect me, someone I could talk to and he would understand that I did not need anything more than just his love. I did not need him to spend a ton of money on me, just time with me was all that I was looking for. I always believed our mother had it wrong—we women could be anything we wanted to be and not just a housewife and baby maker.

I sat at the kitchen table with a bottle of Kahlua in front of me and thought, *Why do people have to drink? What gives this so much power over people?* I opened it and smelled it, and it smelled like coffee. I did not like coffee, but I wanted to know why this had such a power over everyone. I poured a small amount and drank it. Now I thought, *Well, that was nothing.* I took a bigger sip—still nothing. Another even bigger sip. Now I am not feeling well; my head started to hurt. I start thinking to myself, *I don't have control of myself, and that is not a good thing around here, not having complete control of one's self with the kind of stepfather I have.* If William were home, he would have tried something, and I would not have the strength to fight him off. I promised myself I would never do that to myself again. After all, I did *love* myself too much, so I never touched any kind of liquor again. William also loves to take the can of wipe cream and spray all the air from the can into his mouth; he says that you could get a really nice buzz off it. When our mom went to get herself some wipe cream from the can, she found that it was empty and started asking all of us who used up the entire wipe cream from all the cans and put them back in the refrigerator. I told her that her husband would take the can and just spray all the air from the can into his mouth. I told her that he said you could get a nice buzz off it.

I don't know if she believed me or not, but from that moment on, we got the wiped cream that came in the tub and not the cans anymore.

A new school year and no Leonard. I looked everywhere for him; it was odd not seeing him in school anymore. I did get over it after a while, and I finally gave up looking for him, but it was not easy.

I was now old enough to take driver's education class.

I took French as a second language, and Leonard's cousin was in class with me. She would give my notes to Leonard for me. I never got one back. I always got just a message from him through her— always the same thing, call him.

I took the bus to get to my grandmother's place because I was not feeling well and I needed to go home, but I went to my grand-mother's place to wait for my mom to get off work and pick me up. It was raining and had been raining for some time and the streets were flooded. As I tried crossing Lankershim to catch another bus to get to our grandmothers place, I found myself tiring to cross the flooded street, the water was up to almost my knees, and the umbrella did nothing to help keep me dry because the wind was blowing so hard that the rain was coming down sideways.

I got sicker than I already was. My ear got infected again. This time, the doctor gave me a pill and not eardrops. He said the ear-drops were not safe for my ear, even though I told him that is what they gave me the last time and it worked. I was out of school for about one and a half months. I slept most of that time. I was taking something that knocked me out. Every once in a while, I would hear my mom ask her mother (my grandmother) how I was doing.

I finally got well enough to wake up. I tried to get out of bed. I slowly sat up and put my feet on the floor and tried to stand up, I found that I could not walk again. My grandmother was out doing something, so I did not have her to help me, but I had to teach myself to walk again before, so now here I was alone and having to relearn how to walk all over again. I had to use the bathroom; I had to make my way to the bathroom somehow on my own. My grand-mother lived in a trailer, so it was a straight shoot from the couch bed to the bathroom. I had to use the edge of the sink to help get me past the kitchen area; now I had to figure out how to move past the cupboards. They were straight and almost impossible to pass, but I put my body up against the door and hugged the cupboard and then let go of the cupboard with my right hand, pulled with my left hand, and flung myself onto my grandmother's bed that was right next to the cupboard. I hit the bed and bounced right off it and onto the floor. I grabbed the edge of the bed and the dresser to pull myself up; luckily for me, I landed on my back. I got up, turned around, and now I was facing the right direction for the bathroom. I was lucky the bathroom was really small. You did not have to move much to get from the toilet to the sink, so after I was done, I decided to walk straight down the middle of the hallway back toward the bed in the living area. As I got into the kitchen area, I started to feel dizzy and sick. I went over to the kitchen sink in case I vomited. I started to cough, and I felt like I would vomit now. I just kept coughing, and, finally I loosened up what was stuck in my throat and I spit it out into the sink. It was a big blood clot the size of a golf ball. I washed it down the drain, and that is when my grandmother walked in. She said to me, "I see you are finally feeling better." I said yes (I could hardly speak) as I told her what had happened and how I needed to learn how to walk again. I got dressed and asked my grandmother if I could use her tricycle to try and get my legs working again. She said yes, and off I went around the trailer park. I felt like an old person because I moved very slowly at first. The older people around me walked faster than me on the tricycle.

I made it back to my grandmother's trailer, and my mom and sister were there. My mom looked at me and asked me if I was well enough to come home now. My grandmother told her how I had just gotten up today for the first time in two weeks. I slowly got off the bike, and I told her that I was exercising because I could not move. I don't think she believed me, but my grandmother told her to leave me here, and so my mother did. My sister gave me my homework, and for the next couple of days, I had to catch up with all the work I had missed at school.

Leonard had called a couple of times, so after I got some of my homework done, I called him. The first thing he wanted to do was to go out. I told him no. I was just starting to feel better; I was not in any shape to go out. This did not make him happy, but what could I do? I was not feeling well just then, and I needed to recover completely before going out again. I am sure his cousin and him talked. She would have told him that she did not see me at school; after all, I did have her in two of my classes—French class and another class.

Leonard suggested that I work at the UA Theater with him; that way, we could spend more time together. I was seventeen after all, and I should be working and not at home taking care of my sisters (Leonard thought). So one Saturday, I went over to the UA to apply for a job (my very first job). The manager had me take a math test—simple enough—and then after I handed it to him, he looked at me and said, "You're hired."

I looked at him and said, "Really? You didn't even go over my answers."

He said he did not need to and that the only reason I got the job was because I was pretty.

I said, "So if you felt I was not pretty, you would not hire me?"

He said, "No."

I was now working part-time, going to school, and taking care of the two babies (part-time).

I worked the weekends only at first, and I told my boss I could work in the afternoons on Sunday because I attended church in the mornings. He said that would not be a problem.

I could no longer take choir because I did not have the time to spend rehearsing and going to compactions. I told my choir teacher that this would be my last semester with her. She asked me what I wanted to do for a living. I told her I did not know, and she then said that she would miss me because I had such a large singing range. Then she said, "Good luck with your future."

Leonard had never come to any of my shows, and I was getting tired of chaperoning my brother and sister at all the parties they attended. I wanted to do something that was just me for a change of pace. Leonard was there, but he worked in the theater cleaning it and I worked behind the snack stand.

One Saturday night, this very beautiful woman and a man with a long overcoat with its collar turned up, sunglasses, and a hat pulled down to the top of his sunglasses so you could not see his face got in the line to get some refreshments. They walked up to me. Now I can see who this woman was. She asked for a drink and some popcorn. As soon as she spoke to me, I knew for sure who she was and who this man was that was trying so hard to hide himself from everybody.

It was Donna Dixon from *Bosom Buddies* and her husband Dan Aykroyd. As I handed her her order, I whispered to her that I loved her in *Bosom Buddies* and that I did know who her husband was. She smiled at me, and the two of them walked away. They may have thought I would tell everyone that they were here at the theater, but I did not. I knew how hard it is for stars to go out and have a good, normal time among all of us normal people.

I had the pleasure of knowing Mr. Robert Cummings when I was fifteen for a short time. I needed to borrow a hat for a play that I was in, and his son Bob Cummings had the exact hat that I needed. When I asked Bob if I could use it in the play, he told me that I needed to ask his dad if I could use it. I said, "Okay, I can do that. Will he be here after school so I can ask him?"

Bob said no, he walked home and that I would have to go with him.

I walked over to Bob's house with him. Now Bob had never told me anything about his dad, and I had no reason to expect his dad to be Mr. Cummings. Why should I? Normal people never run across stars; that just never happens. We got to his house, and I walked in, and I was met by Mr. Cummings himself. He looked at me and said hi.

I looked at him and then at a big picture of him hanging over the fireplace (the picture was of him, only younger, so I knew exactly who he was), and I said, "I love the movie *Dial M for Murder*."

He then said to me, "So you know who I am?"

I said, "Yes. You must be joking. Of course I know who you are." I then asked him about a hat Bob had been wearing at school and asked if I could use it in the school play I was in.

He asked me to come back tomorrow. With tomorrow being Saturday, I said okay, not sure why, but he said he would give me the answer tomorrow. I told my mother that I had just met Mr. Robert Cummings and I needed her to take me back to his house on Saturday because I wanted to borrow a hat of his for the play I was in.

My mom, of course, told me that I should sleep with his son and get pregnant; that way, I would be set for life. I thought nothing more of what this woman wanted me to do.

The next day, she took me to Mr. Cummings's house and she walked me to the door so she herself could meet him. She then left, and all three of us headed off to Bob's dentist appointment. Mr. Cummings had this nice green-colored Jaguar with a soft tan leather interior.

As Bob went into the dentist's office, Mr. Cummings asked me to stay in the car and talk to him. As we were talking, this woman looked at him and started to come closer to the car. She was bent over. As she got closer to us, Mr. Cummings said to me very quickly and almost whisper-like, "Play along."

I said "What?"

But by then, the woman had come up to the window and said, "Oh, Mr. Cummings, how much I love you," and asked if she could get an autograph.

He looked at her and said, "I am sorry, but I am not Mr. Cummings."

She then looked a little confused. She looked at me, and I bent over closer toward Mr. Cummings and said very straightforwardly, "This is my dad, and yes, he gets mistaken for Mr. Cummings all the time, and I myself and my dad here both love and adore Mr. Cummings and how wonderful an actor he is, and there is no one else like him on this planet."

She smiled and said, "Sorry for disturbing you," and walked away looking even more confused now.

Mr. Cummings said thank you to me, so I asked him about how that affected him. He said, "Sometimes you just want to blend in and not have people recognize you all the time."

I did get to borrow the hat for the play I was in, thanks to Mr. Cummings being as kind as he was.

So when Mr. and Mrs. Aykroyd left the theater after the show, Mr. Aykroyd tilted his hat at me as if to say thank you for not saying anything. I smiled at him as to say "You're welcome."

Then one of the girls I was working with asked me if I knew who that creepy guy was. I looked at her and said, "You don't know?" By now, the two of them were outside the theater.

She said, "What?"

I said, "That is Dan Aykroyd and his wife, Donna Dixon."

She took off to get a better look, and now the people outside were crowding around because of course, they had to be picked up in a limo. The girl ran back in and said to me, "Why didn't you say anything?"

I told her, "Because he was trying not to draw attention to himself, and his wife was just walking around looking as beautiful as ever, and if you know who she is, then you know who her husband is." And I did not need to say anything more.

One day, Leonard and I had broken up over something beyond dumb again when he decided to flirt with another coworker. He got her coffee, and they were laughing as they walked by the snack stand. My friend looked at me and asked if everything was all right (everyone knew that Leonard and I were dating). I told her yes, that we had gotten into a fight and we were no longer dating. It was okay that he was with someone else now. I had left him a letter early that morning in his jacket, so he had not seen it when he was at the ice cream parlor across the parking lot getting coffee for the two of them. I had to run upstairs to get it and throw it away before he saw it. Because of course it must have said something about how much he meant to me and how much he had hurt me by not listening to me or understanding that I too had to spend some time with my family and do as my mother has asked of me. I could not spend all my time here at work and then with him after work. As I got the letter from his letterman jacket, he walked in and asked me what I was doing.

I said, "Taking back the letter I gave you."

He asked me for it, and I said no. H did not need to know what it read because he had already moved on and I did not want to stand in his way. He then tried to take it out of my hand, and I told him to stop. He then pulled on my fingers to get me to let go of the note, so I did. He read it and said, "You are right, I didn't need to know that," handed it back to me, and walked out of the room. I pulled myself together and headed back down to the snack bar.

As the day passed, Leonard and this girl stuck by one another's side, laughing and making sure that when they came out into the lobby area, they would always be very close to one another. I was not a jealous person, and Leonard learned that very quickly by the end of that day. The girl who worked with me asked me what was going on, and she asked me if it was all right if she tried to date him. I said, "Go ahead, just be careful he doesn't like something you are doing and you don't change to make him happy. He will dump you too."

A young man came up to me and asked if they had any opening here at the theater. He wanted to apply for work here. I told him yes. He then asked me if he would be working behind the counter with me. I told him, "Sure, maybe if you are good with counting money," but then I remembered that all it takes is good looks to be working the snake bar, nothing to do with the ability to count.

As we were closing up after everyone was out of the theater, Leonard came in the back where I was helping the others clean up the kitchen area and we were getting everything prepped for Sunday. Leonard asked me what I was doing, so of course I told him I was cleaning.

He said, "No, I saw you flirting with that boy earlier, and someone told me that you told him he should work here with you."

I said, "What do you care what I do or not do? We are no longer dating. This is none of your business—what I do and who I talk to—anymore."

He then said to me that we were still dating and he had every right to know whom I talked to.

I looked at him and said, "Okay, then why are you and Pamela hanging on each other all day and laughing as you two came out of the theaters after cleaning them, almost arm in arm, if we are still dating? Do you think you can just snap your fingers and I will run back to you? Go have your fun with Pamela. I don't need this or you."

Leonard would not let me go home until I said we would be together again as boyfriend and girlfriend. I said, "Fine, but I do not like the way you are treating me, and I will not try to compete for your love with anyone. If you do not love me, then fine, I walk, but if you want this to last, then you need to stop trying to control me. I don't like that, and I know you don't like it when I tell you what to do and not to do." Not that I ever did, because I am not like that. When someone I loved was allowed to get close to me, I needed to feel like I was the only one in their life because they would be the only one in my life.

Now we were dating again. He took me home. I was supposed to call my mom and let her know that I was done and that William needed to pick me up. I called her to tell her Leonard would be taking me home.

My mom told me that William would be picking me up and taking me home and that if she caught me anywhere around Leonard, she would have him arrest for raping a minor (he was eighteen and I was seventeen). I reminded her I was dating him and that we had been dating for a year now. "Why do you have a problem with him now? Because he is eighteen?"

I told her if she ever tried to come after Leonard with the police, I would do the same to her. I would have William arrested for child abuse, and I had a lot on him; she had nothing on Leonard.

The very next week, before I got done with my shift at the UA Theater, I called my grandmother to have her tell William (who was waiting for me to call so he could come and pick me up) to come and get me in twenty minutes and that I would be off at 11:00 p.m. I would then be waiting outside for him. William showed up about ten minutes after I had called to have him come in twenty minutes to get me. I saw him walk by, and I was trying to wave him down, but he was not looking my way. Then about five minutes later, he walked by again, never looking for me behind the snack stand where I worked. He just kept his face looking straight toward the doors and never once looked or even asked where I was.

When I got off, I went outside thinking he was waiting for me in the car. I could not find him anywhere, so I called my grandmother and asked her why he came early. She had told him to wait, but he did not listen to her; he just left. I asked her if she could call her daughter and let her know I still needed a ride home.

I waited about ten minutes and called my grandmother back, and she told me that William had gone to pick up my mother and that if they stopped by here, she would tell them that I was still waiting for them.

Now the theater was starting to close up for the night and I was outside waiting for my mom to come and pick me up. I went back inside to call my grandmother, and she told me that they were on their way to get me. I stopped in the restroom before I went back outside. As I was headed for the front doors, I saw them pull up and park. I walked through the doors, and that is when my mother started to yell at me that I had been hiding from William and that she was sick of my games. I looked at her and told her that I had seen William walk in and then walk out without looking at me or for me and that I did not get off until 11:00 p.m. and he had come early. He, of course, called me a liar, and I told my mom to call her mother and ask her what time I told her to tell William to come and get me. My mom was in front of William holding him back because now he was yelling at me and saying that he saw me run into the one theater and hide from him. I told him, "That is funny because I was working and I watched you the entire time, and you never looked at me. You can even look at my time card to see when I clocked out."

He said, "That proves nothing."

Leonard must have seen me outside arguing with my mom and her holding William back because the next thing I knew, he was outside trying to calm everyone down. That is when my mother told Leonard that if he ever came around me again, she would have him arrested. Now my mom was up in Leonard's face. I was trying to get in between them. This was when my mom told William to grab me and put me in the car. As William grabbed my arm and started pulling me again toward another vehicle, Leonard told my mom to go ahead call the police. The boy who was with Leonard told him, "Dude, no, let them go."

My mom then looked Leonard in the face and said, "See, he's smart enough to know when to keep his nose out of other people's business. Maybe you should listen to him more often." As I got closer to the car, he opened the back door and shoved me in. I almost hit my head on the side of the car. I had to duck my head as I fell into the back seat so I would not hit the car. I ended up lying down on the back seat, and then William shut the door almost on my feet.

William yelled at my mother, "I have her in the car. Let's go."

My mother yelled at me and told me if I ever saw Leonard again, she would have him put in jail and that I should be dating the other guy who was with him. He was smart enough not to get involved and had pulled Leonard back. She kept repeating herself and how I was the one that caused this and that I should have been outside waiting to get picked up and not hiding inside so none of this would have happened. I just kept repeating one thing over and over to her, "Call your mother. She knows the truth."

When she did talk to her mother (my grandmother), she told her that she had told William to wait twenty minutes then I would be off work, but he just left.

Now the next week, when I went to work, the manager needed to talk to me. I followed him into his office, and he told me that he needed to let me go. He then told me it was because of the little incident that happened last week. He told me if I had my own vehicle, things would be different, but I didn't, so he needed to let me go. I looked at him and said "Thank you," and off I went. I stopped to make a phone call. I called my grandmother and asked her if I could stop by to see her because I had just lost my job because of Mom and William and I did not want to go home right now.

I learned to drive. Sadly to say, I did not have a car, but I did have a driver's license.

My older brother Charles was now graduating from high school. I attended the graduation and, then after our father asked my brother if he would like to have dinner with himself and our grandparents, our dad asked me only because I was standing there with my brother at the time he had asked him to go out and eat.

My brother and I followed behind our dad in Charles's car to a restaurant here in Burbank.

We had a nice family dinner, and as we said our goodbyes, my dad handed my brother a card; it had some money in it. My grandmother looked at me and handed me some money and said not to tell anyone she gave it to me. It was only twenty dollars, but it was nice of her to give me something. I gave her a hug and said goodbye to them all.

I was now stuck at home. We watched this TV show called *Dinosaurs*, and the baby on the program had this cute little phrase it would always say after doing something wrong. It was, "I'm the baby, got to love me," so Betty, after anytime she spilled something or wanted something us older girls had, would always say, "I'm the baby, got to love me," then try to take whatever it was away from us or walk away from the spill. When I tried to teach her that she had to help clean up her mess and not walk away from it, our mother would yell at me to clean it up and to leave Betty alone. She was too young, or if she wanted what I had, I would tell her she was too young and that she could not have it. Our mother would tell me to share it with her. So if it was candy or gum, I would give it to her and then she would get sick off the candy or with the gum. It would end up in her hair, then William would have to cut her hair to get it out. The peanut butter trick was not working, nor did the ice cubes trick (freezing the gum and piling it out of her hair). There was just too much of it in her hair for anything other than cutting it out.

Our mother came home from work to find that Betty's hair had been cut. She asked me what happened, and I told her, "You told me it was all right to give her gum. I told you she was not old enough for it, but you insisted that she gets whatever she wants. Remember she's the baby, got to love her? So your husband cut the gum out of her hair."

That was the last time my mother tried to stop me from trying to teach my youngest sister that she did not always get what us big kids had. I would always follow it up with, "You're the youngest, we don't always have to love you. We choose to love you."

That summer, my brother went to work at Universal Studios. I was stuck at home with the babies and my sister for about half of that summer. I too decided I would work at Universal Studios.

Leonard had convinced me to cut my hair short. The last time I had my hair short was when my mother cut it to about shoulder length. I did not attend school for a day (she had cut my hair on a Thursday, and so I only missed that Friday) because I felt I looked too much like my sister Lorraine. I did not like having short hair, but he told me that I would look nice with it short and could I please just do it? I told him I would but only for one year, and if I did not like it, I would grow it back.

I went and get my hair cut. It looked much like Sheena Easton and how she had her hair. He had me wearing miniskirts and heels. I did not like the choices of clothes he picked out for me, but I would only have to wear it when I was with him, and the rest of the time, I could be me and wear what I liked to wear—longer skirts, jeans, shorts, and my vans.

I was working part-time at Universal Studios in Hollywood. I worked crowd control, so they would have me work on the upper lot and the lower lot and sometimes in the warehouse. We would meet at the office to get our assignment for the day when one day, I walked in and saw this blonde girl flirting with one of our co-workers. She was sitting on his lap, and he was trying to push her off, but she just keep jumping back into his lap and started to giggle and laugh, and she was trying to be cute with him. I looked at her. She looked at me. I said to her, "I think I know you. Your name wouldn't happen to be Lisa, would it?"

She said yes, and she then she just looked at me and stood up, and I said to her, "I kicked your ass when we were younger at Calvary Lutheran Elementary."

The boy started laughing. She just looked at me and said, "Yes, I remember you now." She was too embarrassed to say anything more, but when she walked past me, she said, "Renée became my best friend. Now Renée was my friend, but because I was put into foster care as much as I was, Renee and I lost touch with each other."

So I looked at Lisa and said, "Only by default."

They had me work crowd control on the upper lot that day. I was asking how many people were in their party to make sure we filled up the tram. When one of my coworkers spotted this man in line, he was not wearing a shirt. He told the other girl who was working with us, then they both came over to me. The boy told me, "Look, do you see that man with no shirt on? Go tell him he needs to put one on."

I told him, "Why don't you go tell him to put his shirt back on?"

He (the boy) looked at me and said, "Do you see him? He's big." Now this man was big—we are talking Arnold Schwarzenegger big, not round big.

So I walked over to him, and as I got closer to him, the shorter I got. Not only did he have muscles everywhere but he was also tall.

I was talking to the people in the line and just slowly moving my way up to him. I did not want him to think I was coming all the way back to him to say something to him (but I really was). I stopped in front of him; he smiled at me. I just looked at him and then said as sweetly as I could, "As much as we love looking at your chest, I will need you to put your shirt back on. Thank you."

He looked at me and said, "Really?"

I said, "Yes please. You will need to put your shirt on. We cannot have you walking around the park with no shirt on. Thank you," and I smiled at him.

He looked at me then at this little baby in its stroller and said to me, "If I have to put my shirt on, then the baby will need to put its shirt on."

I looked at him and said, "Really?" I then looked at the mother of the baby, took a step back, and said somewhat loudly so the people around us could hear what I was about to do, "Mama, could you please put a shirt on your child? For you see, this grown man will not put his shirt on till you put a shirt on your child, as cute and adorable as your child is without its shirt on. This big baby here is not as cute, and I need him to cover all that up." I waved my hands in front of his chest as I said it. People were now looking at us, so the woman put the shirt on the baby.

I looked at the man and said, "Your turn." Everybody watched him put on his shirt, and I said "Thank you" and walked away.

I got back up to the front where we were asking, "How many in your party?" and then had the people get into lines to board the tram when my coworkers came up to me and said, "I can't believe you did that."

I looked at them and said, "You told me to tell him to put on his shirt, and he would not do it at first because of some baby not warning his shirt. I had no choice but to ask the mother of the baby to put the shirt on her child so that that man would put his shirt on."

The man and the lady were talking as they got up closer to me. I believe he did not think I would ask someone to put a shirt on a baby just to get them to put their shirt on, so as the mother passed me, I thanked her again and then said to her, "Some boys just never grow up." Then I thanked her again and said, "Thank you for helping me teach a big baby to wear his clothes in public places."

She said, "Not a problem." He (the man) did apologize to me for acting the way he had as he walked by me.

At the bottom lot, we worked out in the sun so we were allowed to wear sunglasses. Mine had big lenses to help protect my eyes when I would look up or down. Some of the tourists would stop to take pictures of me; I had no idea why they would what to take my picture. I was just loading up the tram with people and then closing the door. Now sometimes, the door did not always move and I would be hanging from it for about a minute, and then it would slowly start to come down so they could be on their way. I thought they were just taking pictures of me hanging from the door, but the word V got to me as they were leaving, and then I saw more cameras come up, and now the full sentence was being repeated as they took off, "She is from V."

I looked at my coworkers as we stood in the hot sun, waiting for the next tram to arrive, and asked them if they knew what that was all about. one of them told me that one of the tourists had asked if I was from the TV show V, and he said yes. "That's when this stranger started to take your picture." I told him that was cruel of him; he should not lie to these people like that.

He told me, "What can it hurt? He will never run into a real star, and you was the closest he would be to one." So for the rest of that day, people would be taking a pictures of me and asking me if I was really one of the stars from *V.*

I would tell them, "No, I just work here."

The next day at work, I was on the lower lot, and now I had a choice of working out in the hot sun all day or working as an actor for a day. I picked actor (I made twenty-five cents more for the day). Little did I know it would be harder inside the sound studio than outside in the sun.

There were three of us, two boys and me. We showed up on the set, and they walked up through what we were to do and how long we would perform. We would each do three shows and the rest until it was our time again to go on. We got placed inside a space suit, and then they would pick someone from the audience to perform one show with us. Each time we did the show, it was with a new audience member. As they were getting the person into the suite, I would just be standing there in mine. Then while we waited to go on, I would try to talk to the person who was now almost face-to-face with me. They would put our helmets on last so not to scare the person whom they just picked from the audience. I don't think they were told them exactly what it was they had just volunteered for. I told this one guy because he looked a little afraid of what he was going to be doing soon, once they put our helmets on, the stool that we were standing on, we would moved away and we would be hanging in the air, and then he would move away from me. But don't be afraid, they will bring him back.

He did not hear anything I just said to him. They put on our helmets, and once they did that, you could not hear anything but the soundtrack playing of what it was that we needed to act out. We got to the part in the show when one of us gets blown away from the other one and does a little space walk by themselves as they float away from the ship. As he started to move away from me, he grabbed at the box that I had on my chest, and he would not let go of it. As he continues to move away from me, I tried to get his hand off me, because I was not the one who moved, only he was. I am doing my best to make it look as if I was trying to hold onto him, but really I was trying to get him to let go of me. The box on my chest was almost at its breaking point when he finally let go of me. I swung back to my spot, and then they slowly brought him back in and then it was the end. They closed the curtains and they placed the step stools back under us, and they took off the helmets, and this man was scared to death. He told me that he did not know he was going to be moving away from me and that is why he grabbed onto me. I was thinking, *I told you, you would be moving and not to grab me*. I just smiled at him and said "Have a wonderful day."

At the end of that day, the two boys I was working with asked me about that man (the one who had grabbed me). I told them that I had told him what was going to happen as I told everyone when we are face-to-face with these people, but he just did not listen to me and I thought he was going to pull me and my wires were going to break. I did everything I could to get that man's hands off the box on my suit. The two boys thought it was funny. That had never happened to them before. They told me it was because I was a girl and he just wanted to grab onto my chest. I just laughed a fake laugh, and we all headed back to the office at the end of the day.

As I headed into the office, Lisa was in there and again flirting with one of the boys. I looked at her and asked her if I could please get a minute with him so I could go over what it was I would be doing next week. She backed up and I just looked at her and said, "You haven't changed at all, have you?"

We all walked out of the office together, and we ran into the man who was impersonating Mr. T. When we walked out into where the public was, everyone ran over and yelled, "Mr. T, Mr. T, we want a picture with you," so he would stop and take pictures with them. They would sometimes ask me to take it for them, and Lisa would just stand there.

One of the tourists looked at me and asked if I was the lady from the TV show called *V*. As I went on to say no, the man pretending to be Mr. T said, "Yes, she is." Now I was in the pictures with these people.

After they left, I asked the Mr. T impersonator why he had done that. He said, "If they think you are a star and want your picture, who cares? They are happy, and you have made their trip to the US a happier one. No harm in making people happy, right?"

I said, "No, but I am not the one who is impersonating a star, you are."

Then he said to me, "No, you just happen to look like one in your uniform and sunglasses."

Lisa was trying to date this man, even though he was not the one she had been sitting on earlier that same day; that was why we had stopped to talk to him. He told us that he was trying to become a singer and asked if we could listen to his tape, so we went off to his car. We listened to his tape. He had a nice enough voice, but the song he sang was Wham's "Careless Whisper." I told him I liked it, but why was he singing someone else song? Why not sing something he wrote? He never asked me to listen to anything again.

Leonard got this bright idea to help me buy a car and that I should ask my dad to help me with getting one. I told Leonard that my dad would not help me get a car; he said to me that if he could help my brother with a car, he could help me get a car. I told him I would try, but he should not hold his breath. I was not his son; I was just his daughter. I called my father and asked him if he could help me get a car. I was now working, and I needed one to get me to and from work. My dad told me he could not help me. So I asked him, since I was going to be eighteen in two months, if he could please send me my share of the child support so I could then get a car of my own since he would not help me buy one.

Once I got the check, Leonard and I went out and got me a used car. Leonard did all the talking while I walked around the lot. He said, "I did it, you have a car now."

I asked him which one was mine. We walked over to an orange V. W. Rabbit stick shift; I looked at Leonard and said, "I do not know how to drive a stick shift. Why would you get me this?"

He said, "I did not have enough money for anything else on the lot. This was the only one I could afford."

As we were driving back to Burbank, he told me that he would teach me how to drive it. So now I was watching what he was doing and listening to what he was saying about when to change gears and how to do it. He dived to his house, got out and, said to me, "Now it is your turn." He walked away from me and said, "Goodbye."

I get out of the car and asked him, "Aren't you going to show me?" He said he did as he went inside his dad's house. So I got back into my car and sat behind the wheel, thinking to myself, *Okay, I can do this*. I started off without any problems driving down the side streets. *I am doing good*, I told myself. I got to the main streets, and now I was in traffic—light traffic but traffic nonetheless—as I got to a light and I had to make a left-hand turn. I, of course, stalled out, and the car behind me started to honk, and now I was trying to start the car and turn at the same time. I stalled again and then I did it again. This time, I made it. I learned how to get into first gear and make a left-hand turn without stalling. I had gotten so mad at Leonard by now that I was not thinking about what it was I was doing, and I made it all the way to my mother's work without stalling out again. Once I made it safely to her work, I realized I had driven my car the entire way alone and without any help from anyone. I did not approve of his method on how to teach someone how to drive a stick shift, but it did work out for the best, for me.

While I was shopping, I saw a dress in Bloomingdale's that I liked, but I needed to ask my mom for some money to get it. The dress was about one hundred and seventy dollars. So she gave me the seventy dollars so I could get the dress. It was white long sleeves, and it was tight fitting through the middle of it, so it showed off my curves in a nice way; it came down just below my knees. I loved the thing. I wore it almost everywhere we went. One day, we were going out to a church function and I was going to wear my dress, so I put it in the bathroom with me as I took a shower. I wanted to give it a steam bath before wearing it that day. As I got out of the shower and unlocked the door, William was there and pushed open the door. I had a towel around me and told him to get out. He told me that I could not wear this dress and to get something else to wear and started to pull it out of my hands. I told him to let go and that I could wear whatever I wanted to wear. He told me that my mother had told him she did not want me to wear this dress and to wear something else, and he pulled harder. I almost lost my towel, so I had to let go of the dress because I did not want to be standing there in the nude with him in the bathroom with me. I told him after he walked away from me and into his room with my dress that I would call my mother and tell her what he had just done. I got dressed, and down to the payphone I went. I told my mother that if he did not give me back my dress, I would one day soon be calling the police on him for child abuse. Then I walked back up the hill we lived on and told him that when she got home, she would have him return my dress to me. She did not say that to me, but I said it anyway.

When she arrived at home, she did not yell at him. She started to yell at me and told me that she told him to take that dress away from me and that I had worn it too many times. I reminded her that I had paid for most of the dress and that she only gave me seventy dollars for the hundred-and-seventy-dollar dress and that she could not just take it away from me. I never saw that dress again, and when I did call the police on my stepfather for child abuse, my mother stepped in and told the officers that I was just an out-of-control step-child who did not like her stepfather and that he had done nothing wrong. The officer came back over to me and told me to hang in there—I was almost eighteen and then I could just walk away from them both and they could not stop me. I got the same advice from my father when I had asked him if I could live with him. I thought as his daughter he would just want to have me come and stay with him, but no, he said that he did not want to cause any trouble with my mom and that I should just stick it out it until I turned eighteen. I asked him, "Then would you want me after I turned eighteen, or if I were a boy, would you take me in now?"

He just looked at me, and I got up, thanked him for his time, and walked away. My dad was not happy when he found out that my mom was pregnant with me. They tried to abort me before the sperm, even made it to the egg. My mother was always calling me retarded because if they had not done what they did to try and abort me, I (as the sperm) would not have made it to the egg. So here I was asking the other half of me and I, once more, had gotten rejected by the one person I looked like; I did not take after my mother. I had always felt that she found me on her doorstep one day. If you put me next to my father, you would see a resemblance; you would know we were father and daughter, but put my brother next to my father— nothing. They did not look like father and son. We joked about it all the time with Charles. Even our mother told us that she believed our dad's best friend was Charles real father and not the one we all called Dad. It's been a family joke for as long as I can remember. So to have him say no to me was heartbreaking to me.

So back home I went, not understanding why both my parents didn't like me. I must have been this biggest mistake in their lives, but I was the middle child. If they did not want to have any more children, then why did she have my sister?

I decided that I could never trust either of them and I would have to make it on my own.

Thank goodness I was working; this way, I could spend most of my time at work and not at home during the summer vacation.

It was 1986, senior year, and now I was eighteen. My mother could no longer threaten me about sending Leonard to jail.

This was also the year the space shuttle *Challenger* exploded.

I got sick again. This time, I told the doctor that I wanted to get my tonsils removed. I told him that I understood that I would get sick again, but I was now eighteen and I wanted them out. He did not argue with me; he just said, "Okay then." I was shocked that he did not try to talk me out of it. I had just overheard him tell the patient in the other room that they would still get sick and that having their tonsils removed would not help them. Maybe they were younger than me, but the doctor did not argue with me at all.

I told my mother that Leonard would be taking me to the hospital the day of my surgery. She was not happy about it, but what could she do?

Leonard picked me up at 5:00 a.m. and drove me to the hospital and then kissed me goodbye. I looked at him and asked him why he was not coming in to wait with me. He tells me it was because he didn't like hospitals and that he would never go back into one after his mother was dying in the hospital. I looked at him and told him, "I told my mother not to come because you would be here with me, and now you are just dropping me off and leaving?"

He looked at me and said, "Bye."

So I went in, and at some point, my mother showed up and asked me where Leonard was. I told her that he dropped me off outside and told me it was because his mother had died in a hospital, and that is why he would not be coming in and waiting with me.

I was now in the room getting prepped for surgery. My mother had gone, Leonard was no help at all, and I am alone. They wheeled me into the hallway and then put an IV in my arm. The nurse looked at me and told me, "Now this will be cold." I remember looking at him and trying to repeat what he had just said to me, but I couldn't. He told me everything would be fine, and that was the last thing I remembered.

I woke up in my room; there was another girl across the room from me. I believed she was also there to have her tonsils removed. She looked at me, and then for some strange reason—I do not know why—blood started to run into her IV, and that is when a couple of nurses ran in and pulled back the curtain so I could not see what was going on.

I got up out of bed. I noticed that my whole body hurt and that the IV they stuck in my arm had been moved to the middle of my right arm. I also had this numbing feeling in my mouth. I walked into the bathroom, and I looked in the mirror, and I almost fainted when I looked at myself. I looked like a ghost walking. I started to cry, and then I tried to open my mouth to see why it was so numb. There was a big lump on my tongue, and I was shocked to see it. I stared at myself and started to think, *What did they do to me?* I just sat down on the toilet. Now I was thinking, *Okay, the IV has been moved, my arms and legs are sore, and I have a big lump on my tongue.* I must have woken up enough to fight them. They had to strap me down and hold down my tongue—that is why I have this lump on it. I got up walked back to the sink, opened my mouth again, turned on the cold water, and tried to put some cold water on my tongue. The sink was too small to stick my head in it.

After a couple of tries, I just gave up and went back to my bed. The nurse was just moving back the curtain as I was coming out of the bathroom. One of them asked me how I was doing, and I did my best to ask her what had happened to me, but she did not understand anything I was saying to her. I then opened my mouth to show her the lump on my tongue, and all she could say to me was that it would go away over time. She then asked me if I needed anything. I said no and waved her away.

The girl and I tried to talk to one another, but that did not work. I got a call from Leonard that night. As soon as he heard me, he, of course, thought I was in pain and that he would not keep me long on the phone. Turned out that my throat did not hurt at all. It was just my tongue, and I was so frustrated with the fact that I could not talk; I just started to cry. My head was screaming, "I am okay," but my mouth would not let these words come out of it because my tongue had this dumb lump on it. I tried holding my tongue while I talked, but that did nothing to help me. The girl across the room tried to comfort me from her bed, telling me everything would be all right and this was only temporary. I said "Thank you" the best I could and then I went to sleep. The next day was not better at all; every inch of my tongue hurt.

My doctor came in and told me how everything had gone smoothly and that in about a week or two I should be able to eat solid food, but I should take it easy for now. I tried to ask him what happened, but all he could say was not to worry, things would be back to normal soon, just take it easy. I thought to myself, *Easy? I can't even talk—how easy could that be? I can't even yell for help if I needed to.*

Leonard did stop by and visit me once I got home. We sat out in his car, and I tried to talk to him, I showed him my tongue, and then he asked me if I was feeling up to having sex, and he started to lean toward me. I pushed him back and tried to say to him, *Are you kidding, sex now? I can't even talk.* I just grabbed my throat and looked at him. He backed away and said, "Okay, then maybe you should go in then. I don't want to keep you if you are not feeling up to having sex now."

So he left, and I went in. As I was lying in my bed, I was thinking, *What the heck? I just got out of the hospital, and the first thing he wants to do is have sex?* As I was lying there thinking how mad at him I was right now, I started to smell a girl's perfume. Now no one in the house was up and getting dressed, but it was a strong smell and I know it was not coming from the house.

By the end of the week, I was better and now I could talk, and yes, I had a lot to say to Leonard by the time I saw him again. First thing was who was the girl he had taken out after he left me, and what was he thinking—I would just have sex with him because he felt bad?

He tried to tell me that he did not go out after he left me, that he went home. I looked at him and told him not to lie to me. I could smell her perfume, and he knew that I was allergic to perfumes, so it was not something I used.

He came clean and told me that he did take a girl (someone I knew from school) out because I was not the kind of girl you would take to a party and she was. He said to me, "You don't drink or do anything fun."

I said, "Really? I think I would have had a lot of fun at the party. Just because I don't drink, do drugs, and smoke does not mean I do not know how to have fun."

At school, the first thing I did was go up to this girl's boyfriend and told him to be very careful with her; she didn't know how to be faithful. Later that same day, this girl Leonard took out came up to me and started to say how now her boyfriend and her had just broken up because of something I said. I told her, "You did go out with Leonard, right?" She looked at me, and then over my shoulder, I turned to see that it was her boyfriend walking up to us; I think he wanted to hear the truth. She said yes, but he was the one who had called her and picked her up.

I looked at the boy and said, "Enough said," and walked away.

Leonard then came by to ask me what I did. I told him I was just looking out for a friend (the boyfriend of the girl he took out). "She and you like to party together, then the two of you should date each other. I don't need this." He then told me to get in the car because he needed to talk to me. So I did, and we drove to a nearby park to talk. He told me something about how she never got to do anything because her parents are very strict and that her brother, who happened to be the son on the hit TV show *Married with Children*, he gets to do everything. She (this girl) was just trying to fit in, and she needed someone to talk her out, so he was doing the big brother thing with her, making sure that she got home safe—that was all it was and nothing more. They had talked about boyfriend/girlfriend problems and how she thought she was pregnant, on and on about her, and he felt sorry for her.

Lucky for me, by the time I got to my senior year, I had taken most of all my required classes the first half of the school year so that by the second half, I could relax and just do some TA work and have an easy second half of the school year.

I took Leonard to my prom. This one boy in my gym class had asked me to prom, and I reminded him that I had a boyfriend and that the best I could do for him was ask my sister to go with him and then we could all hang out together.

At prom, Leonard and I got our pictures taken, and then we went in to sit at a table. I asked him if he wanted to dance, and he said no, so I went out to the dance floor and danced with my sister and the boy who liked me. We were dancing to Madonna's "Material Girl" when Leonard came over and told me we needed to leave.

I looked at him and said that we had not even eaten yet; he told me again he wanted to go. So I told my sister I would be leaving now.

Leonard and I ended up at a hotel for the night. Leonard made me go up to the window and get the room. He also told me to tell them I was alone, so I did.

At my graduation, my father did show up, but this time he did not bring his parents and he did not offer to take me out for dinner. I asked him if he wanted to go out; he told me that he thought I would have plans with my mom or Leonard. I told him, "No, I told Leonard that I was going to have dinner with you." He then told me that he did not plan on staying and that he needed to head home; he did not want to be away from his parents too long.

My mom came over after my father walked away and asked me if I was going to dinner with him. I told her no, he had other plans. She then said to me, "Told you he never wanted girls and he only loves his son. Remember he took Charles out to dinner just last year?" So now I got to hear it all over again how my father never wanted me and that we girls were nothing all the way home in her car with her, William, and the two babies. We girls were nothing unless we had a man by our side.

I thought to myself, *Don't say a word to her, just let her go off on me. I do have a man, and you don't like him.* She even asked me about Leonard and why I was not with him. Did he not care about me and my big day? I finally opened my mouth and told her, "No, he did, only I told him I was going to spend time with my family and that we could celebrate later." That kept her quiet for a while.

That summer, I worked in the warehouse at Universal Studios; I put price tags on all the items that were going into the gift shops. Not many people got chosen to work in the warehouse; management had to really trust the people they send into the warehouse. It was very easy to take items from there.

So when I showed up, the manager looked at me and told me that they must trust me to send me here and reminded me that if I took anything, I would go to jail. Then he handed me a pricing gun and showed me what to do.

On my lunch break, I would head over to one of the snack bars on the back lot of Universal Studios. On one of my breaks one day, I was sitting at a table reading a book and eating my lunch when the cast members of *Charles in Charge* walked by me and sat down at one of the tables behind me. I could hear them talking and laughing about something, when one of them decided to start throwing French fries at the other cast members. I was thinking to myself, *Please God, don't have then throw any my way,* when one of them said, "Hey, let's dip them in the ketchup." That is when I got up and walked away. I could tell by the way they were acting that they would (by mistake of course) throw some my way, and I did not want to get ketchup on my uniform; after all, I was the one who had to clean it and not some maid.

Leonard and I went out to see *Aliens*, and on my way home that night, alone in my car, this man came up on my left side and slowed down to keep pace with me. If I slowed down, he would slow down; if I sped up, he would speed up. I turned off onto the 118 freeway, and here he came, up from behind me. I looked over my left side and I saw him jerking off and smiling at me as I was coming up to the next overpass to head home on the 210 freeway. I stayed in the third lane, and he was in the second lane. As we got closer to the split in the freeway, I was going to make it look as if I was going to be going on the northbound freeway and not the southbound. At the very last minute, I switched lanes and headed off on the southbound 210, and I watched him continue on the north 210. I was finally free from him. Now I looked around to see if there was a police car on the freeway. But no, I thought to myself, *Where is the police when you need one, especially at two in the morning?* Here I was thinking an alien could jump out in front of my car and I would have to fight it off, but no, something even sicker then and scarier than an alien, a man playing with himself and trying to get me to pull over to help him with it.

I had an opportunity to work at the amphitheater at Universal Studios. This meant I would be working late at night and I could have my mornings off. This way I could hang out with Leonard during the day (if he was off). I worked at the souvenir stand outside the stadium. One night, as the concert was ending, this man walked by the stand, looked at me and my coworker, then walked back to us and asked us what we thought about Velcro. He said he was going to replace zippers with Velcro and wanted to know if we would buy pants with a Velcro front in place of the zipper. We both said yes and that it would be easier to get on and off your pants. He told us his name, but I did not know who he was. Then he looked at me and said, "Look for Joe Boxers, that's me."

I looked at him and said, "I know of Joe Boxers." He smiled and shook our hands and walked away. The young man I was working with was overly excited because of who we had just met and that we helped him with this new idea with this Velcro thing, and anytime we see pants with Velcro, we know that it was because we said we loved that idea. I then cleaned up the stand I was in, and then I would into the vault to count out the money we made that night. Not many of us were allowed in the vault to count money, and they had armed guards to make sure we were not robbed.

Leonard was working at some job with Lockheed in Burbank at the time. He dropped out of college. We had talked about how one of us should attend college and get a degree, so that way, if we did get married and had children, one of us would need to be a role model for them and one of us should have a degree to fall back on and not just get through life in a job that made minimum wage. I told him since he had dropped out of college that I would then have to enroll because I did not want our children to think education was not important. I knew how important it was because I was moved around a lot as a child and I did not get a proper education, and life was hard enough as it was, and then to add, not knowing how to spell and being dyslexic made it harder, but I was willing to go to college. He told me that I should get a second job; this one would be at St. Joseph's Hospital in Burbank. I asked him why. He said because it would get me a better foothold on this "job security thing" I was looking for. He himself had the opportunity to change jobs and better himself. Lockheed would be closing in the Burbank area and he would no longer have a job in a few months, so he decided to apply with the post office. It did not pay him as much as Lockheed when he first started, but I told him, if he did get the job with the post office, he would, after time, be making more money than he was currently getting now, and he was young enough at that time and still living at home. So to make the move now would be a great opportunity for him. He was afraid he would not pass the test. Leonard always tried to get others to help him with everything because he was from Vietnam and he felt he did not speak, read, and/or write English well enough; he would always say he was not smart enough, and I would always have to remind him that he was and that I had faith in him. I told him he should put in a resume for the post office and I would put one in at Saint Joseph's.

I was now working in the mornings at Saint Joseph's in the cafeteria as a cashier and then working three nights a week at the amphitheater at Universal Studios, and Leonard was now working at the post office in Long Beach. I still lived at home.

Charles had gotten into a fight with William over locking his door while he was at college. William would pick the lock to open his door, and then when Charles came home, he would find the door to his room was unlocked and the babies had been in his room. He would get upset and tell William that he had no right going into his room. This upset William, and the two of them got into a fistfight. Now William was about 5'5" and three hundred or more pounds, so when he hit my brother, who was 5'8" and only one hundred and maybe twenty pounds, you know which one of them had the upper hand, and no, it was not Charles. He did not have any kind of training like William; William was in the army reserves. When our mother came home that night and my brother confronted her about the door and how William should not be opening the door without his permission, our mother took William's side; that is when Charles, with the help of our grandmother, moved out.

When the school year started back up for Lorraine, William was now the one who had to take her to school. I no longer could because I was working at Saint Joseph's, and I did not have the time anymore to drive her and the babies to school or the babysitter's house.

Our mother was getting calls from the school letting her know that Lorraine was showing up late for her first-period class. When our mom asked Lorraine why she could not get to school on time anymore, she told our mother that William was stopping by the babysitter's house and he would go in for some time and by the time he came out, she would be late for school. Lorraine told our mother that William was having an affair with the babysitter. Our mother asked him about it, and instead of leaving him, he was now dropping Lorraine off at school first. He told our mother that the women did not have any means of getting to the grocery store because she was babysitting his daughter. William said, so he would then take them to the store and then bring her home with the groceries. My sister said that he was lying because she was sitting in the car while he was inside. But our mother believed him and not Loraine; now he would have to take her to school first. Lorraine was no longer late for school, and now she was no longer a witness to what he was doing behind our mother's back.

One day at work as a cashier in the cafeteria at St. Joseph's Hospital in Burbank, I ran across a red five-dollar bill, and so I traded it out for a green one that I had on me.

I took it into a coin shop with Leonard, and the man told us that even though it was printed in red ink, the face value was still only five dollars, so I take it back from the man and thanked him, and Leonard and I walked out of the store. Leonard did not believe the man and thought he was lying to us, hoping we would just leave it with him. I looked at him and said, "I don't believe that." If he wanted it, he would have tried to get us to leave it with him. Leonard told me it was because he was with me (that is why he did not try any tricks to get me to leave it with him). I told Leonard not to worry about it—that I had it and I was going to keep it. I showed it to my sisters, and then I put it back in my wallet and stuck my purses under my mattress. I went into the bather room, and by the time I came out, William and the girls were gone. I thought nothing more of the five-dollar bill. I grabbed my purse from under my mattress, and off to work I went. It was a weekday, so I did not have to go to my second job that night. I headed over to meet up with Leonard at his dad's house. he asked me if he could see the five-dollar bill again because be believed still that it was worth more than just five dollars. I told him not to worry about it. I was just going to hold on to it; I did not want to trade it in or even try to get money for it. I liked it and thought it was cool. He insisted on seeing it again, so I pulled out my wallet to find that the red five-dollar bill was gone.

Now Leonard was upset with me over this five-dollar bill. I looked at him. I told him, "I believe my stepfather has it, and I will get it back." I asked Leonard why he was so angry about this. He told me it was because he believed it was worth more than just five dollars and he wanted to take it to someone he knows who knows more about this than the person we took it to, to see what the real worth of this bill was, and now, I had lost it. I had Leonard demanding I get that five-dollar bill back. As I was driving home, I thought to myself, *Why did I even trade it out? I should have just left it alone. This bill is not worth all this headache.*

I got home and confronted William about the bill, and my mother stood there, looking at me as I asked him for it back. I told him it was worth nothing more than what was printed on it and that I had already taken it in and to have someone look at it for me. My mom said that William would never take anything from me and that I was lying about this bill and she would know because she went into his wallet all the time and she did not see it and I needed to drop this now.

The next time I was with Leonard, he asked me about it, and I told him that it was gone and that was that, so he would need to just forget about it. My stepfather had taken it, and now it was gone; there is nothing more I can do. He then told me I needed to start giving him my money so he could keep it safe for me; I should not trust William anymore. So Leonard would now get some of my paycheck, not all of it, because when I started to work at the hospital they had me open an account and started saving about 30 percent of my paycheck; they then matched what I put in dollar for dollar. I got to keep my smaller check, the one I got from amphitheater, my part-time job. When I handed Leonard my paycheck, he blew up at me. He wanted to know where my money was going and why I had to put so much of it away. I told him that I had no choice—I had to open an account and start putting money away; it is what they have you do when you work there and have an account in their bank. I did not understand way he was so angry at me about this. I was think-ing, *Now I am saving money at my job and with him—no big deal.* I thought nothing more of it because anytime I needed something, Leonard would make sure I had it.

At some point, he took my rabbit and got me a different car. He surprised me with this new car (it was a used car), a Toyota Camry in a light tan color. I tell him I didn't need a new car, so why would he get me one without asking me first? My rabbit would leak when it rained. I could not wear shoes when it was raining or my shoes would get wet. With this new car, I could wear shoes—no more leaking car. It was nice, but I did not want it.

He asked me to take out a personal loan at the credit union with Saint Joseph's Hospital. I did, and then when I got the check, he asked me for it. He said he would hold on to it for me and that

I would make payments on the loan and then after about six or so months, he would give me the money to pay it off. He said, "This is how you gain credit, and when you pay it back early, then the bank will trust you, so then you can borrow even more money the next time." I give him the check thinking nothing of it and that I would be paying this off soon. So when I made my payments on the loan each month, I would put about twenty dollars extra to it so that I would pay it off even faster. I do not like owing people money, and I do not like credit cards at all. I feel if you do not have the money in cash for something, then you just don't get it. I do understand that when you buy a car, you have to borrow the money, but I would and still to this day put more money toward the bill than just the amount they were asking for to help pay it off faster. When I handed Leonard the cash after I made my loan payment (I would cash my check that way Leonard did not have to cash it or whatever he did with it), he had noticed it was less than what I was giving him before I had taken out this loan; he wanted to know what I was doing with the money. I reminded him that I was now paying off the loan he had made me get and this is all that I had left from my paycheck. I showed him the receipt for my loan payment. He was not happy that I was putting more toward the loan than what the monthly payment was. I looked at him and told him that was not his business how much I gave back to the bank. If I wanted to pay it off faster, that was my choice, not his. I just wanted it paid off even faster than what he had planned. He then told me that I would need to start paying the asking amount on the loan and not put more than that toward the loan. I did not listen to him, so the next month, I did the same; he again was not happy with me. I just looked at him and I said, "It is my loan. I will pay it off however I want." He somehow came up with the money the next month and he went in with me to pay it off. After I paid off the loan, Leonard then told me to ask if I can take out another loan, this time for twice as much than the last one. The woman helping us must have know something was up because she told us that I would need to wait about two months before asking for another loan. Leonard got upset and said to me, "Let's go" after arguing with this woman for about five minutes.

He asked her, "If this is a bank, then why would you say no to people asking to borrow money? We did just pay off her loan, and she should have excellent credit and track record because she always paid on time." We got to the car, and he looked at me and said, "You told her to say *no*."

I looked at him and said, "What? I was by your side the entire time—did you hear me say anything to her?"

"Well, you women have a way of communicating to each other without words."

I looked at him and said, "Yes, because that works so well with you."

He said to me, "I am not a woman. Don't be so stupid."

My sister graduated from high school. I was not there because I was working, but from what my sister told me, our mother almost got arrested for child abuse. She had Nancy on a leash and Betty was in her arms as they were walking across the football field to meet up with Lorraine after the ceremony. Our mother dropped the leash, and Nancy took off running; our mom stepped on the leash, and Nancy fell on her butt and started to cry. This is when someone called the police and they tried to arrest our mother, but she was yelling at the police officer, "What did you want me to do, just let her run so someone could just take her then you would be out here because she had been kidnapped, and not just falling on her butt?" Our mother had both babies with her—Nancy, who is about three or four years old, and Betty, who is two or three, and they were both crying. My mom was yelling at the police officer, and our dad was standing back with Lorraine watching it all. William was not standing by his wife's side with this one because another police officer was keeping him back and away from her, but our mother managed to sweet talk (argue) herself out of getting arrested. My father told my sister the reason they did not take her in was that they did not want to try to put the babies and her into the back seat of the police car. So they let her off with a warning.

This is the summer that David was out visiting with us; Lorraine joined the navy. She had, two years earlier, taken our grandmothers car (when Charles was in choir practice) and driven one of her girlfriends home. She made it all the way back to the school without any problems. Then as she was turning, a police officer came up behind her in his car. She got nervous and made a U-turn on a residential street and hit a parked car. The police officer stopped to ask her if she was all right, and that is when he discovered that she was underage. She was then taken into custody, and when she appeared in front of the judge, he told her she would be paying every penny back to our grandmother for the damage done to the parked car and our grandmother's car.

This was the reason she decided to join the navy; she also could further her education and pay back our grandmother.

Now I was left alone with the babies and David that summer. William had gotten fired from his job at the phone company, and now he was at the house with us.

The time I spent at the house was mostly now spent packing up things because we had to move. David and I started in the garage. William was in the army reserves. One day, they had finally gotten hold of him to let him know that they had some money for him (I believe this was the main reason we did not have a phone in the house). Once he showed up at the reserves building, William was met by two MPs, and they handcuffed him and started to take him away. Our mother was not happy about this and asked what was going on. That is when one of the MPs told her that he had missed some of his service times and he needed to send one week (or maybe two) in the army jail. I then told my mother after she had gotten back into the car, "See, even the army has problems with him. You should just leave him now."

David found some army boxes with ammo and MREs (meals ready to eat) in them, so David and I started to open them and eat the food. We did not eat what William cooked mainly because we did not know what it was and we did not like it. So when it came time to eat dinner, David and I had already eaten. The problem with that was that if I did not eat, the babies would not eat, and if I said I did not like something, they then did not like it. This upset William, and he would tell our mom that I was teaching his daughters to hate his food. She told me that I had to eat his food. I told her no, I did not like it, and I would not eat anything he cooked. I made my own food, and the babies would eat what I cooked, so by the time William got around to cooking, they would not be hungry. William was upset when he found out that someone had eaten his MREs; I never told him who did it.

By the time we moved into a three-bedroom apartment over in Sherman Oaks, William now had to get rid of me. Then it would just be his two daughters and our mom.

One night, Leonard and I were planning on going night fishing, so when I got off of work at the hospital, he took me over to the new place we lived. We had just moved in three days earlier, and I had my own room for the first time, and I would lock the door to my room so that the babies could not get in and mess up my room. The one wall in this room was a sliding accordion door; this door did not lock, so this is how I got in and out of my room. So when I came in and headed to the accordion door (I had to now move some things out of my way because William had but some boxes in front of the door), William starts yelling at me not to use this door and to go around to the other door that was located in the hallway. I told him I had locked it and that I was going to be using this for my door. I did not want the door that entered into the hallway by their door to be open, so I locked it to keep them out.

I then entered the room, and as I was crossing through the room to the side that had the closet, William came busting into the room and started attacking me. I yelled at him to leave me alone or I would call the police on him. Now Leonard was out in the hallway waiting for me so we can go fishing when he heard me fighting with my stepfather. He tried to come in and help me; my mother pushes him out and shuts the door on him. Now Leonard was pounding on the front door and kicking it in. As he came in, my mom yelled for her husband. He got off me because now I was pinned under him half on the bed and half on the floor. When he heard my mom yell for help, William ran out of the room and hit Leonard on the side of his face (cold-cocked him). I then came out of the room, and everyone was yelling at each other. That was when Leonard grabbed me, and we went over to the liquor store to call the police. The police showed up and they talked to all of us, then one of them pulled me over and asked me if my mom was pregnant.

I told him, "No, she is just fat." He looked at me and then asked Leonard if he had hit her in the stomach because she was saying that she was now going to have a miscarriage as she grabbed her stomach (because she said Leonard had hit her in the stomach). He then looked at me and asked me how old I was. I tell him I was twenty. He then told me to get some of my things and never come back. I told him I had nowhere to go. Leonard told me not to worry about that. "And don't even bother with grabbing anything, let's just go."

So we went fishing, and I thought to myself as I sat on the pier, *I am now homeless and have nowhere to go. What do I do now?* Leonard came over and sat down next to me and grabbed the sleeping bag and said he wanted to have sex.

I told him, "No, we are out in the open and we could get arrested."

He told me, "Don't worry, no one is around and they won't know what we are doing. Get in the bag." So we had sex on the pier in the sleeping bag.

Now we spent most of the early morning on the pier, and then we decided to go home. As we were headed to his sister's house, that is when it hit me hard: *I don't have anywhere to go.* I thought that I was going to be homeless, but Leonard asked his sister if I could live with her and her family. I would rent one of her rooms. She asked me what happened and if I could go back and live with my mom. I told her the story and that I did not believe my mom would ever take me back. So she let me rent out the room, but I had to pay her on time. I told her yes, I would, and now I had to call my mom to see if I could go over and get my things. She told me William would have them packed and ready for me when I got over there at 5:00 p.m. My mom told me that I was not to call her if after a week with Leonard, he decided he did not want me anymore. She did not want me to come running back to her either.

I went over to the apartment to see that my stuff had just been thrown out in the yard and anyone could just pick up whatever they wanted and walk away with some, if not all, my things. I picked up what they threw out and called the police for help. They came over. They went inside to talk to William and then came back to me and told me that if I was missing anything to make a note of it and take them to small claims court.

I was thinking, *Nice, I have to sue my mom? Forget that.*

CHAPTER FOUR
Harmony

How wonderful it is, how pleasant, for God's people to live together in harmony! It is like the dew on Mount Hermon, falling on the hills of Zion for there the Lord commanded the blessing, even life for evermore.

—Psalm 133:1, 3

I was now living with his sister Cindy at her house and attending his church. I did not have much contact with my mother anymore; everything was now all about Leonard.

I attended weddings, parties, and church events, and everyone would tell me how much Leonard had changed for the better. I must have been a good influence on him. Leonard did (at least when he was in my presence) not drink, smoke, and use curse words.

When Leonard would come over to his sister's house, he had to sneak around to the back and come in through the back door that led into my room. We were both told that he could not spend the night. If he was going to be spending the nights with me, I would have to move out. His oldest sister was helping me out and not helping him by allowing me to live with her and her family just for the two of us to be together against my mother's will.

We both understood this, and I had promised her he would not spend the nights with me.

He knocked, and I got up, opened the door, and reminded him that he could not spend the night here with me. He told me he would leave, but he just needed to be with me right now because he was upset over something.

As we lay in each other's arms (and anytime we were alone together under the stars), I would tell him, "I need you to promise me that anytime you feel lonely and when people said anything about us being together (your family and friends, my family and friends) anytime they said anything about us being together, I need you to remember this moment, us laying here together, holding on to each other. Nothing else matters but us. You need to promise me you will always come back to this moment. Remember how you are feeling right now, and know that I would never hurt you. Together we work, together we can move mountains. I just need you to trust in this moment and us. Separate us, we do not work. Together, we work. Can you promise me this?"

He said, "You know we will fight."

I told him, "Of course we will fight—that is part of life—but if you always remember how much we love one another right now, here together in each other's arms, nothing and no one can or could ever come between us if you always remember this moment and the love we share for each other."

He then fell asleep in my arms.

I had to wake him up and tell him to get out before his sister and her family got up. I did not want to get kicked out of another place.

I lived with Cindy, Leonard's oldest sister, for about one year before I found out that Leonard had not always paid his sister on time. She stopped me one day and asked me to pay her the rent. I told her that I would have to ask her brother for the money. She looked at me, and then she called me stupid. I just looked at her and said, "What?" I was shocked at the fact that she had called me stupid. She did not know me, so why would she call me stupid?

After work, I met up with Leonard to get the rent money from him to give to his sister. I told him that his sister had called me stupid because I had to get my money from him to pay her.

I asked him, "Why would she call me stupid?"

He told me that she did not speak English very well and that I must have misunderstood what she said.

I told him, "No, she was talking to me, and I understood every-thing she was saying, and she called me stupid. What are you doing, and why are you not paying your sister for me on time?"

He told me he would take care of it.

The next time I saw Cindy, I asked her if she got her money. She said yes. I thanked her again and told her that I appreciated everything she was doing for me and if she needed me to watch her children for her, I would be more than glad to help out.

I would make the boys lunch in the morning and help them with their homework and make sure that they got to bed on time; I did everything I could to fit in and became a part of his family.

Cindy's husband never really said anything to me other than him calling me stupid when I saw him, and he would always just move his head from left to right when I was in his presence. I don't think he liked me very much, but I was a white girl moving into an Asian family.

At work, I also had to deal with the white and Asian thing. Leonard's sister (Renee) worked at the hospital. She worked in the dietary office in the kitchen downstairs, and I worked as a cashier in the cafeteria. When I would go down into the kitchen for my lunch, one of the cooks (a German man) would say that if I married this Asian boy, I would have little Asian babies. I looked at him and told him, "Yes, and you would have little German babies. Do you have a problem with that?"

Renee (Leonard's sister), who worked here, was standing not too far away when I was talking to the cook, and I looked at him and said, "You know Renee and you like her, right? I am dating her brother."

He looked at her then at me. That was when his attitude changed. From that moment on, he did not have a problem with me dating an Asian boy because he knew Renee and he liked her (as a person). Some people just walk around looking at others for their skin color and not for the person they truly are. I never once looked at Leonard as an Asian; when I looked at him, I saw the soul within him. He did have a problem with me being white and so did his family even though they did their best to get along with me. Behind my back, they would talk, and this would upset Leonard a lot.

Leonard would tell me how much his family did not trust me and that they really did not like me. I told him that it did not matter what they said. It was what he was saying and how he felt about me that mattered. I would ask him, "Do you remember I told you no matter what anyone said about us, family or friends, as long as we stayed together and worked together as a team we would be fine and things will work out for the two of us, do you want this to work?"

He told me that people must be thinking to themselves, *What is that white girl doing with such an ugly Asian boy?*

I would tell him it did not matter what other people were thinking about us; it only mattered what he thought, and he was not ugly.

Not only did I felt like I was fighting everyone on this planet to be with him but I also had to put aside what our zodiac signs wrote about how Aries and Virgo did not get along. Aries is the baby of the Zodiac and needed a lot of attention (him). The Virgo was the nurturer and would bend over backward to help others (me).

I would get so overwhelmed with everything and everyone I would drive over to Leonard's mother's grave to sit and talk to her. I would ask her if she felt I was doing the right thing, with being with him and allowing him to control just about everything I did. I would get this warm feeling as if someone was hugging me. I know she understood what I was going through and that she would always be by my side. I did not know this woman when she was alive, but I knew she would always have my back, not like my mother. I would just think of Leonard's mom, and she would come around me and give me a hug anytime I would find myself on the outs with Leonard. One Saturday, when I was sitting in his church, a woman (white) came over to me and put her hand on my shoulder and said, "You will get used to it."

Leonard saw her, and after she walked away from me, he came over to me and asked me what she had asked and/or said to me.

I told him all she had said was that I would get used to this.

He then said to me, 'That must be the future you telling the younger you things will work out." This woman who came over to me was old, but I did not believe that she was me. I just thought that she also loved an Asian man like me and she knew how hard of a road it would be for me. I did, after all, go to a Vietnamese church service and I did not speak or understand Vietnamese.

I no longer worked in the cafeteria. I was now working in the dictation office at the hospital, and I stopped working at the amphitheater at nights. I would take the reports to the patient's charts; I would get the tapes ready for the women in the office who did all the typing of the reports. We had to make sure the reports got into the patient's charts ASAP. That way, if they were being seen by another physician, they would have the findings already in the chart and not have to hunt down the other physician that was working on that same patient.

Leonard and I moved into an apartment together in Burbank not far from St. Joseph's Hospital. His family also moved to a new house in Burbank that same year. The sister (Cindy) the one I lived with bought the house they were living in from her father, and then she rented it out. She bought a house not far from her dad's new house. Renee moved into her own house after she got married; she too lived in Burbank.

We all attended the same church together.

Leonard came home one day and saw that I was wearing a T-shirt. I had just done the laundry, and I had decided to wear one of Leonard's T-shirts around the apartment while I cooked dinner. It was summer, and I was hot. I closed the blinds in the living room so no one could see in. He walks in and started yelling at me and throwing me against the wall and pulling at the T-shirt to get it off me.

I kept pushing him back and yelling at him, "I have nothing on under this, what is your problem?" He just kept pushing me into the wall and trying to pull the shirt off me. I finally gave up, and he got the shirt off me, and I walked into the bed room to put on something. I looked at him and said as I walked by, "I hope you are happy now."

As I was putting on some clothes, the police showed up. One of our neighbors must have called them because of all the noise we were making. The officers came in to talk to me and asked me if I was all right. I told them yes, I was fine. They asked me what had happened, and I told them that Leonard had gotten upset because I was wearing his T-shirt and cooking in it.

The one officer looked at me and said, "You know, mixed couples don't work." Then they left.

I asked Leonard what happened. He told me that the shirt I was wearing belonged to one of his friends and that this friend had a skin disease and he did not want me to catch it. I told him, "First, why do you have your friends T-shirt here and in our hamper, and second, I had already washed it, so you have no reason to act the way you did, and if you had come in and talked to me and not shoved me around, you would have found out that I had just gotten done cleaning it. Whatever skin disease this friend has is now on all our clothes, thank you very much for that." I did not believe his story about the friend and the skin disease. Leonard then asked me what I had told the police. "I told him that you had come in and you were upset because I was wearing what I thought was your T-shirt and you pushed me into the wall and then pulled it off me. Then the officer said to me that mixed races don't always work because they misunderstand what the other one is saying and also how they treat the women in that culture is different than how we treat our women here in the States."

My mother bought a four-bedroom mobile home and moved it to a mobile home park in Action. My grandmother and William's mother moved in with them. My mother had asked me to come up and stay with the grandparents while she and William had to go to Fresno to help with the selling of his parents' house because William's father had died. While they were up in Fresno, William's family got together for a family reunion. While my mother was attending William's family reunion, she ran across some of her family. It turned out that William and my mother were related to one another. William and my mother were distant cousins.

I spent the weekend with my grandmother and William's mom. William's mom had a stroke, so she could no longer walk on her own and she needed someone to feed her. I did not have to bathe her because William did that before he left and they would only be gone for the weekend and he would then bathe her when he got back.

I sat down to feed her. I looked into her eyes, and without saying anything to her out loud, I thought, *Now you know what kind of son you have.* She looked long and hard into my eyes, and I could feel her pain. After I fed her and then cleaned her up, the grandparents would go off for an afternoon nap. I put on some laser-disc movies, ones that I had not watched for a long time: The Beatles' *Sgt. Pepper's Lonely Hearts Club Band* and *The Thing* (1982).

On Sunday, they came home, and I went home after spending some time with the baby sisters, and they asked me about inbreeding; I was shocked at that comment. I did not know they knew anything at all about inbreeding; no one had used that term with them. Our mom came over to us and told me that she and William were related.

I looked at her and told her, "I told you not to marry him. You got lucky that the kids came out normal." I then left to go home.

David had decided to leave his dad in Colorado and come live with our mom.

My sister Lorraine was now married and having her first baby. Charles was doing his editing thing. Charles had gone to college to become an editor for the film industry. Charles always had Lorraine and I perform in his plays as children. We would be acting out something and Lorraine would get bored or she would just get tired of Charles telling her how the scene should go, and then Lorraine would get mad and walk away.

I decide to go back to school and take a typing class. I was about three days into class when I got a phone call from my mother telling me that I had to fly out to the East Coast to be with my sister. Lorraine was now on bed rest. I told my mom that I could not go and that Lorraine would not be having the baby at this time and that I should wait until after she had the baby. Then I could help her out more. I told my mom I had just enrolled in an adult class and it was not refundable and that I could not miss more than three days or I would be dropped. She was asking me to go for one week.

I had vacation time at work. I just did not feel I should go before she had her baby, but my mom bought me a ticket, and off I went.

Leonard was beyond mad at me. He told me, all I ever did was drop my life and run to help my mother.

I looked at him and said, "This is the only time she has ever asked me to do anything, and my sister needs me, and my mom has already bought the ticket. I will be back in a week."

Off to Bethesda, Washington, I went. Lorraine and I went sightseeing. She took me to her job; we had a nice time hanging out together. One day, this big storm came through—lighting, thunder, heavy rain—it was amazing. The lighting would make every hair on your body stand on end, and the thunder would shake the windows because it was so loud. I loved it. I went out on her balcony. Lorraine told me not to go out to far, so I came back in and I just stuck out my head; that way, I could get the full effect of the storm. It woke me up inside. I had not seen a storm like that since living in California, we do not get to experience storms like that. Lorraine had her baby that next week

I got back to Burbank to find that Leonard was going to the gambling casinos now and not spending much time at home with me—not that he did before; it was just a lot less now.

My little brother David had gotten into an accident riding his bicycle to his football practice. A car had hit him, and now he was at Kaiser Hospital, and now our mother called me and she started out with how horrible of a sister I was and how I was not visiting my brother in the hospital. I let her finish and then I asked her, "What was going on? This was the first time I have heard about the accident." I let Leonard know that I was going to the hospital and I asked him if he would like to go with me.

Leonard just looked at me and said, "Off to do something for her again."

I walked out and drove over to the hospital to see my baby brother. I got to his room, and I walked over to his bed and asked him how he was doing. He told me he was fine, then he asked me if I thought he would ever walk again.

I looked at him and told him, "Of course you will walk again. You may not be able to play football professionally, but you will walk again. Maybe you will need to change careers." We both laughed. He showed me his leg and told me that he had a metal rod that ran from his hip all the way down to his ankle. I looked at him and told him, "Not to worry, with non-professional football, nobody cares how funny you look running just that you can make a touchdown." We both laughed again. I went home, and by the next time I decided to visit him again (two days later), he had already been sent home. I do not know how long he had been in the hospital, but the moment I did know, I did spend time with him; that way, our mother could not say I was a horrible sister.

After Williams's mother died, he got into a fight with my grandmother, and she called the police, and they gave my grandmother some information on where she could go to get help. She would soon move out of her daughter's house and out to Lancaster into a living home for the elderly. She had an apartment of her own because she could take care of herself; she did not need the help of anyone. When I found out about the beating and her moving, I told her she should put him behind bars where he belongs. My grandmother said "no it was best that she would just get away from him. I told her okay, but if at any time she needed anything from me, to just call and I would be right up. I went out to her new place to visit with her about a week later, and she still had bruises on her face. William had either hit her or pushed her down; she would never say what happened that day.

I told her what William had done to me and what he had done to Charles and that was why Charles had asked her to help him get out. "We could do something if you wanted to."

My grandmother said no because this was her daughter and she did not want any more trouble for her after all that we had been through already and that we should just stay away from them.

One Saturday afternoon, Leonard and I went over to his dad's house like we normally did on Saturdays. I was not feeling well, and I took a nap on Leonard's old bed—his bed in his and his brother's (Ronald's) room.

As I was lying there resting, Leonard came in and got down on his knees next to the bed and started to poke me. He said, "Are you awake?"

I said, "Not really, but what do you want?"

He then took my hand and placed a ring on it and asked me to marry him. Before I could answer him, he told me that I couldn't tell anyone right now. He just wanted to keep it a secret. I told him, of course, I would marry him, and he gave me a hug then he walked out of the room. I lay there looking at the ring, thinking to myself, *Why doesn't he want us to tell anyone?*

After I got up and came out of the room to join the family for dinner, Leonard's sister (Annie), came up to me in the kitchen and asked to see the ring. I told her I did not know what she was talking about. She then tells me that Leonard had already told her that he asked me to marry him and she wanted to see the ring. I looked at her and I thought to myself, *Leonard told me to keep this quiet, but he told his sisters?* I showed her the ring I was hiding in my palm. I had put the diamond on the inside of my hand so when I made a fist, it would be hidden from everyone. I turned it around on my finger so she could see it. She then told me how lucky I was, and we then joined the rest of the family in the dining room. I quickly turned the ring around so no one could see it, after we all eating and now we were cleaning up, and I was helping with washing the dishes. Leonard came over behind me and asked me what I was doing. I told him I was washing the dishes and helping out—why? He said that I was hiding the ring and not wearing it so everyone could see it. I reminded him that he did not want me to tell anyone about our engagement so I had turned the ring to the palm side of my hand to hide it like he had told me to do.

This only seemed to upset him. He then told me that he never wanted me to hide the ring from his family and that I must think the ring was not good enough for me, I needed something bigger, and I was just hiding it because I was embarrassed to have such a small diamond on my hand. I turned the ring back to the front of my hand and said, "I am not the one who is embarrassed." Then I walked away.

It was now the Christmas season, and I went over to the gym where Leonard was working. As I sat inside the ballroom with him doing nothing, he asked me to help him with checking out basketballs and the pool table.

Some strangers (to me) came over and started teasing Leonard about how now he was wiped. I did not understand what that meant—*wiped*. Leonard told them he would never be wiped by some girl. The guys laughed and walked off. I looked at Leonard, and now I understood that *wiped* meant (to him) that a women controlled their every move, so I said to him nicely and sweetly, "To be wiped by a girl is not a bad thing, and if he gave himself completely to me and me only to him, you would see how wonderful life could be, and that is all this wiping thing means, nothing more." He just looked at me and said nothing.

As we were closing up the park, he turned on the radio. The song "Everything She Wants" by George Michael came on, and Leonard looked at me and said, "This is your song," then he walked away from me.

I asked him as he was walking away, "What do you mean, this is my song? I want nothing from you."

He did not answer me, and so I just kept asking him what he meant by that (still to this day, I do not know what he meant by it), but I think it may have something to do with the line in the song where George sings, "Why do I do the things I do? I'd tell you if I knew. My God, I don't even think that I love you." Every time that song came on, I would always ask him the same question, "What do you mean by giving me this song?" He would never give me the reason, so I looked at him and asked, "Is it because you don't love me? If so, let me know now." He would just sit there being quiet. I told him I needed to know how he felt about me. I told him that if we really loved one another, everything would work out, but if one of us was lying about their feelings, then this would not last. If he thought that he needed to buy me the moon, he was mistaken. I did not want material things; I wanted something much more from him.

I was giving him everything of me, not holding anything back, and this was all that I wanted from him. Every time he would see me talking to some guy, he would always think I was cheating on him. He would say to me, "Now that you have the ring, you don't have to prove you love me. You just wear it to pick up other men."

I would then take the ring off and throw it at him. I would say, "I don't need a ring to show how much I love you. Me loving you comes from inside of me, not with some dumb ring. The ring was to show how much you love me and want to be a part of my life and all you ever do now is tell me that I am cheating on you when you are the one who has always cheated on me. I think you need to take a hard look at yourself before you start calling someone a cheater." I then packed up all my stuff and moved out into the streets because I would rather live in the street than with someone who thought I was cheating on him and did not believe that I loved them. After all, I had moved in with him and given him everything I was making, cleaned the apartment, cooked, did his laundry. I even attended his church, took care of his every need, and this is how he was going to treat me. The ring was not worth all this.

I went and stayed at a friend's house for a week, then I called him and we talked. I told him I did not like the way he thought I was always cheating on him just because I had smiled at the checkout boy at the grocery store. I told Leonard that it was okay to be friendly with people; it did not mean I was sleeping with them. "Am I to think every time you tell me that some lady opened her front door with nothing on, you and her had sex? I would hope you love me enough not to take them up on it and you would then come home to me. I don't like hearing how hard your day was because you had some naked woman at her front door with liquor in her hand asking you to come in and keep her company. That is not easy for anyone to hear, but I trust you and I believe in us. I just need to know if you believe in us as well."

He answered with, "I did not sleep with her."

"Okay, then no need for you to be jealous of me when I am just talking to a stranger. I am not sleeping with him."

I moved back into our apartment. He was still going to the casino; only now he would take me with him. I walked into the casino, and it was filled with cigarette smoke. I did not like to be around people who smoked because of my step grandfather and him using me as an ashtray. I told Leonard that he would have to find tables where they did not smoke and I could then sit with him or I would just stay in the car. Leonard knew I did not like to be around cigarette smoke, so he did agree to sit in an area that was for non-smokers. With me by his side, he won a lot of money. He would tell me I was his good luck charm. We stayed at the casino for a few hours, and I would ask him, "Do you think we can go home now?" I did not like playing card games, so I would just stand behind him being board out of my mind, but I was there for him and not myself.

He would always tell me, "Soon, let me just win a little more, then we will go." He would win big, but he would end up losing most of it because he could not get up and walk away. He always wanted more money; nothing was ever good or big enough for him. I would tell him that was good enough for now and that he could always come back on a different day and win more. He would tell me, "That is not how this works. I am hot tonight."

I would then pull up a chair and sit behind him; I would try to get in some sleep but never really fell asleep, so finally, at about 3:00 a.m., we would go home. He would be upset with me and complained how I could not stay awake long enough for him to hit it big.

I asked him, "How much did you win tonight?"

He told me he had won six thousand dollars.

I then said, "How much did you walk in with?"

He said, "Three hundred."

I then said, "I think you won big tonight."

He then said, "I would have had more if you did not fall asleep."

I said, "How many times did you have to win to walk away with what you now have on you? Did you have it then lose it many times? Did you just hit it big that last time? We spent from 9:00 p.m. to 3:00 a.m. at the casino for you to walk away with six thousand dollars? Seems to me that you did win and lose a few times, and this last time, you walked out with something to show for it—not everybody can say that. Most people lose everything on them then take out loans to try and win it back. You got lucky that you did not have to do that. You walked out with more than you went in with, and if you always remember to get up and walk out with more than you walk in with, then that is a win, or even if you just break even, it is not a loss to me, it is a win, because now you can still eat and pay your rent on time."

Leonard told me that I just didn't understand.

I told him he was right, I didn't, because I knew how hard it is to work and make money. This gambling thing, if you play it right, is easy money; you just need to know when to get up and walk away.

One year had gone by without us even talking about when and where we would get married.

My mother told me if an engagement went past a year, then we would never get married. I told her I was not going to push Leonard into marrying me. This was something we would decide together.

Leonard never liked my mom and made it very clear to me that he did not want her anywhere around his family. So this made it hard for us to even talk about when we would get married, for he did not want her to be a part of it, and I was not going to leave her and my family out of it. He would remind me that she made it hard for us to be together and that William had hit him, and if he ever saw William again, he would have to hit him because he had never gotten the chance to defend himself. I looked at him. This was the first time I heard Leonard say that when he turned to hit William, my mother had stepped in and he had hit her. I told him she was still my mother and my family had every right to see us get married. I would not be walking down the aisle of the Catholic Church either. So we never really ever talked about it again.

One day, we were at his uncle's house, and Leonard started talking about having kids. I told him that I was not going to have kids out of wedlock. His uncle said we should run off and elope in Vegas. This would solve all our problems.

About three months later, Leonard told me he wants me to go out to my mother's place and start planning our wedding. He wanted to invite his dad over to our place and have a long talk with him about us getting married. I tell him I did not want to go and stay with my mom, but if he needed some time with his dad, I could just leave for the day and then come back later that night. He would have all day to talk to his father, and I would not have to be with my mom over the weekend. Leonard told me if I loved him, I would do this for him. I would go and visit my mother for the weekend and he would talk to his dad, and then his dad would allow us to get married.

I told him, "I am only doing this for you and no one else. I packed up some of my clothes, called my mom, and told her I will be staying with her this weekend so we can start to plan for my wedding."

I got to my mom's place in Action, and my sisters were happy to see me. I spent some time with David. It was nice being with him again.

We all hopped into our mom's car, all but William, to start shopping for things I was going to need for this wedding. My mom starts asking me where we planned on getting married. I tell her that I would like to get married at Calvary Lutheran Church where I had spent my childhood. She tells me that Leonard's dad would not allow that and that Leonard would have to get married in the Catholic Church and that I was sinning against God marrying someone of the Catholic faith. I told her, "No, God doesn't care that we marry outside our faith, only that we love Him and that we stay faithful to Him." My mom then asked me about what religion we would raise the children in. I told her, "Leonard and I have already talked about this, and if we have a girl, she will be baptized in the Lutheran faith, and if I have a boy, I will allow him to have him baptized in the Catholic faith." I thought since I was a girl, I could help my daughter get to know her father in heaven through my faith because I did not know much about the Catholic faith. Leonard would then have to help his son know his father in heaven through the Catholic faith because he had grown up Catholic and understood it. My mother told me I was sinning and that I should rethink all this. I asked her, "Do you want to make my wedding dress or not?" She said yes she did, so I told her no more talk about religion and me sinning.

So we spent the rest of the day looking at patterns, and I finally found one that I liked—next would be the material. I did not find anything that I liked, but I told her I could always return next weekend and we may find something I like. I am not one who likes to go shopping, so finding the right pattern was a milestone for me.

Before I headed for home on Sunday afternoon, I spent some time with my brother. I asked him why his bedroom door was missing, and he was just about to tell me when the babies Betty and

Nancy ran in to the room to tell me that David had a girl in his room and that their dad took the door off because David would always keep it closed and William told him he needed to leave it open even when he did not have a girl in his room. David did not listen, so William took the door off. David also told me when Lorraine was out visiting our mom with her baby, William would peek in on her when she was in the shower. I told David that he would try that with me when I lived with them and that he (David) would need to be careful and try to stay out of trouble. He told me he understood and I asked him why he did not go back to live with his dad. He told me even with William being the way he was, this was better than his stepmother back home.

I was hoping things were not as bad for him as they had been for me.

When I walked into our apartment, Leonard was not home. I had called him before I left my mother's place to check and make sure I could come home. I walked into the bedroom to start unpacking my things. I noticed a small package on the floor, and the bed was not made.

I picked up the package to discover that it was a condom. Leonard and I never used condoms, so I did not understand why I would be finding one in our bedroom. As I was looking around for more of them, Leonard walked into the apartment. He came running into the bedroom to find me standing there with the unused condom in my hand. I asked him what this was and why would I find it in our bedroom if he had spent the weekend with his father.

Leonard told me that he did not have the chance to talk to his dad and that he had let one of his friends use the apartment to entertain a girl.

I told him, "You sent me to my mother's house to start planning our wedding and you don't tell your dad we are getting married, and I am to believe that you did not stay here with another girl and that you let one of your friends stay here so he could sleep with some girl? You must take me for a fool."

He then told me no, that his friend liked a girl that his family disapproved of and that the only way they could be together was if they used our place.

I say, "Sounds a lot like us, only we found time to spend together, whether it is the back seat of your car, the pier, the game room at the park, and even the pool locker room. We never had to borrow someone's place."

He then told me that he is the only one of his friends who had a place of their own, and if I trusted him, I would know he did not cheat on me.

I told him we would find out in nine months.

CHAPTER FIVE
Marriage

Marriage *is* honourable in all, and the bed undefiled:
but whoremongers and adulterers God will judge.
> —Hebrews 13:4

About one month after I was sent away to plan our wedding with my mom, Leonard called me while he was at work to tell me to run out and buy a dress. We were going to head over to Vegas to get married this weekend. I told him I had to work on Monday. Monday was a holiday, so he had a three-day weekend.

I was now working at Builders Emporium. I had taken a job working in a doctor's front office. When I was being interviewed for the job, I told the women that I did not have any experience working in the front office. She told me that I would mostly be filling like I was already doing at St. Joseph's Hospital. She told me not to worry—they would train me. Leonard was not happy about this. He told me to take a week off from my current job (at the hospital) and not just quit altogether, because this may not work out for me. I did not listen to him; I just quit the hospital and started work at the doctor's office.

I was there for about one week; none of the older women would help me or train me. They told me it was not their job to train anyone.

The doctor (I was now working for) asked to see me in his office. He asked me how I got the job, and I told him. He then told me this was not the place for me and that he needed to let me go.

I said thank you to the doctor and left. Leonard reminded me that he had said not to quit the hospital job, and now look, I had nothing.

One week later, I was working at Builders Emporium—not a real glamorous job but a job nonetheless.

The dictation office at the hospital closed about one-and-a-half years later. I knew they would be closing, and so I was looking to get out of there anyway. I just quit before they could let me go. Leonard said that they would have had to pay me benefits and they would have had to move me somewhere else with in the hospital and that they would not have just let me go.

I told him, "No, they would have just let me go. The other women that worked there had more seniority over me, and they would be giving them the opportunity to move to another department."

Leonard called me and told me that we would be going out to Vegas to get married and to take his credit card to find something to wear, I told him I would find something that did not cost him too much money.

Off to Kay Mart I went, looking for something to get married in. I called my mother and told her she did not need to make my wedding dress that Leonard and I were headed off to Vegas to get married. I asked her if she would like to come but she would need to bring Grandma with her. She said she would. I gave her the address. Leonard's uncle had given us a card to a chapel in Vegas where we could get married, so I just read it off the card to my mother. I asked my mom if she could call my dad and brother for me (I did not have their numbers to call them and ask them to meet me in Vegas).

I found a nice, simple half-white and half-blue long-sleeved dress that fell below my knees. Very nice, clean, simple dress made out of cotton.

I got everything ready to go so when Leonard got home, we could just leave.

He ran in and asked if I was packed and ready to go. I said, "Yes, I am ready to go, but you will need to get your things together. I did not pack anything for you." He was upset because I did not get anything out for him, but I did not know what he wanted to wear.

He grabbed what he wanted, and off we went. We had to first stop by his uncle's house to pick him up because he was coming with us. I was not told that Leonard's uncle was coming with us. I thought to myself, *We do need witnesses, so why not?* And I did not tell him that my mom would be meeting up with us in Vegas.

We made it to Vegas, found a hotel room (yes, one), and the boys told me to stay there as the two of them took off to hit the casinos. I fell asleep waiting for them to come back. Leonard did not tell me he was running off with his uncle to gamble all night. Once I got up in the morning, he was still not in the room. I took a shower, and then I get dressed and ready to go. They came in at about 8:00 a.m. Leonard took a quick shower, and his uncle crashed on the bed.

We made reservations at the chapel to get married at 9:00 a.m. I did not know my way around Vegas, so I had no idea where this chapel was. We made it to the chapel just as the other couple was coming out. It was just after 9:00 a.m. now. The lady asked us if we had a marriage license. We said no. She sent us over the city hall to get one. Leonard and I headed out of the chapel as my mom was walking up the walkway. Leonard did not stop to say hi to her, and I told her, "We need to run over to city hall to get a marriage license. We will be back," as I ran by her.

As we were driving to city hall, Leonard had some choice words for me. I let him yell because I knew down deep inside, he was just scared and he needed to take it out on someone and I was the only one in the car. When he calmed down enough for me to say something, I told him, "You have your family here, and by the way, he did not come with us, and we need a witness for this. I asked my mother to bring my grandmother with her. I also asked her to ask my father and brother to be here today with us. I don't know what happened because I have not talked to her, but when we get back, I will ask her where everybody else is."

We finally got to city hall after going the wrong way and Leonard being too angry at me to hear me tell him he made a wrong turn. We walked in, and at any moment, he could have said no to this and walked out. I was half expecting that from him with the way he was acting. When we got up to the counter after filling out the paperwork, the women then asked the two of us, "Is this really want the two of you want?" We both said yes, and then she stamped it and handed the paperwork to me, and now off we went, back to the chapel to get married.

It was now 10:15 a.m., and they had to take another couple that had made reservations after us go before us because we were not ready. The women gave us more paperwork to sign, and then my mother took it and signed it as a witness to this union, and then she said to us, "It is bad luck to get married as the hour hand is going down. It will be good luck for us because now the hour hand will be going up."

We stepped into a room, and the wedding planner asked us some questions about how we wanted the ceremony to go. I told her that we both believed in God and that it should be a very religious ceremony or however much they could make it one for us. This woman then looked at Leonard and asked him if he also wanted God's blessing. He said yes, and I said, "As many times as you can say 'May God bless you always and forever' in the ceremony would be fine."

The wedding planner then handed me a bouquet of flowers, and my mother asked her where Leonard's flower was. She said Leonard did not have a flower because we did not purchase that package. We had gotten the one we could afford. My mother then took a rose from my bouquet and got a pin from this lady to make him a boutonniere.

We took some pictures in an empty chapel, and then now it was our turn to get married.

They walked him into the chapel, and I stayed out in the hallway. Then the doors opened and down the aisle I went. William was videotaping this; I did have a video copy of the nice, happy, cheerful event, only I never picked it up from my mother, so she still has it even to this day.

Now we were married, and that was when William walked up to Leonard and said, "Let's bury the hatchet."

As we got into our car, my mom told me she had bought a cake. I told my mom that we needed to get back to the room we got for the night to pick up Leonard's uncle because we only had it for that one night and we had to go and check out of the room and get him. She told me she would keep it for me, and I told her fine, I would be up to get it at some point; I just did not know when.

Off we went to pick up his uncle and get our stuff. Leonard looks at me (as he is driving us back to the hotel) and with an evil tone says to me, "I own you, and I can do whatever I want to you." All I remember thinking at that moment was jumping out of the car and getting hit by the oncoming traffic. I thought I had killed myself. This thought was so clear that for a moment, I did believe I jumped out of the car, but reality sank in, and I looked at him and said, "I can do whatever I want to you then because now I own you." I was not as evil about it, more of a joking type of tone; he looked at me with eyes that could burn a hole in you. I just smiled at him. I turned my head back out the window and took pictures of the casinos we were driving by.

We picked up his uncle, and then we headed over to one of the casinos so the two of them could get in some more gambling before we headed home. I had to work the next day, but Leonard had it off, so he did not care how long we spent in Vegas.

We now all headed over to the casino. As we walked in, his uncle and I took some pictures together by the palm trees. Leonard and I did not get any pictures together because he did not want to.

We went out to where they had this big tank. This tank had dolphins in it; one even had a baby. I could not believe my luck. I loved dolphins, and to be able to see them in the desert on my honeymoon was an amazing moment for me. I even took a picture of the dolphins, and then I walked over to where Leonard was to get some pictures of him; the one picture I managed to get captured him in the normal Leonard state of mind. I will describe it to you now. He was standing next to his uncle ordering something, and I called out to him, and as he turned to look at me, he swung the brown paper bag he had in his hand toward me. Now if I were closer to him, he would have hit me with it, Lucky for me, I wasn't close to him. Now I had a nice picture of him and this ugly expression on his face as if he were saying to me, "Leave me alone, b——!"

We then headed back into the casino so Leonard could gamble some more before we headed home. He told me that I could play the slot machines while he waited for a spot to open at one of the black-jack tables. As we waited in line to get some change to play the slots, I spotted the machines that had the zodiac signs on them; each slot matching had one zodiac sign. I knew enough not to use the Virgo machine because I was the Virgo and I would not win off it. Aries was taken right now, but I knew once it opened up, I would need to run over to it and I would win something on it. I played on one of the open slots till the Aries was freed up. I wanted to play the Aries one because I had just married the Aries and I know it would bring me luck. After I dropped in a few coins (they were dollar coins), Leonard walked over to me to see how I was doing. He walked away from me for about one minute, or it felt that way, then he came back to play the machine with me. That is when I looked up to see if the Aries machine was open. It was, and I just walked away from him. I dropped two coins in at a time (two dollars). Leonard then walks over to me, and he dropped in one and then I would drop in my two. He told me to slow down because we were almost out of coins. He dropped in one, and then I dropped in two. He went to tell me again to slow down, and as I looked at him to say okay, the machine started to make a noise, and the lights started to flash. A big red one on the top of the machine was going off and making a loud sound. I started to look around because I did not believe that I had just won something. This was the first time I had ever won anything in my life and it was my first time playing these things. I was trying to guess at what number it would stop at—two hundred, two fifty, three hundred, three fifty—when a guard that had come up behind us said to me, "You just won *five* hundred dollars."

I was like, "*No*, five hundred dollars? Cool."

The guard walked with us over to the cashier, and I handed them all my winnings. Then the cashier asked me if I wanted to keep two of the coins; I said yes. I gave one to Leonard's uncle, and I still, to this day, have the other coin from that day.

Leonard then took my winnings and went to the blackjack table and sat down to play. I was just so happy to have won something and to have that one dollar in my hand; that made me happier than anything else that day. I did not care that he took everything I had won and used it to gamble. It was his money I used to get the coins anyway.

After a short time at the table, Leonard got up, and we then went out to a very expensive restaurant to eat before we headed home. Leonard had won a lot of money that weekend. It paid for everything, and he still had a chunk of money to take home. How much he never told me, but he did say it was a lot, and after all, I did win five hundred dollars of that on my own. Not bad—we had a nice wedding and won some money and now we were headed home to start out lives together. I told him, "See, as long as we stick together, there is nothing that can stop us. Look at all the good fortune today."

I went into work that Monday after we had gotten married and filled out paperwork to change my last name with the payroll department, and the next stop would be the DMV and Social Security.

My boss looked at me and said, "Congratulations, no honeymoon?"

I told him we had gotten married in Vegas and I had won five hundred dollars off a slot machine and that was good enough for me. "Yes, no honeymoon."

We worked hard at making a baby now (every night). I thought I was pregnant the month after our wedding, but it turned out to be a false alarm. The nurses at the doctor's office told me when you worked as hard as we did to get pregnant, it didn't always work out the first time, and maybe I and Leonard should slow down a little.

I told Leonard I had gone to the doctor's office and it turned out I was not pregnant and that we should take it easy; after all, we were still young and had plenty of time.

Leonard did not listen. If we were both home on the weekend, all we did was stay in bed and have sex. I think we ordered food so I did not have to stop and make us something to eat.

Two months later, I went to the store and bought a home pregnancy test. I did not bother with the doctor's office this time because it was too depressing to have them come back and tell you, "You are not pregnant."

I was home alone one Saturday. I got out the home pregnancy test, and then I went into the bathroom to pee on the stick. I left it on the bathroom sink, and then I went into the kitchen to make myself something to eat. I went back into the bathroom about thirty minutes later to find out if I was pregnant or not. One line meant "Yes, you are pregnant," and two lines meant "No, you are not pregnant." It had one line, and I was beyond happy. I wanted to call Leonard and tell him the good news, but I thought maybe I should wait for him to get home so I could see his face when I told him.

He got home, and I asked him about his day. He seemed to be a little tired and not in a good mood, so I told him that I had something to tell him as he walked into the bathroom (I left the stick on the sick so I could show him). He walked out of the bathroom with the stick in his hand and asked me what this was. I told him, "It is a pregnancy test, and it reads we are pregnant."

He said that he did not believe me and that he needed to see the box. I walked past him and pulled the box out of the trash can in the bathroom and handed him the box. I said to him, "Do you believe now?"

I think he must have been in shock or something because he did not say anything to me. I finally walked over to him and hugged him and said, "This is what you wanted."

I don't remember him saying anything to me.

I had to visit the doctor's office now once a month to make sure everything was going along smoothly with the pregnancy.

Leonard, for some reason, thought that he was not the father of our child and that I had cheated on him. He would say to me (daily) that if this child did not come out looking like him, he would know the truth—that I had cheated on him. I would pray every day and night that this child growing inside me would come out healthy, strong, and looking just like its dad.

Every month, I would ask Leonard if he would like to go with me to one of my doctor's appointments. I got to hear the baby's heartbeat, and I thought he would like to hear it for himself, but he did not take time off from his job to come to any of my appointments. I told him I could schedule a time and date so he could go and then we could spend the day together after the appointment. I was going to buy a stethoscope so he could hear the baby's heartbeat, but as I was walking to the store, I told myself, "Why? If he did not want to come to my appointments, then why should I want to share this with him?" so I walked home. He never came to any of my doctor's appointments, even when I thought I was going to lose it. I started to bleed—not much, but it was enough for me to call the doctor's office, and they told me to go home because I was calling from work. They wanted me to get off my feet and rest. Then I was to come in and see them in the morning if the bleeding did not stop.

Leonard came home and found me on the couch with my feet up. He asked me what I was doing home so early, and I told him that I may be having a miscarriage. He did not come over to hug me or anything, he just said "Okay," then he took off to his second job, the one with the City of Burbank.

I walked to my doctor's appointments because I did not like having to drive Leonard's truck around town. I was driving his truck to work because it was a gas guzzler. We did take it out mud roping this one time. Leonard told me to get in behind the wheel. I get out into the middle of the mud track, and I pulled off some really nice donuts. I had everyone on the track yelling and shouting at me, then Leonard told me to stop and I did. I opened the door to the truck, and I hear one young boy yell "It's a girl!" and that was when I stepped out and I heard the crow start chanting "It's a girl!" and clapping their hands. I took my bow, and Leonard told me to get back into the truck, only on the passenger's side; I think I upset him because no one cheered for him. He had raised the truck up and he had put on these really big tires on it—that was why he took my car to and from Long Beach, because it got better gas mileage than his truck.

I told Leonard as my pregnancy went on that one day I would not be able to climb into this truck anymore and that maybe we should think about getting something that was more for a family because we were not single people anymore; we were about to become a family. He told me he did not want to get a minivan—he was not that kind of person—and I told him that my car (the Camry) would be just fine for me but that he would have to find something for him to drive to and from work.

We went over to the Toyota dealership to find a new truck that we both could be happy with.

He told the car salesman he did not want a minivan; minivans were for old men and he was not an old man.

The car salesman showed him the Forerunner; it was still a truck, but it had room for up to five people and the truck was low enough for me to get into.

So now he had to sell his baby (the truck), and we bought the Forerunner. This was the start of changing our lives forever— the family car and then a house at some point down the road. This should have been the happiest time of our lives, but Leonard was not that kind of person. Always keep in the back of your mind that I was being verbally abused by him every day with him saying I was cheating on him. I was praying very hard that this child would look just like him and nothing at all like me every day.

Leonard would spend more time at the casino now and less time at home with me. If I had the day off, he would take me to the casino with him; only now he did not care that I did not like the cigarette smoke and he would sit at the table where everyone was smoking. I kept my head down and my mouth covered with my shirt, so that way, I did not breathe in all of the smoke. He would look at me and ask me what I was doing. I told him, "I do not want to breathe in all the smoke, and I am using my shirt to help keep out some of the cigarette smoke." He told me to stop because I looked like a fool doing that. I saw another person in the casino doing the same thing as me, and I told him I was not the only one in here who was coving their month. I told him, "Look over there." He told me to put my shirt down and to stop making a fool out of myself. I got up and I asked him for the keys to the truck, and then I walked away.

I sat in the truck and finally fell asleep when he finally came out so we could go home. He told me he did not win and that I would need to make that up to him. I told him, "No, you did not sit in an area where they did not smoke, and I was choking in there, and if you want me to come sit with you, you will need to sit in an area where I can sit with you and not choke to death on cigarette smoke."

He decided to be nice to me and take me to the Halloween Hunt at Knots Berry Farm for Halloween that year. Elvira was going to be performing, so I said yes.

That was a big mistake. I took that day off so I could get some sleep, but no, Leonard decided to take me to the casino and leave me there all day, and then when he got off work (at the post office in Long Beach), he would be back to pick me up, and then we would leave from there to head over to Knots Berry Farm. He told me it would be easier to get me from the casino then having to drive all the way home and then all the way back out to Knots. I reminded him that I did not gamble and that I did not like this idea. He told me as he dropped me off, "Don't lose any of it, you need to win." I went in, and thank goodness not many people were in the casino at 7:00 a.m., but they did not have a lot of tables open either. I sat down at one that was in the non-smoking area, and I started to play blackjack. I was not good at it because I hated having to bet money. I didn't even like to make bets on anything in life (in general). So as I sat there playing the game, two men came around me and started to place their bets based off my hand. They had seen that I was winning money, and so they decided to play with me. As we played, they would bet more and more money. I would pick up the cards, and if I had 15, I would pass on picking up another card. The men next to me and the one standing behind me both just held their breath as I said "Pass." They both knew what I was holding because I had held the cards face up as I told the dealer to pass on me. The next card was something I could have used. So now it was up to the dealer—what would he get? They had to hit on 16. So when the dealer pulled his card out for himself, he got a queen, which made him over so everyone won that hand. The two men could now breathe again. It came time for me to be the banker, and I would always pass on it. The one man who was standing behind me said he wanted to be the banker, so I told the dealer we would be the banker this time. The banker was the one everyone is trying to win. So it was my cards they would have to beat. The dealer passed out the cards, and I picked them up. I showed them to the man behind me, and he said he would leave it up to me. I showed it to the man next to me, and he just smiled at me.

I did not know what to do. I think I had something like 19. So I just said "Pass" to the next card. The man behind me put more money down on the table, and I then started to sweat. I was already nervous about losing my own money but now his money as well, and he put a lot of money down on the table.

So after I passed on the card, the dealer then gave the card that I would have gotten if I had taken it to the person next to me. It was a 10, which would have made me over 21, and the two men were very relieved that I had passed on that card. After the dealer had gone around the table, the dealer then took his cards, and I believe the house busted again, so a lot of the other players won that hand as well, and the man behind me hit it big, He said something to me like "Good job." He took his money and left. I sat there all day. Sometimes I would win and sometimes I would lose, but every time, I would win back the money Leonard had given me, I would put it way and only play with the money I had won. By the time Leonard had gotten to the casino, I had lost everything that I had won, but I still had the money he gave me. Leonard found me asked me how I was doing, and I told him that I had just lost the last of the money I had won. Now he was thinking I lost everything, and he started to say to me that I spent all day here and I lost everything. I tell him I did not lose the money he gave me, just the money I had won. "I still have the money you have give me."

He took the hundred dollars and placed it on the table, and he won. He then told me, "That is how you do it."

I told him, "I am tired and we need to go."

Then he said for me to get up, and he then sat down and played a couple more hand just to loss what he himself had won. He did have to pull out his own money, and he did win the hundred dollars back, and off we went to Knots Berry Farm.

I told him after we got into the car, "See, not so easy." He then tells me that after spending all day there, I should have walked away with something to show for it. I told him I did. "I did not lose your money, and I was even up the one hundred dollars a couple of times, but I had to do something to pass the time away waiting for him to get off of work and pick me up." I told him to never leave me there again if he didn't like the way I gambled.

We got to Knots Berry Farm, and we went to see the Elvira show. After the show, I bought a life-size poster of Elvira. Leonard asked me what I was going to do with that.

I told him I was going to hang it on the door in our bedroom.

He told me no.

I told him most men would love to have this up in their room, and here I was going to be the one who put it up for him. He did not like the idea at all, but I did it anyway. I loved the poster, and when you had our bedroom door closed, you could see her lying in her coffin; it was cool. Leonard would never close our bedroom door, so when he was not home, I would always have it closed.

Every day, I was hearing how this baby should come out looking like him or he would know I was cheating on him, so when we were at church, all I did was pray to God, "Please make this child look like him and healthy." I did not listen to anything the father was saying, not that I could even understand him because it was a Vietnamese mass, so I would just sit there talking to God and asking him to watch over me and the baby, and also the people here at this church. I looked around, and I saw statues everywhere. I was told that we should not kneel before any other God and we should not build statues, but the Catholics had them everywhere, even in their homes. I sat there talking to God and asking him to watch over them because they did not know what it was that they were doing. They even had prayer candles. You would have to drop in money, then you would light a candle so that the saints would grant your wish or prayer. I would tell God some of us still needed to have something that they could see; some of us didn't know how to just believe without seeing like Doubting Thomas did. But that didn't make them sinners and you just needed to be a little more patience with them.

Leonard was upset that I had a life-size poster of Elvira on the door in our bedroom, and he wanted me to take it down. I told him to grow up. "It will not kill you to have a picture of a woman on our bedroom door."

He then went out and bought a fish tank—not any fish tank, it held up to 250 gallons of water. He wanted to make it a saltwater fish tank. I told him I didn't think this was a good idea, but he told me he wanted it, and so now we had a 250-gallon fish tank.

As we moved it into our apartment with the help of some of his friends, the owner of the building came by and talked to Leonard about this tank. We were able to keep it, but now we had to give the owner of the apartments a two-hundred-dollar security deposit for any damage caused by this fish tank.

Leonard bought two baby sharks, a lion fish, some clown fish, coral, and a sea anemone, much like the real ocean.

I had nightmares about that tank; I would see myself floating in it. The tank was wide and long enough to hold a human body. I told Leonard that I felt very uncomfortable with that tank being in the apartment. He told me this was for him and it helped him relax after a hard day at work.

The funny thing about that was, I was the one home alone with it, and I would lie on the couch watching the fish and thinking to myself that one day, I would be the one swimming with the fish.

I would have to turn the TV on to help me get those thoughts out of my head.

Leonard and I would talk about what was going to happen after we had the baby, as far as me going back to work or if I would stay home and take care of it. After I looked into some day care programs and we found out how much it would be to put the baby in one, we decided that it would be better if I stayed home and took care of the baby. We did not know what would happen to our baby if we put it into a day care center; we did not want someone else raising our child for us. I told him if it was a girl, I would be baptizing it in my faith, and if it was a boy, he could baptize it in the Catholic faith. He said nothing to me at the time.

When his dad asked me about baptizing the baby, I told him that if it was a girl, it would be baptized Lutheran, and if it was a boy, I would allow him to be baptized Catholic. This upset my father-in-law.

Leonard came running into the kitchen, where I was now help-ing with cleaning the dishes because we had just eating with the family. We always went to his dad's house on Saturday, we would go to church and then have dinner as a family.

Leonard came up to me, yelling, "What did you tell my dad?"

I looked at him and said, "What did I tell your dad about what?"

Leonard then told me, "You told him you were not going to baptize the baby Catholic."

I looked at him and reminded him that that was something we had decided already. "I do not understand why you are so upset about it."

Leonard then told me, "We never came to any such arrangement," and that I had to go and apologize to his father and tell him I would baptize the baby Catholic even if it was a girl." So off to the living room I went to tell my father-in-law that I would baptize the baby boy or girl Catholic. This made my father-in-law very happy. I, on the other hand, was not happy.

I looked into signing us up for a Lamaze class. I paid for it like I was paying for my prenatal care.

He went to the first class with me, complaining about it the entire time as we were driving to the class. I asked him, "Do you know anything about giving birth? I don't, and I would like to take a class so I can be prepared for what is going to happen to me and my body."

We got to the classroom, and Leonard ran into one of his friends, and they started talking.

He finally got around to introducing me to his friend and the wife, only because we were all there for the same reason.

We all sat down, and the teacher went around the room, asking the couples to introduce themselves to the class so we could get to know each other a little better.

She told us before we started introducing ourselves that with the first baby, "Labor can take up to twenty-four hours or longer, so don't think this will be a walk in the park." We needed to think about what may upset us with our husbands, and the smallest of these things would set us off. "And, husbands, you need to understand your wife may start yelling at you and may even call you names. She doesn't mean it, and that is part of the course."

Leonard looked at me and said, "You better not yell at me."

After we all introduced ourselves, the teacher then asked all of us how long we planned on being in labor. She got to me, and I told her, "No more than one hour." She smiled and said that with the first one, it might take longer than that, so then I told her, "No more than eight hours."

We then take a break; I came back into classroom after using the restroom. We all sat down again, and this time, the men were asked to massage our lower backs. This would help us in childbirth, and this would give the man something to do to help them feel like they were a part of the whole birthing experience. Leonard looked at me and said, "I have to touch you." I looked at him a little confused. I lay on my side so he could rub my back. He made it look like he was touching, me but he really wasn't. The teacher was up walking around the room and showing the husband how they should be rubbing their wives' backs. She came over to us and told Leonard that he would have to rub harder than that. Leonard now had to get closer to me, and then he said to me, "Did you forget to take a shower today? You smell."

I was so embarrassed. I told him yes and that I had even taken one before we came to class. The teacher must have heard us because she then told us that even our scent would change. "If any of you have a dog, you will notice that the dog will treat us women differently. Some of you will have to send the dog away during the pregnancy, or the dog may become overprotective of the woman."

After class, we went home, and on the way home, Leonard told me he would not be attending another class with me. I told him, "Then who do I go with? I can't go alone. You are in this with me whether you like it or not. I need you by my side. I paid for this class, and I need it more than you." All he could say to me was he was not going back; I should take my boyfriend.

Leonard still spent most of his time away from the apartment and me. Some mornings or when he came home to change in between jobs or the casino and I would catch a glimpse of him, he would always remind me that the child growing inside me had better come out looking like him.

He had lost a lot of money, so he asked me to call my dad and ask him for money. I told Leonard that I was not close to my dad and that he would not just lend us money just because I asked him for it, and if he wanted money from someone, he should talk to his own father. He told me that it was about time I get to know my father, and if I wanted to stay in the apartment with him, I had to come up with the money somehow. I was still working, but all my money was going into a bank account that had both of our names on it and he would spend everything in our account.

I asked him what had happened to all our money.

He just looked at me and said, "Call your dad and get the money."

Leonard left, and I called my dad. I asked my dad if we could borrow some money. My dad told me that we were now adults and we needed to budget our money better. I then told my dad that I thought we had, but I guessed Leonard had lost more than he thought he would at the casino and we did not have the money for rent, and that I was pregnant and I had only called him because Leonard told me to call you and this was not by my choice because I knew you would not help us. If I did not at least try, then Leonard would be upset with me. My dad told me that we needed to make better decisions, and I should sit Leonard down and ask him if he was really ready to become a dad. He also asked me if we had gone to his dad and asked for money. I told my dad, "No, but I did tell Leonard he should ask his dad because I am coming to you." We said our goodbyes, and I then went off to bed.

Leonard woke me up to ask me if my dad was willing to help us. I told him my dad said no.

Leonard then left.

When it was time for me to go on maternity leave, my coworkers threw me a baby shower. Leonard dropped me off at one of the women's homes. I asked him, "Aren't you coming in?"

He told me, "This is not a place for men, it is just for women only." I looked at him and reminded him he was the father of our baby and he had every right to be at this party.

He just drove away and told me he would be back later.

We had to move now because we could no longer afford the apartment. Leonard told me we had to move so we could start saving money.

We moved into his sister Renee's house. Now she already had one child and was pregnant with her second child.

The fish tank went to his dad's house, and our furniture came with us to his sister's house. Luckily for us, we did not have much.

One night, Leonard decided to take me out on a date. We went to a seafood restaurant out in Redondo Beach on the pier. I told him I did not want seafood, but in we went.

We finally got a table, and he ordered all his favorite seafood. I told him I did not like to eat seafood, and he said to me, "You girls are always saying no but you really mean yes." He then tried to get me to eat some of the crab that he had just ordered. I told him that I was just going to sit here and not eat anything. He looked at me, and then he told me to eat some of it. He had just spent a lot of money; the least I could do was help him eat it. He told me that he had asked Sandra, a girl from school we both knew and were friends with, here to this restaurant and asked her if he had any chance with her. Sandra was about to get married, and Leonard had always wanted to marry her. She told him that he was about to become a father and he was already married and both the church and her family would not allow this union between the two of them.

I just sat there thinking to myself, *I must be his second choice. He really never wanted to marry me, and he just couldn't get this other woman he loved to marry him because they came from different backgrounds.*

Now I really did not want to eat anything, and he just kept on eating like he had done nothing wrong; He told me he would never have told me this, but because he loves me, he wanted me to know that I was not his first choice and that I would always be second to her. Then he said, "See how much I love you? I don't hide anything from you, and I will always tell you the truth."

I did everything I could do to fit in with his family and to become a part of his family. I learned how to cook Vietnamese food. His sister told me that they didn't measure anything and I would have to learn how to cook by taste only. Lucky for me I had been cooking my whole life and cooking by taste was easy for me, so I learned how to make the food Leonard had grown up on.

His sister told him that I made dinner. He looked at me and told me that from here on out, I was to cook Vietnamese food only, no more of that American crap.

One night, Renee asked me to help her out in the kitchen. I was about eight and half months pregnant, and she was five months pregnant.

I got up and walked around the coffee table and in front of the TV to go into the kitchen. I did not want to pass right in front of Leonard, who was sitting next to me on the couch.

As I started to step up the stairs to go into the kitchen, Leonard grabbed me by the throat and lifted me off the ground. I made some very weird noises as he was choking me. His sister heard me and came over to the doorway and yelled something at him in Vietnamese and he then dropped me. He told her that something had just come over him and he had to grab me and try to kill me. He even said to her, "Look at my arms. Something went into me, see the goosebumps."

I walked up the two steps and into the kitchen and thanked his sister for stopping him. She told me that he did not mean anything by choking me and that it would not happen again. I told her if she had not been here, he would have killed me. "Thank you for saving my life."

That was all that was said about that. That night, when we were in bed together, he told me that he had been possessed by an evil spirit and that he would never have done that to me if this spirit did not take over his body.

I really never fell completely asleep with him next to me anymore. I learned at a young age not to fall into a deep sleep. I would sleep with my feet hanging off the side of the bed so I would feel someone trying to sneak up on me. They would touch my feet, and I would be awake. I would also wrap the blanket around me, so if someone did try to hurt me, they would have a hard time getting to me with the blanket around my body. I would always wake up before they could get it off me.

Leonard did not like the way I sleep because he could never get to me when I was sleeping. I would always wake up before he could hurt me or sleep with me.

He was still spending a lot of his time away from the house. One morning, at one AM I told my child that if they wanted Daddy to stay home with us, they would have to come now because come 5:00 a.m., he would be going to work.

My water broke right when I got done thinking that. I told Leonard it was time and that my water had just broken; I need to go to the hospital.

He got up and ran into his sister's room to tell her I needed to go to the hospital because I was about to have the baby.

They came back into the room, and I was in the bathroom trying to clean myself up and I was going to be removing the sheets from the bed because I had made a mess and I wanted to clean it up. Renee told me she would take care of it and I should just get in the car and start heading over to the hospital. I thanked her, and off we went.

It was 1:00 a.m. on a Monday, and Leonard was driving slower than a snail. He hit every hole in the street or it felt that way to me. I told him he would need to go faster than this if he did not want to deliver the baby by himself in the car.

He told me he had to drive the speed limit because he did not want the police to stop him for speeding. As he said this to me, a police car went by us. I asked him, "Are you about one block away from the hospital?" He just looked at me. I said, "Do you understand that it is early in the morning and we are headed to the hospital? I do believe that if they see us driving fast toward the hospital, they would understand that we were in a hurry for a reason, and if they follow us, they will see us drive into the hospital driveway and see me get out of the car, and they will know what is going on, so run the red light, it is okay," because now we were stopped at a red light waiting for it to turn green.

Leonard ran the light, and the police car did not even turn around to give him a ticket or to see what was going on.

We got to the hospital, and they put us in a room and placed the baby monitor on me; this way, they could monitor us from the nursing station. I keep telling the nurse I needed to get up and walk around my back and the back of my legs were hurting me and I could not lie in this bed anymore. She tells me that it was because I was close to giving birth and that was why my back and the back of my legs were hurting me. They did not want me up and walking around the room at all, so I told her I needed to go to the bathroom. She put the sidebar down so I can get up. As I walked toward the bathroom, I had a bowel movement, and I made a nice trail from the bed to the bathroom.

I was sitting on the toilet and thinking to myself, *as much as this feels better, I cannot have my baby in the toilet.*

I went back into the room and lay back down in the bed, and they strapped me in again. This time, I rolled over onto my left side and curled up in a ball. I was hurting, but I could not be on my back, and they would not let me up to walk around the room.

The nurse came back into the room and told me I needed to lie flat on my back. I told her it hurt too much to do that. She then told me that I should start my Lamaze breathing; she then asked me if I had attended any type of Lamaze class. If so, then this would be a good time to start my breathing. I told her that we had dropped out of class because someone here did not want to touch me.

I asked her if I could get up and go to the bathroom again. Off I went again, and I had another bowel movement as I was walking to the bathroom, Leonard said to me, "What did you eat for dinner?"

The nurse told him that this was normal and not to worry—everything would be okay.

I found myself sitting on the toilet again, feeling much better but not wanting to have the baby in the toilet, so I got up and headed back out to the bed. I sat on the edge of the bed, and the nurse was trying to get me to lie down. I slowly moved back on the bed and lay down.

They hooked me up again, and I lay there in pain, so I started talking to God, "Please let me see the sunrise before I give birth. I was going to name our child, if it was a girl, Aurora and dedicate her to

God. *Aurora* means God's first light, and this was my first child, and it was because of him that I had made it this far.

As I was lying in the bed again, curled up in a ball on my left side, Leonard was trying to get some sleep in, but the baby monitor was beeping, and with each contraction, it was making the meter on the machine go higher than the last time. He told me to get up. "You need to see this, this one is stronger than the last one."

I told him to give me a minute. "I cannot move right now, as soon as I am feeling better and the pain stops, I will get up, I then asked him to help me out of the bed.

He told me to forget it; I had missed it. "Next time, move faster."

I rolled over on my back, and the pain started again, and he got up and started telling how this one was really a strong one and I needed to get up now if I was going to see it. At this point, I just gave up on him. He did not understand that I was the one that was having the contractions and that the machine was only recording what was happening to me. As soon as this one was over, he again got mad and said to me, "Forget it, now it's over."

The nurse came in and tells me not to lie on my side, because they were having trouble monitoring the baby's heartbeat and that I needed to stay on my back. I told her, "It hurts too much to do that."

The nurse then told me to breathe anytime I felt a contraction; I needed to breathe in and out at a slow and steady pace. I looked at her and told her "I feel pain all the time." I did not understand what she meant about the contraction thing. So now I was breathing in and out a little too much because she walked over to me and told me that I was hyperventilating, and she then handed me a brown paper bag. She asked me if I wanted an epidural. My mother had told me, "If they ask you if you want an epidural, tell them no. They could paralyze you by mistake." I looked at her, and she told me that my time for one was running out. She needed to know now.

After the pain subsided, I told her, "No, thank you."

The nurse told me I was very close to having the baby and that I was nine centimeters now, whatever that meant. I was not going to have this baby without seeing the sunrise. I was lucky enough to be in a room with a window, only the Disney Studio was across the street and I did not see the sun until about 8:30 a.m. or so, and that was when I told God that I needed my mother and I called out to her in my head.

I then gave birth to our daughter. All I heard was Leonard saying that she had blue eyes; the nurse then told him all babies are born with blue eyes and that would change soon.

Leonard then walked over to me with the baby, and she was crying. He tried to hand her to me, and I was in no shape to take her from him. I told him, "Just talk to her, she will stop crying," so he did just that, and she stopped crying, and then they, Leonard and the nurse, took the baby out of the room. The doctor was trying to get me to give birth to the afterbirth (the water sac), but I was too tired and just wanted to lie there doing nothing.

The nurse tells me that they had my mother on the phone, and they handed me the phone. She asked me how I was and what I just had. I told her, "A girl, six pounds and seven ounces, the normal size for a baby." The doctor was still trying to get me to give birth to the afterbirth, so I told my mom I had to go; I was not done yet.

I got off the phone with her, and now I had to push to get this afterbirth out of me.

They took me to my room, and then they brought in my daughter to me. Leonard went home, and it was just me and the baby now.

In the morning, they brought in the birth certificate for us to fill out. I filled in her name as Aurora, and then he gave me a middle name for her. The middle name was a Vietnamese name so that way, the family had a name to call her. I wrote it in, and then the lady took it down to the certificate office so it could get recorded.

Leonard's two sisters were there at the time I filled in the birth certificate. They asked him what we had just named our daughter, and he told them, "Aurora."

That is when one of his sisters pulled him out into the hallway, and I overheard her tell him, "You are really going to let her name your daughter after toilet paper?"

He came back in very upset and started to yell at me to change her name now. I told him, "We have discussed this, and you had no problem with it before, and now you do? I will not change my daughter's name. You know how much that name means to me and why I gave it to her."

He picked up the telephone and was about to slam it into my face, and as he was picking up the phone, I saw the lady in the bed next to me jump out of her bed and then look at me with fear in her eyes, so I told him to put the phone down; I would call them and have them change the name. I was too embarrassed at the time to be upset with him.

I called down to the birth certificate office and had them change the first name and to use the Vietnamese name as her middle name on the certificate.

Leonard was home for a week on paternity leave. He helped out with cleaning his sister's yard. He even helped with the baby; he allowed her to sleep on his chest while he was sleeping on the couch and doing the laundry. Renee, his sister, caught me taking pictures of him cleaning the yard and sleeping with our baby; she asked me what I was doing.

I told her, "He has never helped me. I want to have pictures so that in the future, we can all look back and say look, he does know how to help." He did listen to the doctors when they told us, "No heavy lifting and no sex for about a week." We had to allow my body to heal.

My mom stopped by to visit with her granddaughter. She asked me what I had named her. I told her Samantha.

She looked at me, and I took a picture of the two of them together on the couch.

My mother then told me that Samantha was jaundiced and that I should get her out into the sun; this would help her and make her healthy.

I told my mom that she was not jaundiced because her eyes did not have a yellowish tone to them. She was part Asian, and their skin coloring was different than ours; she was just fine.

My mother left to go home. I looked closer at Samantha, and I did not see any discoloration. The next day, I did play with her outside; she was almost a week old now.

On her first doctor's visit a month later, I asked the doctor about her being jaundiced. He told me she looked just fine to him, and being jaundiced was something you could spot really easily— yellowing around the mouth, nose, and the whites of the eyes.

I told him, "I know all that, but my mother scared me, and I just wanted a second opinion."

It was now time to have Samantha baptized. The only way the Catholic Church would baptize our child (because I would not become a Catholic myself) was if we decided to renew our vows within the church. No big deal for me—we were already married and had been for almost one year now.

That morning, my sister-in-law said, "This is your big day."

I said, "Yes, it is. Samantha will be baptized in a religion I know nothing about, but I do know that God will overlook that and watch over her because this is something I have already asked him to do long before she was even born."

Renee looked at me and said, "No, today you get married."

I looked at her and said, "We are already married. Did you think I am the kind of person who would get pregnant out of wedlock?"

Renee did not say anything more to me.

We lied to my mother about the date of the baptism; Leonard did not want my mother or anyone from my family to attend it.

My mom had asked me when I would be baptizing Samantha. I told her it would be the week she just happened to be out of town. This was the only time the church was open, and I could not wait any longer for Samantha was one month old now, and I wanted to get her baptized before she got any older. "You know, Mom. You always get the baby baptized one month after they are born." We really had her baptized the week before she went out of town. I believe that was the last time I saw my mother; she was moving to the East Coast to be closer to her favorite daughter, Lorraine.

I was kind of sad to hear that she was moving, but I knew it would make things easier for me and Leonard if she was not so close to us.

Leonard always thought I would drop everything and run to be by my mother's side; she thought that I did not want her around, and that was because Leonard controlled my every move.

At the baptism/marriage, it was just his family with us. This was a private baptism; we did not have it during the regular church service mainly because we were renewing our vows that day.

After it was done, Leonard's family handed me an envelope with some money in it. They told me to hold on to it and whatever I did, to not give it to Leonard. I told them I would do my best. They told me it was not much, but it was something for the three of us.

Once Leonard, Samantha, and I got into the car, he asked me for the envelope. I told him, "Your family told me to hold on to it and that this was something I needed to put away for the three of us."

He looked at me and repeated it to me slower, "Hand me the envelope."

He opened it and said, "This is it—this is all I am worth." It was one thousand dollars.

I told him, "Does the amount bother you? It shouldn't—money is money and we can build on that. If we put it away by the time Samantha gets older, it will have grown."

He looked at me and told me, "You don't understand. They don't like you, and this small amount of money from them proves it—it is a slap in my face."

I just looked at him and told him I loved him and Samantha loved him. "That is all you need, the money means nothing."

So he kept the money, and then he went out for the night.

I received a rather big check in the mail shortly after quitting my job at Builders Emporium. I was thinking I should put it away for Samantha in some college trust fund or buy her some books and educate her now so when she grew up, she could get a good career that made her some good money.

I decided to buy her books. Leonard asked me where the books were coming from. I told him that my mother had gotten her a subscription to the Disney baby book club. I knew if I told him I was buying them, he would ask me for the money, and then I would have nothing for my child.

I was able to get her about six months' worth of books before the money ran out.

He was back to saying that I had a boyfriend on the side and he was the one buying the books for our daughter.

We were using his sister's crib for Samantha. Renee got a new one after her second child was born four months later. Someone gave us a stroller. All the clothes we had were from his older sisters and their girls. We did get some new clothes for her, but we really didn't need to with all the girls in the family, and babies don't need much when they are young.

I would sing and read to Samantha most of the day. We would go out for long walks and look at all the bugs, birds, anything to entertain me. We would walk just to get out of the house.

This was the first time I did not have to get up and go to work. I had all day and night to myself. Samantha was an easy baby. She stayed awake during the day with some little naps (I would nap with her), and she slept all night. She would wake up at 5:00 a.m. on the dot. Her daddy's little alarm clock is what I nicknamed her.

She was no trouble. I, on the other hand, was so nervous about everything, and I could not understand why I had this uncontrollable need to clean her all the time, change her diaper every time she peed.

Leonard told me that diapers were made to hold more than just the one pee; she could wear them longer and she would still be okay. I would change her about five or more times a day, and with every change of the diaper, I would clean her. I gave her diaper rash because I cleaned her all day long by putting her bottom under the running water and then drying her off with the towel every time.

I would put an ointment and powder on her to keep the pee from touching her skin, not realizing that it was causing her to get diaper rash because I was washing her bottom with soap and water and not using the towels they have to wipe the baby's bottoms.

I had to allow her to air heal; I would open up the diaper so her skin could heal when she was sleeping. I learned that babies don't really pee too much when they sleep, or mine didn't. I had the diaper still on her, only it was just under her bottom and not on the top part of her. You can't do that with a boy; they wake up and with the air touching them, they pee. Girls are a lot different that way.

There was something going on inside me that I had to call my dad and ask him what our mother did to us as small children. The need to stay by my daughter's side and clean her all the time was so nerve wracking it was all I could do, and when I was not next to her, I would have horrible thoughts of her getting hurt. She couldn't even move to hurt herself, but I could not shake this feeling that kept coming over me.

I would try to just be in the other room cleaning or cooking, and I would have to run in the room and check on her to make sure she did not move or stop breathing. During the night, I would wake up just to make sure she was still breathing, and when I thought she was not breathing, I would pick her up and bring her into the bed with me. Leonard would ask me what I was doing; I told him I could not hear her breathe. I move the crib next to the bed and removed one side so I could easily get to her in a heartbeat.

My dad told me, when I called him, that our mother would sit on the bed and talk to her friends in New Jersey and not clean or feed us. He would have to come home on his lunch break to clean us and feed us. He said that I would always be crying when he walked into the apartment and my mother told him that it was because he was around me. They both told me that I did not like my father as a young girl; I would always start crying when he came home. I told my dad, "Did you ever stop to think I was trying to tell you I was being mistreated by this woman?"

He told me no, he never thought of it that way. "I did walk in and you and your brother were both covered with shit." She did not change our diapers.

I told my dad, "It's funny what the body will remember when we are young. They always say that we won't remember anything as a small child, but I seem to have remembered it all without knowing what it was until I had a child and became a mother."

I made a decision right then and there not to keep hurting my child the way I was, by washing her as much as I was and to allow her to get dirty. I would not change her diaper when she peed once; this would not kill her. I learned I would change her when I could feel the diaper full from the outside and not stick my finger inside to see if she peed.

This was a big weight off my shoulders, and I felt better after I talked to my dad and found out how our mom would neglect us when we were younger. I know now that I was not perfect, but I did not want my child growing up with the same anxieties that I have or had. I did not want to make the same mistakes my mother made.

I did want Samantha to wear a dress every once and a while so I could get some cute pictures of her. Every time I put her in a dress on her, she would scream. She started this after her first birthday. I think it may have had something to do with the time she touched the iron and burned the back of her hand. Renee's husband was ironing his clothes for church when Samantha crawled into their room and touched the iron with the back of her hand. Both Renee and I ran into the room, and I grabbed my daughter and ran back out into the kitchen where Renee and I had just been, to run water on the back of her hand. Leonard came out of our room to see what had happened. I showed him Samantha's hand, and Renee's husband said he did not see her and he was sorry. Leonard looked at me and said, "I blame you for this."

I looked at him and said, "What? I was out here getting everything ready for her birthday party, and you were with her."

He then told me if anything more happened to her, he would blame me and I had better watch her better. I did not understand at that moment what he was trying to say to me; I just shrugged it off to him being scared.

We headed over to his dad's house after about a half hour of me running the water on Samantha's hand to get it to stop hurting her and her screaming at me. I knew burns from an iron take some time to stop hurting or burning because I had burned the palm of my hand with a curling iron. I had been curling my sister Nancy's hair one day because she wanted to have curly hair when Betty one came into the bathroom and wanted the iron so she could curl her hair. As it started to fall and hit her in the face, I grabbed it—the iron and not the handle—so it would not hit her. I burned the whole palm of my hand, and I held on to it and threw it into the sink. I put my hand under the running water. But we had to get going, and my mom came into the bathroom and told me to wrap things up. I told her I had just burnt my hand and that I would need some help. I could not just get up and go now. My mother handed me a bag full of ice and said, "Let's move now." A bag of ice doesn't work on a burn. So I understood the pain my child was in, and I would not move until she was no longer crying every time I took her hand out from under the water, no matter how long this would take. Leonard had some burn ointment, and he rubbed it on her hand, and she seemed to calm down. He worked for the city and he had taken a CPR class and a first-aid class so he knew what to do in case of an emergency. He just did not act as if he did. He just got angry with me about this, and on the way to his dad's house, he told me that if I allowed this to happen again, he would take it out on me. I reminded him that she was with him and I was in the kitchen and that he should have been watching her and this was just an accident and she was fine. He then told me that if she ended up with a scar, it would be my fault.

When we got back home after her party, I would hold her hand and tell her how sorry I was for hurting her. I asked God if he could take this pain from her. I felt as if I was the world's worst mom because this was my daughter's first birthday and now she had this burn on the back of her hand.

We got back to Renee's house. I put Samantha in her crib and raised the crib wall to go into the kitchen and help my sister-in-law. I was standing at the stove when I saw my niece call to someone. She was standing in the living room looking toward Leonard's and my room, and right then out of the corner of my eye, I saw Samantha walk over to my niece.

I had been working with Samantha for some time now to get her to come away from the walls and walk over to me but with no luck, and then here with my niece, she got out of her crib and walked over to her without using the wall.

I asked my niece, "What did you do?"

She looked at me and says she just had called to Samantha and she had walked to her. Now my niece is four years old. I said to her again, "I understand that, but how did you get her to walk to you without using the walls, and how did you get her out of the crib?"

My niece told me that Samantha had climbed out of the crib, and that is when she saw her and called to her.

I was like, "OK," so I picked up Samantha and put her back in the crib and stood there to see what she would do. Samantha would just lie in the crib and not move. I stood there for five minutes and nothing.

I walked out of Samantha's view to see what would happen if she did not think I was watching her.

Then I heard it; she landed on the floor, and then I heard the pattering of the little feet moving toward the living room.

I was shocked to see my baby girl climb out of the crib and then just get up and move as fast as she did out to my niece; she would never do this for me.

I have to admit I was a little hurt to know she did not want to walk for me. After all, I was the one teaching her. I wanted her to walk to her dad on her birthday; turns out she walked to her cousin.

I was glad that I did get to see her walk. It may not have been her first step, but it was the first time she walked.

I don't know where Leonard was, but with Samantha walking now, he did not act as if it was a big deal. I told him that night that I was hoping he would be the one she would walk to or that he would be home to see it. He told me, "Why, are you jealous that she did not walk to you?"

I told him, "No, but I was hoping that you would be the first one she walked to. It would have been nice to see her walk to her daddy and you could then pick her up. I was here, and I did see her walking, and maybe she will do it when you are home, then you will be able to watch your daughter walk to you."

I rolled over and away from him, and I started thinking to myself, *God, how do you do this? This unconditional love you have for all of us? I feel hurt when my own child prefers to be with her cousins and not with me, but I am not angry or jealous about it. I was being selfish, hoping that she would at least walk to one of her parents first. Every other kid runs to their parents, but mine runs to be by her cousin's side. Every morning, I would find Samantha in my sister-in-law's room, not wanting to be with me and her dad. It hurts to know that my own child turns away from me and I just have to let her go. God, you must have a lot of patience with us. So many of your children turn away from you. You don't get angry with them or try to hurt them in some way. You just wait patiently for them to come back to you. God, I know that I have been asking for patience all my life, but this is the time I will need it the most. I know my child loves me. I just need some patience with her because she doesn't like being stuck with just me all day long and her cousin is her size. I get it. I just need patience with all the rejection I will be getting from her as she grows up. I understand you more now, God, I see a lot of you in me, and I will take each rejection at a time and then just give it over to you. This child is dedicated to you to look after and guide, and I will need to trust you with her. Amen.*

From that moment on, I did not let the rejection of my child hurt me inside anymore. I trusted God, and he always got me through everything.

I developed a small cyst on the right side of my neck; I was told this was normal after giving birth because I had not gone to the doctor's office early enough to have it removed in the office. I had to be admitted to the hospital. It was a one-day procedure, meaning I would be admitted to the hospital in the morning and then go home after the procedure later that same day. I was a little nervous about this procedure because now I had a small child at home. Samantha was about a year and a half now.

I woke up in the recovery room, and things were going well. Leonard brought Samantha with him, and they came into the recovery room and asked me if I was ready to come home. The nurses told him not just now, but they would be releasing me soon.

They handed me my clothes, and I walked over to the changing room to get dressed. We headed over to his father's house to have dinner.

About two weeks later or so, I went to the doctor's office to have the stitches removed. I asked him if the cyst would come back. He told me, "Not in the same area." He had cleaned it out, and it was nothing to worry about.

The three of us moved out of his sister's house and into her converted garage. It was two rooms. One was used as our sleeping and TV room; the other was the bathroom and kitchen.

Leonard would have me take the fiancé of one of his younger sisters (Tammy) to his doctor's appointments. He (Donald) suffered from migraines, and he went in to see his doctor about once a month for a shot. So now I was the lucky one; I got to take him to his appointment. As we headed home after he got his shot, he asked me if he could take me out for lunch (you know as a way of saying thank you for helping him out). I told him no, I had to get Samantha home and to bed. I did not want to tell him that I really felt uncomfortable around him and Leonard would never forgive me for going out with his sister's fiancée.

I dropped him off at my father-in-law's house because that is where he and Tammy were staying. He had Tammy ask her dad to move out of his room so that Donald and she could have it. I never really liked Donald from the beginning; he just rubbed me the wrong way. Then when he asked Tammy to ask her dad to move out of his own room in his house, that just sealed it for me. I could not be around someone like that.

So when he asked me to have lunch with him, I could not tell him the truth—that I found him disgusting and a bit of a baby.

Leonard was still spending a lot of time away from us. On one of his outings, he crashed the Forerunner. He did not tell me what he had been doing at the time of the accident. I found out when some strange man had called us and asked for Leonard and I told him he was not home. I took a message for Leonard to call this man. He asked me who I was, and I told him I was the wife. That was when I found out that he had been hit by a semi truck. It was a rainy day, and Leonard was in the fast lane on the freeway when he hit a puddle and hydroplaned across two lanes and the truck driver could not slow down in time, so he hit Leonard on the passenger side right in the middle of both the passenger side doors; they were smashed in. This truck driver told me he did the best he could to slow down, but my husband had been driving too fast in that outside lane, and when he hit the puddle of water, he just took flight; there was no way to avoid him. I told him I understood and thank goodness no one was hurt. This man then asked me if we had insurance on the truck. I told him, "Sorry, no, we do not have any insurance on the truck."

He asked me again, and I repeated, "No, we do not have insurance on the truck." He then hung up.

I asked Leonard about the accident, and he told me that yes, he did hit a water puddle and hydroplaned. He said it did not matter how fast he was going because he would have hit it and the same outcome would have happened even if he was driving slower. I said, "Okay, as long as you did not get hurt. What are we going to do with the truck?" I could still drive it, only I had to use the doors on the driver's side of the car, and I did not like trying to get Samantha in and out of the truck on the driver's side because that would put us both on the street, and a car could easily come by and hit us as I was trying to get her either in or out of the car. I would climb into the back seat and then close the door, so that way we would both be safe inside the car, and then I would open the door to get out of the car after I put her in her car seat.

Leonard asked me to call my father and ask him if he had a car I could buy off him. The truck had disappeared one day, and I had no means of getting around town anymore. I told Leonard that I would now need a car to take Samantha to her doctor's appointments and that I would like to know where the truck went.

My dad worked as an automobile mechanic out in Ventura at a dealership when I was younger; he now had his own place. We drove out to his shop in Ventura.

Leonard talked to him about his shop and asked if he needed someone who could help him run the place with him, like to be his partner. My dad told Leonard that he already had a business partner, the young man who works with him. When he did decide to retire, he was going to allow this young man to buy him out.

Leonard stayed in the car as I went into the DMV to sign all the paperwork for this car my dad was selling to me.

As the three of us were waiting in line (my dad, Samantha, and myself), my dad asked me how things were going, and I told him, "Fine." I thanked him for allowing me to buy this car off him and that I really needed it now that our truck had gotten into an accident and somehow it disappeared. He told me that if it were me asking him for the car, he would never have sold it to me; it was only because Leonard had asked him for it. He then tells me he never wanted any more children after my brother was born and that I was a mistake. I was in shock; my heart stopped, and I almost started to cry. I could not believe that my own father would not sell me a car just because I was a girl. He had given or helped my brother with his car, and to this day, our father still works on my brother's car that he had given to him. The car our father helped my brother with is a 1963 Plymouth Belvedere; the one he sold me was an old Plymouth that had some ailment issues.

After we got the car registered in my name, we all went out into the parking lot, and I walked over to get into the car with Leonard, and I told him, "Never have me ask my dad for anything again. He doesn't like me and never will, and I am okay with this." Leonard handed me the keys to my car, the Toyota Camry that we had drove there with, and he would drive the Plymouth home.

Samantha still spent a lot of time with her cousins in my sister-in-law's house. Then they sent her back to me, and she was always upset and crying when she had to come home and be with me. Once her dad got home, she was happy, but then he had to go to his second job.

I gave her a bath and she played by herself while I fixed dinner. She liked to talk to the rice bag. The rice bag had a picture of a Buddha on it. I thought nothing of it when I caught her talking to it. Lots of kids have imaginary friends. Leonard, on the other hand, was a little freaked out by it; he said she was talking to a ghost.

I told him, "No, she just wants someone her size to talk to." So I told him I wanted another child. I wanted Samantha to have a playmate for life.

I was now pregnant, and Leonard's sister Tammy was upset with me. She got up in my face and very angrily asked me why I had gotten pregnant again.

I did not say anything to her, but in my head, I was asking her how this is any of her business. I just walked away from her.

I was back to Leonard telling me that he knew I was cheating on him and if this baby didn't come out looking like him, he would know this to be true.

That night, after having his family members upset over the fact that I was pregnant again and Leonard starting up on me that I was cheating on him, I thought to myself, *What have I done? Another nine months of listening to him tell me that I am cheating on him and his family not happy about it?* But I reminded myself why I wanted another child. I did not want Samantha being left out all the time. His family did not accept her like they had Renee's daughters; they treated her differently, and I did not want Samantha thinking she was less than her cousins. I wanted this child, and I would go through all this nonsense with Leonard thinking this was not his child again just so that Samantha would have someone like her to play with. So every night, I would pray to God, "Please let this one look just like him and make sure it is healthy and has all its toes and fingers."

I was now driving the car my dad had sold to me. I was taking Donald to his appointments, and I was also now taking my father-in-law to his doctor's appointments.

Leonard's family members would tease Leonard on how I was sleeping with the mailman. I now had to take everyone and myself to the doctor's appointment. Leonard was harder on me about this child coming out looking like him. I thought it was bad the first time around, but now with the family members helping out the way they did, it just made it harder on me, and he was full of anger and hatred when he said it now.

When I was eight months pregnant, Leonard decided to come with me to one of my dietitian appointments. I was gestational diabetic with my second child, and for some unknown reason, Leonard took me to the hospital to meet up with my diabetes doctor.

She asked if we wanted to know the sex of our child. I told her yes. I looked over toward Leonard and then back at the monitor. I heard her say, "It is a girl." I was extremely happy, but with the look on her face, I could tell something was going on. She walked over closer to me and asked me if I was going to be okay.

I told her, "Yes, we already have the clothes for a girl. She has an older sister at home."

She looked me in the eyes and asked me again, "Will you be all right?"

I was a little confused to what she meant by that. I was not the one looking at Leonard's face when we were told the sex, and this doctor of nutrition was. She almost held me down on the bed asking me if I was going to be okay. I got up and told her, "I have a girl at home, and we have everything we need. Not to worry, I will be fine."

When Leonard and I were walking out of her office, I asked Leonard if he was okay with having another girl. He wasn't saying anything to me, so I just kept on telling him that we had everything we needed; we did not have to go out and get new clothes or boy things. We were going to have another girl, and I was really, extremely happy about that.

We got into the elevator, and the doors closed. This is the first time I took a good look at Leonard's face, and I asked him if he was okay. He said nothing to me, and as we were standing in the elevator going up, I could feel this cold chill from him. It hit me like a ton of bricks—our marriage was over.

From that moment on, he was even more distant from us.

I went to my last doctor's appointment one week before the due date; the doctor told me that if I did not have the baby by that Monday, we would have to induce labor.

Renee had had to induce her labor, and she told me, "Whatever you do, make sure you give birth naturally. You do not want them to induce your labor."

She told me, "You have no control, and the body just takes over."

I told her, "I will do the best I can, but I don't think it is up to me. This child will come out when it is ready." Only because I was already big because I was gestational diabetic and they did not want the baby to stay inside me longer than the nine months.

So the night before her due date, I started with heavy contractions. We left Samantha with her aunts at my father-in-law's house, and off to the hospital we went. His father lived about five blocks away from the hospital, and this time, I was in no hurry to get there. My water did not break or anything like that. I was just in heavy labor, and one of Leonard's sisters told him to get me over to the hospital.

It was a Sunday, and we were all at his dad's house for dinner and the football game.

As they admitted me, the contractions slowed down and then stopped altogether. At about 10:30 p.m., the nurse came in and told me that if I did not go into labor by 12:00 a.m., they would send me home. I did have an appointment to be at the hospital the next day (Monday) to be induced.

Leonard must have misunderstood the nurse because he left and went home. The nurse came back in and told me that they would be releasing me and that I should be back here by 8:00 a.m.

I asked her if I could use the phone. I needed to call for a ride if they were going to release me. She then asked me where my husband was; I told her that he had gone home.

The nurse was upset with me over this; she told me that she had told us that they would be sending me home at 12:00 a.m. I just looked at her. She then handed me the phone, and I called my father-in-law's house and asked for Leonard to come back and get me. They told me he was not there at the house, that he had gone out. I told my sister-in-law someone needed to pick me up and take me home. The nurse came back in and asked if I had found a ride home. I told her yes and that they helped me get dressed. She told me to go home and take a nice bath and relax and to make sure I kept my appointment here tomorrow morning. As I was getting into my sister-in-law's car, my contractions started again. She told me not to have the baby in the car, as we are both now headed back to my father-in-law's house.

As I got out of the car, Leonard's younger brother ran up to me and started telling me how Leonard had taken his best clothes and has taken off. I was in between contractions and not saying much to him. Once the contractions stopped, I looked at him and asked if I could use the phone. I called Leonard's pager and put in our emergency code; this way, he would call me as soon as he could.

He called, and I was not a happy camper. I asked him where he was and why he had to change his clothes to go out. Leonard's sister was trying to get me to be quiet as I was yelling at Leonard. She reminded me that it is 1:00 a.m. and people are sleeping. I told

Leonard to get back to his dad's house now. I hung up, and I looked at his sister and told her I was sorry if I was making a lot of noise, but I was in labor and my husband was out painting the town red.

By the time Leonard came to get me and Samantha to take us home, it was about 2:30 a.m. I get home and cut off the hospital tag because it was bothering me and making my skin crawl. I took a cool shower because I was sweating so badly.

I got out of the shower and I dried myself off, but because I was sweating as badly as I was, I could not fully dry myself off.

I put on a long shirt and got into bed. I did the best I could to fall asleep, but I could not. I was now dripping with sweet and in a lot of pain. I looked at the clock, and it was now 3:00 a.m. I rolled onto my left side and tried to sleep. No good. It was 4:30 a.m., and I was trying to get Leonard up and take me back to the hospital because I felt there was something wrong and I would feel better being at the hospital. Leonard told me to call someone to take me; he was tired and did not want to get up. I shook him and said, "Get up now, I need to go to the hospital."

He rolled over and told me to call his sister.

I called his sister (Renee) and asked her if she could take me to the hospital. I needed someone to take me now, and Leonard was not going to get up and drive me this time. Renee told me that she would take the baby and Leonard could then take me to the hospital. I told Leonard what his sister had just told me—that she would take the baby and that he needed to get up and drive me to the hospital. I moved the phone away from my face so she could hear him tell me, "No, I am not taking you, and I will stay right here and watch our daughter." His sister told me to meet her husband outside; he would be driving me to the hospital.

I walked out to the front of the house and got into the car. My sister-in-law's husband drove me to the hospital. He then helped me into the wheelchair and took me in. We were met by three nurses, and he then handed me off to them and told me, "Good luck."

I thanked him, and as I did, one of the nurses asked him if he was coming up with me. We both at some time said, "This is not my husband/wife," and they just looked at me. I thanked him again as they took me off to my room.

The nurse asked me if my husband was going to be coming up later. I told her, "No, he is at home with our older daughter, sleeping. That is just my brother-in-law dropping me off."

As they got me into the bed, the one nurse looked at me and asked me where the tag was. She said, "I just sent you home."

I told her as they were hooking me up to the monitor, "You told me to go home and take a nice, cold bath. Only the tag was irritating me, and I took it off."

They were tiring to stick a needle in my arm for the IV, but because I was so wet, they could not get it into my arm. They did get it to go in on the side of my arm right at the wrist, just below my thumb.

They had about ten nurses in the room telling me not to push because they could not deliver the baby.

They kept telling me that I needed to stay on my back and to stop rolling on my side; they could not hear the baby's heartbeat. As they rolled me back onto my back, I heard one of them say to another, "Get the crash team up here now." They told me to stop pushing and to wait for the doctor. It was 5:00 a.m. when I got into the bed at the hospital, and by 6:00 a.m., I had given birth.

My daughter decided that she would come out still inside her water sac, so she ripped me in two. I could feel the doctor sewing me back up while the crash team took care of her.

This little Asian nurse walked over to me so I could see her for the first time. I looked at her and then the nurse, and all I could say was, "She is so big. That came out of me?"

They took her away, and then the doctor finished stitching me up. They all left the room. I was now really starting to feel the pain in my arm from the IV. I called to the nurse to come back into my room and remove the IV from my arm. The nurse walked in, and I told her if she took the IV out, I would get up and use the restroom. "Just please get it out of me because it hurts."

She then walked over to my left arm where they stuck the IV and saw that I was still all sweaty and that I was in a lot of pain; I almost fainted when she lifted my arm. She then called for someone else to come in and remove the IV. I thought I would die when they were removing it. I had gotten goosebumps all over my arm when they lifted my arm to remove the IV from it. She also said, "I can see that this is very painful for you because I see you are reacting to me just touching your arm." They removed it, and I then asked if I could use the restroom. One of the nurses reminded me that I would need to use the water bottle and tap-dry myself and not wipe because they had just stitched me up and they did not want me to rip myself open again. I had forgotten that. So I did as she said. When they brought me the baby, I was told that she weighed ten pounds and eleven ounces and she was twenty-two inches long. I had prayed for her to come out looking like her dad because he told me daily he would know if I cheated on him if this baby did not look like him. I also prayed that the baby would be big because I knew that Samantha would want to play with it, and if the baby came out small like Samantha was (seven pounds, eight ounces, twenty-one inches), she may hurt the baby if she tried to play with it, so I did tell God to make sure this one looked like its dad but also make sure it would be big, and God heard my prayers.

It was about 4:00 p.m. by the time Leonard and Samantha came to the hospital. Leonard asked me if I could go home now. I told him I did not know; I would have to find out.

Leonard's father came with them. His dad asked me whom I thought she looked more like; she looked like Leonard, but she did take after me just a little. My father-in-law said yes, he too believed she looked a little more like me. I think it was because she was so round and lighter in color than the other babies in the family.

She also was born with both the white babies' red neck and the Asian babies' blue butt.

We named her Natalie, and we also gave her a Vietnamese name for the family.

They said we could go home after Natalie checked out to be healthy because again, I was gestational diabetic and they had to make sure she was not diabetic.

Leonard drove us all home, and then he left. I was now at home with two babies, and we all got into the bed and went to sleep.

I had Samantha on one arm and Natalie on the other arm. My arms were out as if I were nailed to a cross with a kid on each one of them like they were the nails on my cross.

Two weeks later, it was Samantha's third birthday; her god-parents were kind enough to throw something together for her. Samantha's godparents were Leonard's oldest brother and his wife.

Two weeks later, we had Natalie's baptism, only this time we did not have a private one; there were about six other people with us having their babies baptized. Leonard's oldest sister and her husband were picked to be Natalie's godparents this time. I did not have any say in who was going to be Natalie's godparents and/or Samantha's.

Leonard took Samantha in the church, and I was still in the car getting Natalie ready for her big day when I saw an envelope stuck in between the passenger seat and the center counsel. My first thought was Leonard did care about me and his new daughter, so I opened it and started to read it. It was a beautiful card with a nice, warm beach scenery on the cover. It read something like this (in ink, not the card itself): "I can't want to be with you again. Every moment we spent together I will treasure. I had lots of fun with you last night. Counting the moments we are apart."

I just sat in the car. I could not believe what I was reading. I did not read what the card had printed on it because I was just too stunned at what I had just read.

Everything within me turned cold. My worst nightmares were coming true, and here it was in my hands. Leonard came back to the car to get me. He opened the door and asked me what I was doing. I looked at him, and I showed him the card. He told me he had never seen that before. I started to read it to him. Meanwhile, I was getting out of the car, and his sisters were standing close enough to us to hear me read how this person could not wait to see him again and that she had lots of fun with him last night.

He told me this card was not his and he had never seen it before. His sisters told me not to make a scene because we needed to get inside the church to baptize Natalie and Leonard would never cheat on me because that was not who he was and if he said he had never seen that card before, then he had never seen it. "Okay, let's go."

As I was standing on the steps of the altar in front of the church with Leonard's oldest sister (Cindy), I looked at Leonard sitting next to Samantha and I was full of hate. I had to look away and just look at Natalie and try to listen to what the father was saying to us.

With this open baptism, they only had room for one parent and one godparent on the steps, again because there were six other families with us.

I kept looking at my baby girl and thinking, *Please God, get me through this. I cannot be angry now. This is the most important time of Natalie's life, me having her join you in spirit forever, and I am not in that holy place right now. I need you to watch over her and guide her in this church I do not believe in. I just need you to help me focus on this moment in time and let me not be so full of hate.*

After the ceremony and we were all outside taking pictures together as a family, I noticed Leonard was staying far from me.

Tammy came over to me and told me that Leonard would never cheat on me. I just looked at her and said, "Are you sure? Because he is never home with me or the children. I would be very careful with what you are about to say to me."

Donald walked over and said, "See, Tammy, she forgives him for cheating on her. Why can't you do the same?"

I could not believe my ears. Donald knew Leonard was cheating on me, and Donald was cheating on Tammy.

When we got home, I asked Leonard who she was and why he felt he had to cheat on me.

He told me he was only doing this to prove to his sister that Donald was no good for her.

He did it all for his sister, and this girl meant nothing to him, and he would never see her again. He then told me that he did not like the way Donald was treating his sister. He did too many drugs, drank, and cheated on her. I told him "Donald only did that because you were by his side doing the same thing, and if that kind of behavior was not good enough for your sister, then why was it good enough for me?" "Don't I deserve a husband who is going to be faithful to me, someone who doesn't drink, smoke, and do drugs? Is Tammy that more deserving of someone who will treat her with respect than me?"

He looked at me and said, "Are you jealous?"

I told him, "No, I am not jealous. I just want someone to love me the way you love your sister."

One night, Leonard was out, and the girls and I went to bed. He came in and grabbed me by the ankles and pulled me to the end of the bed. I was trying to get away from this unknown person when I heard him say he needed some more good luck; I recognized his voice at once. He then forced himself on me. Once he was done, he handed me a large sum of money, all one-hundred-dollar bills, and he told me to hide it from him. "Whatever I do, don't give it back to me or tell me where it is."

He then left, and I started to quickly count this roll of money he handed me. I counted out sixty-five one-hundred-dollar bills, then I stopped and hid it away. I still had a lot more money in my hand, so I put that roll in a different place.

I crawled back into bed, and just as I was falling asleep again, Leonard came in. It was about an hour or two later; he grabbed me and asked for the money. I told him calmly that he told me not to give it to him. He then got very angry and started to yell. Now the girls were sleeping and I did not want him to wake them, so I gave him the smaller of the two rolls of money. He looked at me and asked me, "Where is the rest of it?"

I told him, "I do not know what you mean. This is what you gave me, there is nothing more."

He now got up in my face and was spitting on me when he talked. He told me, "I know how much I gave you. Give it to me." So I got up and got it for him. He then counted it.

I told him, "It is all there." He handed me back a small amount, and this time, I did not count it because I knew it would be gone by daybreak.

He then came back one more time, and this time, he went right to where I hid the money the first time and took the rest of it.

In the morning when the girls decided to get up, I got up and started looking through the dresser drawers, hoping that maybe he had left a hundred-dollar-bill behind (but no, nothing). To my luck, he took it all.

He was being more careful with not leaving money in his pockets now. He also was not paying his sister Renee rent. The bills were being paid late, and I had strike rules on when I could call him.

I was getting tired of him gambling all night and then being away all day when the girls and I had nothing in the place to eat. Natalie was still breastfeeding, but I still needed to eat, and so did Samantha.

Every once in a while, I would find twenty dollars in the wash after cleaning his clothes. I would then walk the girls up to the grocery store and get something for us to eat for dinner.

I always had to ask him for money. Sometimes he would take us to the grocery store to get food, but most of the time, I would ask his sister if she had anything we could eat.

I developed some bumps on the walls of my vagina. I went to the doctor's to find out what it was; these blisters hurt more than anything words could describe.

The doctor had to take a sample to have it tested, so he scraped the inside of my vagina wall, and I almost fall off the bed; the nurse was trying to hold me down on the bed.

He told me he was done and he would be right back and to go ahead and get dressed.

Now the inside of my vagina was on fire, and I could hardly move. I got dressed, and I sat back down on the bed.

He came back in to tell me that I had herpes and that I would need to contact all my sexual mates.

I told him I was married and had been for five years now; I was not sleeping around. He just looked at me and walked out of the room.

I got up, and now I had to pee. I walked into the restroom and I sat down to pee. As soon as I did, I jumped off the toilet because it hurt. I thought for a moment I was going to hit my head on the ceiling in the bathroom; that is how high I thought I jumped.

Now I was trying to figure out how to make the pee run down the right side of my vagina wall and not the left where the doctor took the sample from. There was no way to do that, so I held on to the sides of the toilet and finished peeing.

I got back home and I told Leonard, "You gave me herpes. Who are you sleeping with?"

He just walked away from me. I had to go back to see my doctor because I had gone into the emergency room the night before.

My doctor looked at the chart and told me, "This is not herpes II. It is herpes I, and with herpes I in a herpes II area, it is not herpes." Meaning that I did not have the virus, I would just break out if my partner had a cold sore and then we had sex. I told her he did not have a cold sore at the time. She then told me that it was something he carried within his saliva and that if he even had the smallest of cracks on his lips, I would break out.

I went home, and now I was afraid to touch Natalie, so I wore gloves when I had to bathe her and change her. I did not want to give my child herpes at such a young age.

I started looking through the phone bill because I knew he had been cheating on me; now I had the proof. I found a number that repeated in the hours when he told me not to call him. He had gotten a cell phone, so that was why I could get in touch with him if I had an emergency at home, only he had the cell phone, not me, so if I was out, he could not get a hold of me.

I called the number that kept showing up on the bill, and I talked to the young lady who answered it. I told her who I was and that she would need to go to the doctor's to make sure she did not have AIDS because I just got out of the hospital and I found out that I had AIDS.

She tells me she was not the one sleeping with Leonard, that it was her girlfriend. I told her again, "Then you—or I mean your girl-friend—had better see a doctor because I now have AIDS, and I have the paperwork to prove it to her, or I mean your friend."

I then hung up the phone with her, and about five minutes later, Leonard called me all upset over telling people he had AIDS. I let him yell at me, and when he was done, I simply asked him, "If you were not sleeping with this girl, then why you are so upset? I believe you are sleeping with her, and that is why you are so upset with me. I now know the truth because if you were not sleeping with her, then you would not be calling me this upset, and how did she get your number, and why is it that she can call you during the hours you tell me not to call you?"

He did not say anything more to me other than he was not cheating on me.

I told Renee that I now had herpes and it was because of her brother and he was cheating on me with some Vietnamese girl. She looked at me and told me that Vietnamese women don't sleep with married men.

I showed her the card from this other women, and she looked at me and said, "Vietnamese women do not do that."

One day, the car I bought off my father despaired. Leonard had taken it to his second job, and then he did not come home with it. I asked him what happened to my car. He told me that he had sold it to a woman who needed it more than me. I look at him and said, "She needs the car more than me? I have two young children whom I need to drive to their doctor's appointments and the grocery store and she needs it more than me, are you sure? That car my dad sold to me and not you, you can't just up and sell it."

He then told me he could do whatever he wanted; it was his money.

I walked over to the WIC office in Burbank to see if I could qualify for the program. WIC is a program for low-income families—women, infants, and children. I took in my husband's pay stubs, and the women behind the desk told me that he had made too much money for us to qualify for the program. I sat there, and I told her how he spent all his money gambling and I did not have food in the house to feed my children. I was in tears asking her for help.

She did allow me to go on the program, but it was just for the three of us. I told her I understood. She also said the Samantha would not be eligible for the program at the age of five. She was four now. I told her I understood and that I would do my best to get off the program as soon as I could. This way, they could give what they were giving me to another women and her children. I took a meal preparation course and a dietary class as well because that is what this program was about, how to prepare and cook healthy meals for your children and not go out for fast food all the time.

Leonard had to buy me a new used car (because he sold the one we bought from my dad); this one was an old red Mercedes. I do not like the color red, but I had no choice. The salesman was telling me how lucky I was to have such a loving husband, I looked at him and said, "Yeah, luck!" The salesman then walked away from me.

Leonard was not happy about my reaction to the car salesman. He said, "Why can't you just be happy?"

I told Leonard that I did not want to be fake. I did not like the car, and I did not want it. "You will get rid of it in time."

We drive it over to his family's house to show it off. Annie, one of Leonard's older sisters, came outside to look at it, and the first thing out of her mouth was "What a beautiful car, and it is a Mercedes—nice." I just looked at her and smiled; I did not say a word. The old owner of the car left a pillow in the back window that read something about loving his wife so much that he bought her this car. Leonard told his family this was the reason he bought this car for me, because he loved me and I did not appreciate him. I thought to myself, *No, they just wanted to get rid of that old pillow, so they sweet-talked him into buying the old thing.* It had nothing to do with me. It had everything to do with him showing off to his family. He was never around and he was not paying his bills. Renee was not happy about this either, but she did not say anything.

Samantha was now enrolled in preschool; she loved getting away from me for the four hours a day. I would drive her and my niece in the afternoons to the local preschool.

We qualified as a low-income family, so we did not have to pay for the preschool.

One afternoon, after I picked up the girls from preschool, Natalie was in the car seat, and it was placed in the middle, so that way, the two older girls could sit next to a window. As we were heading home, we passed the high school. It was close to the end of the school year, and all the seniors were outside in the front of the school to take their yearbook picture. There were about twenty cops out front directing traffic. As we made the left-hand turn to drive home, Samantha tried to get up and look at all the police officers. As I was driving down Burbank Boulevard heading home, I saw her, and I was telling her to sit down. I moved my hand down by my right side, and I grabbed her foot and I was holding on to it so that way, she would not be out of her seatbelt and/or standing, looking out the back window.

When I got to the bottom of the hill, I saw a police offer behind me with his lights on. I pulled over. He asked me to step out of the car. He then told me why he pulled me over. I told him that my daughter was in a seatbelt and all he needed to do was look into the car and see it for himself. He would not do that. He then asked me to open my truck. I did, and the officer found a second license plate in the trunk of the car. He asked me about this second set of plates. I told him we had just bought this car and I did not know anything about them; I did not even know they were in the trunk.

He then told me that it was illegal for me to have two sets of plates for the one vehicle, but he could tell that they were personalized plates and that maybe the other owner did not know they could take them with them when they sold this car.

I did not say anything more to him about the plates, and he then gave me a ticket for not having a seatbelt on my child. I told him again, "Please look into the car. You will see she does have a seatbelt on." He handed it to me and told me to have a good day.

I was going to be in trouble once Leonard got home. I saw he was not happy about the ticket and he told me I would have to fight it. I told him he needed to go the DMV to hand in the extra plates in the trunk of the car.

I went to the courthouse, and I paid the ticket, and I asked them about fighting it. The clerk then gave me a court date to come back.

I had to show up in court sometime in November.

I took Samantha and Natalie to court with me to fight this ticket. Natalie was asleep, thank goodness, for most of the time we were there. As the day passed, Samantha fell asleep and Natalie woke up. I had to leave Samantha sleeping in the court room and run out into the hallway to call my sister-in-law (Renee) to come and pick up Natalie. I kept walking in and out of the courtroom till my sister-in-law showed up to take Natalie home. I sat back down, and finally, I was called. I was the last case for the day on the judge's list. The officer stood up and told his side of the story to the judge. He also told the judge that I kept trying to get him to look into the vehicle, and then the judge looked at me and asked me to tell my side of the story. I told the judge the officer had it right, but he did not know that I was trying to get my daughter to sit down by pulling on her leg. I told the judge that if I had gone up and over my shoulder, he would have me in here for child abuse because he would have seen my arm and mistake it for trying to beat my child. They all just laughed, and then he dismissed the charges and told me that I would be getting a refund in the mail.

Now it was closer to Christmas, and Leonard took the money and went gambling. I told him he needed to start paying his sister rent; he just walked out the door.

I now started keeping track of all the money that he was throwing away. I took his paychecks and added them together, and I took the bills we had and added them together, then I took the income and subtracted the bills, and he was throwing away about two-thirds of his income. I showed him how much money he was just throwing away, and he told me, "Do not concern yourself with this. You did not make the money, I did, and it is mine to do with as I want."

I told him, "The only reason we moved in with your sisters was so that we can save money. You are always gambling it away. How are we ever going to move out of here?"

We did not have a TV, so I spent a lot of time outside with the girls. We walked every day to the grocery store to buy food. I would walk around the store with the coupons that WIC had given me to get some food and formula for Natalie now that she was no longer breastfeeding. I would slowly walk around the store, and I would talk to God. I would tell him, "Please one day let me be able to walk around a grocery store and not have to count my pennies. I would like to be able to just walk in, get what I need, and walk out without having to count or think. Do I have enough money for that?"

When I found money in the dryer, I would stop at the ice cream store and buy Samantha and I some ice cream. I would share mine with Natalie because she was still young and it was not good to give babies ice cream, they could get the runs eating too much of it.

Leonard was asking me where I got the money to buy the small amount of groceries that I did buy. I told him I was on the WIC program; he did not believe me, so I pulled out my card and showed him. He still did not believe me and asked me if I was cheating on him.

I told him, "No, here is my card, see?"

I had to walk over to the WIC building once a week to check in and get more food vouchers. Leonard did not like me using the gas in the car, so the girls and I walked everywhere. The only time I took the car out was to take my niece and Samantha to preschool and then to pick them both up from preschool.

The trip over to the WIC building would take up the morning because the building was on the other side of Burbank. It would take me two hours to walk over there and then one hour at the building and then the two hours to walk home. I would be pushing both girls in the stroller. Sometimes Samantha would get out and walk, but it was a long trip, so she would get tired and crawl back into the stroller with her sister.

Leonard would come home at night when the girls and I were asleep. He would sometimes force himself on me, and then we would leave.

One time, when he decided to take me, he tried to put a dildo in me. I moved away from him and asked him what he was doing. He told me that he wanted to see if I noticed the difference between him and the dildo.

I told him, "Of course I do, I would have to be insane not to." I told him that he had better get that thing away from me or he was not going to be getting anything. I got up before the girls and I took it outside to throw away. Renee happened to be standing there when I did it; she looked at me funny. I told her, "This is what your sick brother is up to. I am not into toys." Then I put it in the trash can.

CHAPTER SIX
Darkness and Light

Woe to those who call evil good and good evil, who put darkness for light and light for darkness, who put bitter for sweet and sweet for bitter.

Woe to those who are wise in their own eyes and clever in their own sight.

Woe to those who are heroes at drinking wine and champions at mixing drinks, who acquit the guilty for a bribe, but deny justice to the innocent.
—Isaiah 5:22–23

Samantha was very much a tomboy, and she loved to climb trees, play in the dirt, and spend lots of time riding her bicycle. One day, when she was outside playing, she fell and hit her face on a tree root that was above the ground.

She came running into me, crying. I stopped the bleeding, and then I put some ice on her month to make it feel better. I told Leonard that Samantha had fallen, and he told me if she had any damage to her teeth, I would be paying for it; he would hold me fully responsible for this.

I took her into the doctor's office the next day to see if maybe she had done some damage to the nerves in her mouth because now her gums were this kind of gray discoloration and then her two front teeth had turned gray. The doctor told me that he was not sure if she had done damage to her nerves; he said we would have to wait and see once her permanent teeth came in.

I told Leonard what the doctor told me—that we would need to wait for her permanent teeth to come in; the doctor had no clue if she had done any damage to her teeth.

Again Leonard reminds me that if anything bad has happened to her teeth, he would put full blame on me and this was my entirely my fault for not watching her. He meant this; he was very angry and up in my face when he said this to me. I told him, "Kids fall and get hurt—that is part of the package. You can't stop them from getting hurt. Did you ever get hurt? I know I did. You learn from it, you get up and dust yourself off and do it again."

He just looked at me with hate in his eyes. Leonard turned to walk out, and I told him I had had enough and that if he went out again tonight, the kids and I would not be here when he got back.

He walked right by me as if he didn't hear me.

I yelled at him, "I am not joking. You choose to go out or you choose to be with your family— which one means more to you? Your choice, but remember, we will not be here when you get back."

He closed the door behind him. I was just standing there, looking at the door, waiting for him to come back in.

I packed up some clothes for the three of us; off we went after waiting one hour for him.

I drove out to my grandmother's place in Palmdale. As we drove out to her place, this overpowering urge came over me to just run the car off the road. I saw it so clear in my head, the three of us rolling down the steep hill and dying, but then I started to think, *Wait, what if just one of us lives, like Natalie? How could she survive without me? Or if only I survive, then how could I live with myself If I kill my babies?* I snapped out of it and told myself, *No, he doesn't control me like that. I am in control. Leonard wouldn't even miss us. We need to live. He is not worth it. My kids are worth more to me than him.*

We made it safely to my grandmother's house, but because she lived in a retirement place, we could not stay with her for more than one week.

That night, I prayed to God, "Please let Samantha's permanent teeth be white." I saw an image of God touching her teeth, and then I heard they would not be straight. I said, "That is okay with me. Just make them white—that is all I care about right now. We can make them straight. We can't make them white."

In the morning, my grandmother asked me what I was going to do. I told her I didn't know. I did know that I could not just go back and keep living the way we were. He needed to stop living a life that we didn't exist in.

I called Leonard's dad that night to tell him what had been going on, and I asked if maybe he could help me with his son. All I got from my father-in-law was, "I did not raise him like that. I can't help you."

My mother called and told me that she would have three tickets at the airport for us. She was going to send the three of us to David's house, and then from there, we would drive over to Lorraine's house.

I told her, "Fine, just let me know when we have to leave."

I called Leonard's cell phone, but he did not pick up. I told him it was over and that I would be leaving in the morning.

He showed up at my grandmother's house and he wanted in. I told him (through the door), "Will you give up everything you are doing? Will you give up the girls, drink, gambling?"

He told me he could do whatever he wanted and that he would not change anything.

I then said, "We have nothing more to talk about. You need to go."

He told me he would not leave, but then my grandmother told him, "If you do not leave now, she will get security out here and they will escort you off the grounds."

He left.

My mother called me the next day and told me, "The tickets will be at the airport tomorrow." I thanked her, and we spent the last day with my grandmother and we made it a good one. As much as I was dying inside, I knew that I needed to get away from him. I needed him to understand how it felt to be alone.

He was never around or interacting with the girls.

The day we were heading to LAX to catch our flight, I stopped by his sister (Renee's) house, where we lived, to pack up some more of our things to leave for good. As I walked into the kitchen area, I ran into the ironing board. It had been left up, and his best suit was missing; it looked as if he were happy to have us gone.

The three of us headed over to the airport. I parked the car in the overnight lot. I started to think, *He is going to have to pay to get his car out of here if I park it in the lot.* And then I said to myself, *Who cares what he has to pay to get his car back? This is not my problem anymore.*

As I found an empty spot and parked the car, the song "Listen to Your Heart" came on (by Roxette), "You've built a love but that love falls apart. Your little piece of heaven turns too dark." I waited for the song to finish because at that very moment in time, I was finally standing up for myself, and it was something I needed to hear before I left him because I was feeling those exact feelings at that time. I needed to listen to my heart and tell him goodbye.

I walked over to the check-in desk, and I checked the girls and myself in. They told me that I could keep the car seat with me because I was holding it, but if they needed to give that extra seat to a passenger, they would then come and take it and put it in with the other luggage under the plane.

Once I got past all the security, I called Leonard to tell him where to pick up the car. I also told him he would need to bring cash with him to get the car out of the lot.

He didn't say, "Please don't go" or "Stay, we can work this out." He just started yelling at me about something which just made my heart sink, and now I knew I was doing the right thing, and I said goodbye and hung up.

We got on the plane, and they placed us up front. This was the first time the girls and I had been on a plane.

Another mom sat down with her child, and an older woman was next to us. I had the car seat still with me at this time, but I did not place it in a chair because I was not sure if I was going to be able to keep it.

Then the flight attendant came over to me and asked me for the car seat. I had Natalie in my arms, and Samantha was next to me in her own chair. Once the plane took off, Samantha started to cry, and there was no stopping her. I did everything I could to get her to stop crying. The flight attendant tried to give her some crayons, some water, gum—you name it, they were trying to help. Even the older lady next to me asked if she could help by taking Natalie so I could hold Samantha and maybe that may calm her down. I thought to myself, *This woman can't run away with her, so why not?* I handed Natalie to her, and I picked up Samantha. It did help for a short time, but then we started to descend, and she would start crying again. As the passages got off at the first stop, a lot of them were giving me a nasty look.

We then took off and back to Samantha crying again. Now I heard from the other passengers, "Can't you get that baby to stop crying?" The flight attendant came over to me again and asked if she could walk around the plane with Samantha. I thought to myself again, *She can't just run off with her,* so I handed Samantha to her and they walked to the back of the plane. Samantha was still crying. The flight attendant brought Samantha back to me because now we are about to descend again. This time, as the other passengers were getting off, they made rude comments to me like, "Maybe you shouldn't be flying with such a young child, can't you control her? I hope you are getting off here."

The other women with the baby and the older lady got off; I was riding this all the way to the end.

We took off, but now we had the entire front row of seats to ourselves. I let Samantha get up and walk around.

The flight attendant came over to me with some Sprite to see if we could get her to swallow and that may help her with the presser building up in her ears. Samantha would just push it away from her mouth without drinking any of it. I would never think about giving my child soda, but when you are on a plane and everyone around you would like to kill you, you do whatever you have to do to help the situation.

We finally landed, and I waited for everyone to get off the plane before even moving. They were happy to be getting off the plane, and once again, they were giving me dirty looks.

I finally got off the plane, and I walked over to the luggage area. I could tell from all the faces in the baggage area the people who were on the plane with us; they were talking and pointing at me and shooting me looks of disgust and shaking their heads.

You could not tell that Samantha had been crying for the past three or so hours; she was happy to be back on the ground.

My younger brother David came up to me and hugged me. We grabbed my bags and the car seat, and off we went to his place.

As we were driving to his place, someone in another car yelled out to him. I asked him who that was, and he told me that it was his wife's friend. I then asked him if I was going to be meeting her and his boys. He told me that Lynn and the boys were with her parents this week, so I would not be meeting them on this trip.

We got to his place, and he was tired because he worked the night shift, so he was going to lie down. "But if the phone rings, answer it. But don't wake me because I do not want to be disturbed."

I made the girls something to eat, and then we sat down to watch TV. The phone rang, and it was David's wife, Lynn. She asked me who I was and why I was at her house. I told her that I was David's oldest sister and that I was here with my daughters and I was hoping to meet her and the boys. She told me that she was visiting her parents; she then asked if she could talk to David. I told her that he told me not to wake him but I would try.

I knocked on his bedroom door and told him that Lynn is on the line and that she needed to talk to him.

He finally came out of his room and we talked; I asked him if everything was all right.

He told me yes, her friend had told her that she saw me with another woman, so she thought I was cheating on her. I told him I fully understood that—here was some woman showing up in his car and house that no one knew about; of course she wouldn't like that.

Our mother called the next morning and wired some money to David and me. I told my mom that we would need about six hundred dollars to drive over to Lorraine's house.

David looked at me and told me it would not cost us that much to drive to Maryland from Ohio.

I told him whatever was left over, he could have it. "You do need to drive back? We do need food and drinks for the drive, right?"

Later that day, after picking up the money, we headed out for our road trip. We stopped at the store and grabbed something to drink and eat in the car and fill up the gas.

As we were driving, he told me that I was the only reason he was walking. I said, "What do you mean by that? I did nothing." David told me that I was the only one to visit him in the hospital and that Mom had told him he would never walk again (the day of his accident), and when he asked me, I said it with such firm conviction of certainty that I knew I would walk again.

I told him, "Mom told me that she was the only one visiting you and that I was a bad sister for not visiting you."

He then told me, "No, you were the only one to visit me, and she never once came to see how I was doing after I was admitted."

I was in shock; this was all news to me. He then asked me if I knew Mom's recipe for the lasagna she would make. I told him, "Mom never made the lasagna, I did."

He laughed and said, "No wonder she stopped making it."

I gave him my secret ingredients. Then I told him, "I will need to kill you now," and we both started laughing.

We got to Lorraine's house, and we all went out for dinner before David headed home. I drove us from his house to Lorraine so he could sleep and then make the trip home later that night.

Lorraine was in the middle of a move herself, so I helped her move to her new place, then she tells me that I can't stay here with her. She rented this house for her and her two children, and she could not just add us to the lease. I called Leonard, and we talked things over. He said he would change and that he would give up the gambling and spend more time with me and the girls.

Lorraine gave him her address and told him the best and fastest route to her house and that he should take Highway 40 straight out to her place.

He made it to the East Coast in three days.

He arrived, and I was placing all our bags in the car, and Leonard was talking to my sister.

Lorraine walked over to me and told me it was too soon for me to go back. I told her, "I can't stay here. Can you help me get a job?"

She said, "No, so then I need to go back." She then told me that he was high on something; he has not slept in three days.

I said goodbye, and off we went.

Leonard asked me to drive once we hit Highway 40. He said all I had to do was stay on the 40 and we would end up back in California.

As soon as we switched places, Natalie starts crying.

Natalie had to sit with me in the passage seat because Samantha was in the car seat in the back, and we only had the one seat, and some of our luggage was also in the back seat as well as the trunk. So I would hold Natalie up front with me.

Leonard could not get Natalie to stop crying. I told him it was because she did not know him, and here was his opportunity to get to know her.

After about thirty minutes of her crying, he told me to pull over, and we switched places again.

The minute I took her from him, she stopped crying. I looked at him and said, "See, she just needs to get to know you."

As we were driving, he told me he was falling asleep. I told him to pull over; I could drive.

He told me "No." He said that I should give him road head and this would help him stay awake.

Now both girls were asleep, and I told him, "No, how is that going to help? Natalie is asleep, and I can drive. Pull over."

He pulled my head over to him and shoved it down to his waist and told me to give him head. I was not in a position to do anything. I did what I could, and then he got mad at me for not doing it right. I raise my head and move away from him, he then told me he would need to do it himself.

This same routine with us trying to switch driver and Natalie crying and him trying to get me to give him head happened three different times on the way home, each time with the same outcome. I was always doing it wrong. I told him I could not get down on the floor in front of him. I was coming at him from the side, and I had Natalie in my arms. Of course I would not be able to do it right.

We made it home safely as I was unpacking the car. He told me if I ever did that again, he would call the police and tell them I kidnapped his kids.

I looked at him and told him calmly, "Are we getting a divorce? I was just out visiting my family who has never seen our children."

He just walked away from me.

We had to claim bankruptcy because of the accident Leonard had with the truck driver. He was coming after us for payment of his truck, and we could not afford to pay him. One of Leonard's friends told him that if he claimed it in bankruptcy court, he would not have to pay for the accident.

We were in the room with other people who were claiming a chapter 11 bankruptcy. They called us up and talked to us, and then someone from the stereo store stood up and asked Leonard where the stereo was that he had bought; the store wanted it back. Leonard told the man from the store that he had sold it at a pawnshop. The man asked him which one, and Leonard told him he did not remember, then the man left. I was told to keep my mouth shut when we were in this room. Leonard said he would handle everything.

When we got into the car, I looked at him and asked him, "The stereo system that man was talking about, isn't it the one we still have at home?"

Leonard said yes, but he did not want to return it.

I tell him, "That is stealing, and you should return it to the store."

Now Samantha was in kindergarten, and I was taking my niece to school in the morning. I had a red wagon, and I set all three of them in it. I then tied a big umbrella to the side of it with a bungee cord so that they could have shade from the sun as I walked them to school.

One morning, as Samantha was brushing her teeth, I heard her start yelling, "She broke it." She came running up to me saying, "She broke it, she broke it."

I asked her, "What did you break?"

She said her tooth.

I told her, "No, baby, you are growing up and you have to lose your baby teeth. That is what happens when you become a big girl."

She was crying and saying no, and then she said she was not going to school.

I told her, "Everything will be fine, and yes, you have to go to school."

I got her to school, and I pulled her kindergarten teacher over, and I told her what happened this morning and asked her if she could help make Samantha feel better today. She said she would make it a special day for her. I thanked her, and then Natalie and I headed home. By the time I got to school to pick up Samantha, she had forgotten about her tooth and was laughing and playing.

Leonard kept his promise and he was no longer gambling, but he was now spending more time at both his jobs. We did see him a little more than we used to.

I was no longer getting WIC because he had decided to feed us, and I started looking into programs that helped first-time home owners qualify for a house of their own.

One Saturday, when Leonard was off, we headed over to a seminar to learn how to qualify for a house.

The program was running through how to cut back on spending and how to save your money, things of that matter. They also told us about some other programs out there that claimed to do the same as they did. As he was running through their names, he told us not to write them down. I wrote them down because two of them I had heard of before, and if this one did not help us, the others might.

At the end of this seminar, they then asked us for a small deposit. Leonard was not one who parted with money that easily to strangers who claimed they could do something for you for a small fee.

We got in the car, and he was not happy about this program. He started up with me on how this was a dumb idea. I looked at him and I asked him, "Does *Fanny Mae* and *PERS* ring any bells?"

He told me, "No, why should it?"

I told him, "Because these two programs are for first-time home owners, and PERS is through the government. I see it on your check suds. I know how to get in touch with them."

He asked me how I knew about the other groups and why this group would even mention other groups that did what they did, only for free.

I asked him, "Did you hear what they said when they mentioned the other groups? You must not have been listening. They said not to write down the names of the other groups."

He then said to me, "Yeah, so?"

I told him, "When someone tells you not to write down the name of their competition, you do, and then you call the competition, that's what."

We got home, and during the week, I started looking into these programs. PERS would not help us because of the bankruptcy, but Fanny Mae would. We had to wait eighteen months before we could make any big purchase like a house.

During that summer, Samantha lost her front teeth, and the permanent ones came in. They were white and thick. They were the whitest teeth I had ever seen; all I could do when I saw them was to thank God for making them come in white and thick.

They were crooked, but that was okay. I told God if he made them white, I could make them straight.

At the start of the new school year, Leonard and I started looking for homes. It had been eighteen months now since we had filed the chapter 11, and now we could start looking for a house. I don't know for sure if Leonardo had saved up any money, but he was willing to look for a house and finally move out of his sister's converted garage.

We had been living with his sister for seven years by the time we finally moved out.

We sold the Mercedes and bought a suburban because I told his sister I would pick up her two children and Leonard's cousin's two children and watch them. I would not charge Leonard's sister to watch her children because I was now paying her back the money we owed her for living in that converted garage without paying her.

Samantha was now seven and Natalie was four when we finally got a home for all of us.

Leonard apologized to me for having us live that way for so long.

We get a two-bedroom house with a nice big backyard for the girls to play in.

Natalie started preschool, and I now had some free time to clean the house, do yard work, clean and iron his clothes, cook dinner, and all my chores.

We had a push grass mower, so it did take me some time mowing the grass. I would mow it, and then I would have to rack up all the cut grass. I would move some of the cut grass to areas of the yard that were not as healthy as the other side of the yard. That's why it would grow and make the side that was not as healthy healthier.

It would take me the whole morning to cut the front and back yard. By the time I was finished, I would have to pick up Natalie from preschool. We would come home, and then Natalie and I would play and do the laundry together. Then we would drive over to the elementary school to pick up all five children at 3:00 p.m.

Their parents came to pick them up at around 5:00–5:30 p.m.

I would help them with their homework, and I would be making dinner for Leonard so that way, when he came home he could eat, shower, and then be off to his second job.

When he got home at 12:00 a.m., he would wake me up to have sex. After we had sex, I would get up and take a shower. He caught me doing this and was very upset with me. He told me, "What, you don't like having my smell on you, that you need to get up and wash me off?"

I told him, "No, I just did not want to get a breakout. I always break out with herpes after we have sex if I don't wash myself."

He then said something like, "Yeah right, you just don't like my scent on you. You have to shower me off you." (He used foul language.)

So the next time we had sex, he lay in bed watching me. I just rolled over and fell asleep. In the morning, I got up, and sure enough, I had a breakout (herpes). I had two blisters.

That night, he woke me up again to have sex, and I told him no, I was tired. He told me, "How you can be tired? You do nothing all day."

I told him, "Today was house cleaning day," and that I had spent all morning cleaning and then I had taken care of six kids in the afternoon.

He then forced himself on me, and all I could think about was me breaking out more because now he was going to pop the blisters I already had.

I got up to take a shower, and he was not happy with me at all. I told him I already had two blister, and now with us having sex again, they would spread.

He started saying that I was cheating on him again. I was so done with this cheating thing that I said to him, "You are right, I am cheating on you. The man I am cheating on you with loves me so much more than you that he allows me to stay with you, have your children, and always make sure I have what I need and all the money in the world. That is how much love the man has for me."

I turned to walk away from him; that is when he hits me. He hit me on the back of my head. I turned around and looked at him. I said, "Do you feel like a man now?" I just got into bed; my head hurt, and I prayed to God that I did not die tonight from a concussion or some kind of head injury.

Leonard would always make sure he hit me in places that would not burst.

I would get up at 5:00 a.m. and make him his coffee and lunch.

When he stopped taking his coffee with him, I would then just make him his lunch, and when he would stop taking his lunch, I would just stop doing it for him altogether.

He would get upset with me, and I would remind him, "If you do not take the coffee and/or your lunch that I have made for you fresh every morning, I would no longer make it for you. I do not like the smell of coffee, and I do not drink it, so if I have to get up at five a.m. with you and get your lunch and coffee for you so you can just run out the door and you decide not to take it, I will no longer make it for you.

"You are the one who will be deciding if I have to get up or not. I only do this to help you—this is not for me. I would love to be able to sleep until six-thirty a.m. and then get up and take care of the girls, but because I love you, I get up with you and sometimes before you to make sure you get to work on time."

He just looked at me, and then he told me that he did not like the way I made his coffee. I told him, "That is all you need to say to me. You tell me how you like it, and I will do my best to make it that way or you can do it yourself. I never made coffee before and I don't know how you like it without you saying something to me."

So now I had worked out a schedule for me. On Mondays, I would clean the house; Tuesdays, I would do the laundry; and Wednesdays, I would iron Leonard's work clothes. On Thursdays, I would mow the grass and put out the trash, and then on Friday, I would bring in the trash cans and do more cleaning around the house. That way, I would have time to spend with Leonard and the girls on the weekend.

Leonard injured his knee on the job when someone's dog got loose and chased him. He twisted his knee as he was running from the dog; he had to jump into the back of someone's pickup truck to get away from the dog.

Now he was at home with me, and I had to take care of him. We went to see the doctor, and they took x-rays and an MRI. He would need to have surgery; he tore his meniscus and ligament. The doctor gave him something for the pain.

Now he spent all his time in bed sleeping. When he got up, he was mean. He started yelling at me and calling me names. I asked him if he needed anything, and he just pushed me out of his way and walked into the kitchen. He made himself something to eat, and he grabbed a beer. I asked him, "Where did you get the beer because it was not in the refrigerator the night before?"

He told me he could have alcohol in the house if he wanted. It was his house and I was not paying for it.

I told him, "I do not like alcohol in the house, you know this. We have talked about this many times before. I hope you do not drink it in front of the girls. That is something I do not want around them and your smoking. If you could, please not do that in front of the girls."

He told me he only smoked in the car when he was driving—it helped keep him awake—and he could drink whenever he wanted.

Leonard's family had this running bet that I would get pregnant again (they never said it to my face, but behind my back, I did hear them) now that we had our own house. Leonard always wanted a boy, and I told him when he learned to appreciate the girls, then I would think about it. He was heartbroken when he found out that the second one was another girl. I could tell he really wanted a boy. In reality, I was not going to have another child with him. I had the two, and with how hard of a delivery I had with Natalie, I did not want another child. I had herpes and did not know if I could have a safe delivery, and I did not want to have a C-section. With the way he was hitting me, I did not want to bring another child into this mess.

I developed heartburn with Samantha's pregnancy, and with Natalie's pregnancy, I developed acid reflux, and with him home and strung out on whatever drug he was on made my acid reflux flare up. I had to deal with him being angry when he would finally wake up. I had to take care of everything around the house, the children, and the dogs he had just brought home one day. I would throw up in the morning. He told the girls I was pregnant.

The girls asked me if I was pregnant, and I told them no. He would look at me with darts in his eyes (as if I were calling him a liar). They then asked me if I was sick. I told them no, I was all right. I told Leonard to stop telling them that I was pregnant. I was not doing that again, remember?

Then once I started my period, Leonard would be very upset with me, and sometimes he would hit me again on the back of my head. I would pray to God at night, "Thank you. I do not want another child. Please don't allow me to get pregnant again."

Every month I didn't get pregnant, Leonard got angrier and angrier with me. He hit me and always on the back of my head; he hit me so hard that I got whiplash. We had to go over to his dad's house to eat, and I told him, "I can't move. I do not want to go."

He then started up on me on how I was going to stay home and cheat on him. I just didn't what to fight anymore (I was already hurting), so I got into the truck.

We get to his dad's house, and I sat down on the couch. They called me in to eat, and I told them, "I am fine, I don't want to eat."

Annie came over to me and asked me how I was doing. I told her that her brother had hit me and I couldn't move my neck. I was not in any mood to eat right now; I was in too much pain. Annie then walked away, and the next thing I knew, Leonard was now yelling at me to get up and eat. He came over to where I was and got up in my face and said, "Why would you tell her I hit you? I did no such thing."

I looked at him and I asked, "Then why do I have whiplash right now after you punched me in the back off my head?"

He said so sweetly to me, "I don't know. Maybe you fell and now you are blaming me? Get up and go in the other room and eat. If you tell anyone else that I hit you, then I will kill you when we get home."

I just sat there for a while, and then I got up and joined the family. I just sat with the family, not saying anything and not eating much because my neck and head hurt too much to eat.

After a year in our house, Leonard decided to refinance the house. I told him that would not be a good idea because we had a low interest rate, and the monies for the land tax are being kept in impound for us with the bank, and if you decide to refinance, then you will need to make sure it is an impounded loan. We cannot afford to come up with the land tax in November and then again in April if we do not have someone set it aside for us.

Leonard told me that the bank was getting all our interest on that money and not him. He told me he knew how to save money. "This is not your decision. I pay for everything around here, not you."

So we refinanced the house, and the first thing he did with the money was go out and buy himself a convertible Mustang.

All I could think of at the time was, "God, please let us be able to come up with the property taxes."

He also traded in the red suburban for a newer white one.

Leonard's dad had an aneurysm, and the family had all gathered at the hospital. They had to remove some of his skull to allow the brain to swell up; they told us if they did not do this, he could have brain damage, so the older brother and sisters said yes to the operation.

As I was sitting in the waiting room, I started to pray, "God, this family is not ready to let go of their father. Could you and your wife, Mary, watch over him and give him back to them? They would be lost without him."

He made it through this aneurysm with no major side effects, but with the second one about a year to the date later, he did not do as well. He lost some of his memory. He could no longer speak to me in English.

This made it easier for Leonard to yell at me in front of him, because his dad no longer understood us when we took Leonard's dad out food shopping. On one occasion, we took his dad to a bird show to get him some birds for the big walk-in cage Leonard had gotten him after his second aneurysm. Leonard bought him the birds and the cage to help keep him busy during the day. So as we were walking around looking at all the birds, I saw Leonard in a light I had not seen him in for some time now. He was walking around with a big smile on his face. He was talking to everyone to the point where he and this woman started talking about him and how kind and sweet he was. She looked at me and asked me where I had found such a sweet man, and before I could answer her, Leonard told her that we had met in high school. So she looked at me and said, "Oh, how cute, you are high school sweethearts."

And Leonard's said, while grabbing me to hug me, "Yes, yes we are."

I just remembered looking at him and thinking, *Why can't he be this nice to me all the time?*

He then looked at me and said, "Can't you say anything nice about me?"

I snapped out of my thoughts and said, "Yes, it's nice."

We got to the car, and Leonard put the top down. I reminded him that we had live birds and they could not survive all the wind on the freeway in these small cages. "Could you please put the top up?"

He placed the birds in the back seat with me and told me if I let just one die, he would kill me.

I told him, "If you drive with the top down, you are killing the birds, not me, so don't even think about it."

He gave me this evil look, and so now I had to place myself on the tops of the cages that were on the floor of the car so that the wind didn't hit them from the top. I did not have a seatbelt on because I needed to use my body as a shield. Leonard's dad had one of the bird-cages on the floor between his legs. Leonard loved to speed. I kept asking him to slow down, and the minute I did, we would just speed up, so I just gave up on him.

We made it to his dad's house safely. All the birds survived the car trip. I could tell from his dad's face he knew something was up between Leonard and me. I just smiled at him and took his birds into the house for him.

Leonard spent more time at home and not at his first job. He was still working at night with the city job. He was high on whatever pain pills they gave him for his knee. He spent most of the day asleep. I would check in on him to make sure he was still alive.

Now that he was back to work (and on light duty) at the post office, Leonard's sisters told him I should go back to work because the girls were in school and we needed the money.

Leonard told me that I should start looking for work now that Natalie was in kindergarten and Samantha was now in third grade. I reminded him that he told me when we first decided to have kids I would stay home and raise them. He told me that they were not at home and they were at school now and I needed to get a job.

I went to the girls' school and applied to be a yard duty guard. I had to go and get a live scan. They had to take my fingerprints and run them through the Burbank Police data bank. They did a background check and drug testing, and I passed with flying colors. I didn't do drugs or drink; I didn't have a criminal record.

Leonard would go to his day job about two days out of the work week, and then he would spend the other three days at home. He had now picked up a new habit; he was now watching porn when I was at work (part-time with the elementary school the girls attend).

When I and Natalie would get home, we would catch him watching it. I opened the front door to find him in the living room and the porn on the TV. I told Natalie to stay outside so I could go in and turn off the TV, and then I would tell her to come in after the TV was off. I did not want my child to see any of that.

Leonard would wake up and curse at me, "What the f—— are you doing?" I told him we were home now and Natalie needed to get her homework done. She did not need to have the TV on right now. He got up and walked by me, then after he passed me, he hit me in the back of my head.

I just stood there thinking, *Nice, I get hit because you have a problem with porn.*

Now when we had sex, he told me that I was doing everything wrong. I asked him, "What do you mean I am doing this wrong? You never complained before." I then asked him, "If you think I am doing this wrong, then you must be doing it right with someone else?"

He pushed me off him and said, "Never mind."

After almost a year of waiting for workman's comp to pay for his surgery, he was now scheduled to go in, only because he had taken too much time off. He no longer had any time, sick time and/ or vacation time, so he need to ask his co-workers (at the post office) if they would donate some of their time to him so he could have his surgery.

Once he got enough hours from them, he decided to BBQ for them. One Saturday, we all drove out to his job in Long Beach so we could BBQ for all his co-workers as a thank-you to all of them who had given him some of their sick and/or vacation hours.

He sets up the BBQ and started to cook the meat we bought for the employees that gave him hours. Things got going and he started taking in the cooked food into his co-workers' and left the girls and me outside to continue cooking for him.

It must have been time for everyone to start their routes because people were coming out of the building as if it were on fire; they would walk by me and ask me what I was doing. I would tell them that Leonard was saying thank you to all the coworkers that had donated hours to him. Some took food; some did not. I had no clue to who helped him and who didn't; I didn't know these people like he did, and he was now inside doing whatever it was he was doing.

I just kept cooking and handing out the meat that was done to anyone who would take it. The girls were getting tired of sitting around. I told them I was too, but we were here to help Daddy, so we needed to do what he had asked us to do, and that was to cook the meat and pass it out to his friends. I would hand the food to the girls, and they would then give it to the people walking by us.

I was wearing a dress; it showed off some cleavage, not much. They had a staircase behind me so as the men walked up the stairs, they could look down my dress. I could feel them doing this, and every once in a while, I would turn so that I would catch them, and they would then walk away smiling at me.

These men would walk up and down the stairs multiple times, and I would stop what I was doing, turn, and watch them. They finally just gave up and left.

Leonard came out of the building, and he was upset with me. He started in with, "Why are you so angry with everyone?"

I asked him what he meant by that.

"I am the one out here in the heat of the summer and cooking for your coworkers, and where are you, inside? While I am out here and your little friends are trying to look down my dress. That's okay? Stay out here with me and cook—this was your idea, not mine."

He told me that they had asked him to work and that I had to smile more at everyone. As he was saying this to me, some of the women who worked in the office came out to get some food. They asked me what was going on, and I told them, "We are Leonard's family, and we are here to say thank you to all the people who donated some of their time to him so he can take off the time to have his surgery." They asked me what I had left. I told them I had just started cooking up the last of the chicken wings and that was all I had, then we were done. They asked me to hold on to it for them and that they would come back. I gave my girls some chicken, and then we waited for the woman to come back.

They came back out, and I handed them the chicken. I asked them, "I know you don't know me, but was I mean to you?" They just looked at me.

I tell them that Leonard told me that I was not being nice to some of his co-,workers and I was not smiling. It was hard to cook, hand out food, talk, and smile the whole time so someone told Leonard I was not being nice to them. They smiled and told me that I should not worry about it; the people who worked here were a little off themselves. We all laughed. They went back inside, and I started cleaning things up.

Leonard came out and told me he was almost ready to go home. I told him the girls and I were tired and hungry. We did not eat much of the food we were making for his friends.

He put the BBQ on the hitch on the back of the suburban, now that it had cooled down.

He drove the truck off the lot, and he parked it in the street under some trees and then went back into the building. We were just about to fall asleep in the truck when he finally came out.

He got into the car and didn't even say thank you to us for doing all the work for him. He started driving us home. I reminded him we are hungry, "And could you please stop somewhere so the girls and I can eat?"

He must not have heard me. He dropped us off at home, he took a shower, then off he went. I had to now cook something for us and clean up everything from earlier that day.

He got home later that night and started poking at me. I knew when he started poking me, he wanted sex. I told him I was tired and I was not in the mood to have sex with him. He just kept poking me. I told him no.

He was like, "Come on, I need this. Look, you get him hard just by doing nothing, and you are the only one who can do that to me."

I told him, "No, if you had stayed and helped me and seen what your friends were doing, then I would not be this tried and maybe I would want to have sex with you, but you dragged us out there, then you went inside and left us for over four hours to cook for people we did not know and then left us in the truck with no food and water. Thank you, but no thanks." So he started to poke me again. I told him that would not get me to have sex with him; it would only make me even more upset with him.

He finally stopped. He got up to go out in the living room, and he turned on the TV. The sound was really soft, but the light for the TV kept me awake. I got up and walked out to the living room. I saw what he was watching. It was porn from the porn channels on the TV. I sat down with him and watched the porn. I told him, "Look, he has already come. Listen to the noise, it doesn't match up with what they are doing. The sound has been dubbed." I then told him this was so fake. "Look, he has come again, then a couple of scenes later, look again." Leonard then told me to go back to bed. I was ruining this for him.

I told him, "If you are going to sit up and watch porn, then you can never touch me after. I am tired of you telling me that I am doing it wrong. This porn you are watching is fake, and humans do not have multiple orgasms. Remember, you watch porn, you don't get the real thing."

He then said to me, "Let see who can go without sex the longest."

I told him, "Game on."

You never challenge a woman to who can outlast whom when they are pissed off at you for sitting up all night watching porn and then trying to get some from their partner and then during sex tell their partner they are doing it wrong.

He went without sex for one month before he broke down and asked for it again. I told him, "I win."

He then told me that I was sleeping with someone because I could not go without it for that long. I told him he was sleeping with someone because I could keep going without sex, and if he wanted, I would show him just how long that would be.

He then just walked away from me. I told him, "That means this is still on. No sex for you tonight?"

He then called me a b——.

I said, "I didn't hear that. What did you call me? I am not a b——, you are. If you had treated me better, I would then be nicer to you, and maybe you could have sex with me more often, but to hit me and curse at me and put me down all the time, I am just giving you back what you are giving me."

Monday was the day Leonard had his knee operation. He had not eaten since 1:00 p.m. on Sunday. I left the girls with Renee and Leonard, and I headed over to the hospital in Beverly Hills.

We checked in at 7:30 a.m., and then we have a seat. I planned on staying with him till he got a room, and then I was going home so I could take care of the girls. He did not say anything to me about not leaving, so I thought we would just stick to the plan. As the morning turned into late morning, and he was becoming cranky. The nurses put him in a room. It was around 9:30 a.m. now. We were in the room, and I told him I was going home. He started yelling about how long this was taking and what was going on. A nurse came in and looked at us. I told her he was hungry and he got like this when he had not eaten.

She asked him if he would like an IV drip; he agreed to it. He then got into the bed, and they hooked him up. He asked the nurse as she was putting the IV drip in him what was taking so long; she told him that his doctor never came in before 10:00 a.m. That was the wrong thing to say to Leonard. He then started to yell at her, "Why would you have me show up at 7:30 a.m. if he doesn't get here till ten?" He used some swear words as he was talking to the nurse. She then walked out of the room.

I told him he would need to calm down; he told me not to tell him what to do. I told him I would be going home once he headed over to the prepping room and I would be back in the morning to pick him up.

Two nurses were now ready to take him down to the prepping room. I followed them, and then I stayed in the waiting room to just make sure I could leave now.

One nurse came out and started calling for me. I walked over to her and told her, "I'm here." She looked at me and told me that my husband was calling for me. I looked at her and asked, "Am I allowed back there?"

She looked at me and said that they were going to let me stay with him here in the prepping room, but I could not follow him into the operation room. So in I went. I could hear him complaining. I walked into the little area they had him in.

They had him in the middle area. I believed there were only the two other people in the room with him and they had curtains hanging from the ceiling to give the patients some privacy. But with him yelling and complaining about everything, the other patients were getting upset.

The nurses thought with me being his wife, I could calm him down. I was standing next to him and trying to get him to be quiet; he would just yell at me. I told him, "You are making the other people in the room uncomfortable, and they too are headed into surgery, so could you please just turn it down a little?"

He just looked at me and closed his mouth, but I could tell I was going to pay for this later. I stood there with him till about 10:30 a.m. The nurse came over to me and told me Leonard's doctor was in and that they would be taking him in soon.

I watched one of the patients leave, and as they went by the area where Leonard and I were, he just looked at us. I don't think he was very happy with all this drama right before his surgery.

The doctor came in and let Leonard know he was here and that he would be starting shortly. Leonard was very calm and sweet-talking once he saw the doctor, not the real him, the one the nurses and I had to deal with all morning.

They start to wheel him out of the prepping room, and he told me I needed to stay with him and I had better be here when he wakes up. The nurse told me I could not go into the operating room and that Leonard would be fine. I told him, "I cannot go with you, but I will stay here."

I called Renee and asked her if she could take care of the girls for me. "I will not be going home, Leonard wants me here."

I was not prepared to sit at the hospital all day. I got some cookies and nuts from the vending machine, and then I just sat in the waiting room all day. The keys to the car were in his pocket when they put him in the room, and the nurse took his things and locked them up. I did not have keys on me, so even if I wanted to leave, I couldn't, and I didn't have much money on me, so I couldn't even go to the cafeteria to eat. I found a chair far from the others in the room and just sat there all day. I read all the magazines they had and watched some TV. The evening news came on, and now I knew it was now 5:00 p.m., and here I was, still waiting. I finally decided to get some rest and close my eyes; that's when Leonard's doctor came out and sat down with me. He told me things went well and that Leonard would be fine; he then showed me the pictures of his knee.

I called Leonard's sisters to tell them he was fine and they could now come over here to see him if they wanted. I got to talk to my girls and tell them, "Daddy is fine, and we will be home soon."

Renee and Tammy came to see Leonard with Leonard's dad. Tammy came in with her dad and spent some time with him, then Tammy came out in tears, saying how much he looked like their dad. Tammy just looked at me. I looked at her and I told her, "I have not seen him at all. You and your dad are this first visitors he has had today, and only two of us can go in at a time." So I looked at Renee and told her she could now go in and see him. Tammy had nothing to say to me; she just looked at me. I turned to go sit down, and that is when Renee came out and called me back; she told me he wanted to see me.

I went in and walked over to his left side and told him, "I am here." He asked me something, and I told him, "The doctor told me that you were going to be fine. He repaired everything, and he did not have to put in a cadaver's ligament because the doctor repaired yours." Leonard was relieved to hear that. He was nervous once he heard that he would have a dead person's body part in his.

I could tell that took a lot of anxiety off him; a calmness rolled over his face.

Leonard's dad and I left the room because now it was time to take Leonard to his room for the night. They told me that I could come back in the morning to get him. Leonard told the nurse as we were walking away from him that I would be staying. His sisters and dad went home, and I sat down again, waiting for them to put him in a room. They came to get me from the waiting room and up to his room I went. They asked me if I wanted a bed. Leonard told her I did not need it; the chair will work just fine for me. I looked at the nurse and told her, "I will be fine, thanks."

They put Leonard in a device that moved his knee; it would make it bend and then go straight. He would yell every time it bent his knee; he would say that it was ripping. The nurse came running in, and she told him, "He is fine." He told her it was ripping.

She said, "No, you are fine," then she gave him something that made him fall asleep. He woke up and asked me if I was still awake.

I said, "What, did you need something?" I got up and helped him get up so he could go to the bathroom. I helped him into the bathroom and then I walked out. He started to yell at me to come back and help him. I told him to use the bars, and when he was done, I would then help him back into bed. I was not going to stay in the bathroom with him as he peeped or whatever he needed to do. He starts yelling for me again, and I asked him, "Are you done?"

He said, "Yes, now come in here and help me." I helped him back out to the bed, and we placed his leg back in the machine. The nurse came in and checked on him; she gave him some more meds, and out he went.

In the late morning, the doctor came in and talked to Leonard and then discharged him. Leonard told his doctor that he felt his knee ripping every time the machine bent it. The doctor told him, "That is normal. It is your muscles relearning how to stretch, and everything is fine."

They placed Leonard into a wheelchair, and they brought the car around for us. I got in behind the string wheel, and he got in on the passenger's side.

He got in the car (Mustang) and off we head for home. I felt like a vampire hitting the sun for the first time since yesterday.

I missed a whole day, and now I had to take care of him. As we were driving home along San Vicente Boulevard, Leonard started to yell at me that I was hitting all the bumps in the road and asked if I could drive slower. I started to think, *Now he knows how I felt when I was pregnant with him hitting all the bumps in the road.* I then heard him say, "Are you listening to me?"

I told him I was driving slowly and there were no bumps in the road. "You are being extra sensitive to everything like I was when I was pregnant and I thought you were hitting all the bumps in the road."

He then told me, "No, this is different now. Slow down and stop hitting all the bumps. I know you are doing this to me to get even, now stop." I did not listen to him, and I just kept driving; he complained the entire trip home.

We got home and I helped him into the house. He told me he wanted to stay on the couch. So I helped him to the couch.

A home nurse came to the house later that same day to drop off a knee machine for him (just like the one he had in the hospital) and a cold water ice cube care box machine. They set him up on the couch, and they showed us how to fill up the ice box.

The nurse left, and I was stuck with him. I told him I had to run out and get his medicine. I told him, "I will be back," and I asked him if he needed anything before I left. He did not say anything to me, so off I went.

I came back home, and now it was time to get the girls from school. I checked up on Leonard, and he was sleeping, so I went and got the girls. I picked them up and told them that Daddy was asleep on the couch, so they would need to be quiet when they came in.

We got inside, and the girls looked at their dad sleeping on the couch. I told them, "See, he is fine," and then they went into their room and I started to cook dinner.

Leonard had to work his knee at least three times a day for about ninety minutes. We kept the ice cube machine full of cold water twenty-four seven. I had to make eight ice trays every time we had to refill the cube. He spent about six weeks sleeping on the couch and eating when he woke up. Every once in a while, he had to get up and use the restroom, but he had to do that on his own. I had the bed to myself. I could hear him up at night watching TV. At this point, I didn't care that he was watching porn. I knew he would not be getting up and poking at me to try and get me to have sex with him. This was the first time I had gone months without a herpes breakout. I was more than happy to have him live out on the couch.

But like all good things, it did come to an end.

The home nurse that had been checking in on him once a week told him he no longer needed the machine and that he would need to get up and walk around, and if he felt he needed a knee, brace then he would need to order one. They could have a sports knee brace made to fit him.

So he ordered one, and now he was up and moving more. He was still taking his pain meds, but now I was not sure if it was the meds the doctor gave him or something else he was now taking.

A couple of months went by, and now he was up and crawling around on the floor, looking for something.

I could hear him ripping at the carpet, so I got up and asked him to stop. He didn't hear me. I bent down, and I touched him. I told him to stop. He still didn't hear or seem to know I was standing there asking him to stop. He was sweaty to the touch, and his eyes were wide open and dilated.

I tried to pick him up. He did not budge, and he just got out of my arms and moved around me. He slowly started picking at the carpet again.

I just gave up on him, and I went back to bed.

In the morning, I asked him what he was doing last night.

Leonard said, "What are you talking about? I wasn't doing anything last night."

I told him he was up and pulling out the carpet. I walked over to the fireplace and show him the spot in the carpet he had been pulling on.

He told me it was not him and that I was the crazy one.

I looked at him and told him, "No, I am not crazy, and you need to cut back on the meds the doctor gave you. You were up last night doing things you don't remember doing, and you may just hurt yourself, and I can't help you."

He just walked away from me.

My sister Nancy called me and asked me if she could come and stay with us for a few months. I told her I would have to talk it over with Leonard, but I did not see any problems with her coming out here and staying till she finished school. She was in her last year of high school, and she only had about six months to go.

We picked up Nancy from the airport in Los Angeles. We got home, and I had her put her clothes in the drawer we had cleaned out for her, and she could hang some of her things in the closet with the girls' clothes.

After I got my girls off to school the next day, I asked Nancy what was going on. I did not want to ask her in front of my children because I was afraid of the answer. I knew it had something to do with her and our mom fighting over something, but what, I did not know.

She told me that her father would make her have oral sex with him and she did not want to do it anymore. She would get into arguments with him (William), and then he would lie about what he was making her do to him to our mother, so that was when our mom kicked her out of the house and she had nowhere else to go (our mom did buy her a ticket here).

I took her over to the police department so she could report the abuse to the authorities and she would have a police report if at any time she needed to take him to court. She would have something on him.

She would sleep with Natalie on the bottom bunk. We had bunk beds for the girls, and Samantha, who was older than seven, slept on top. The bottom bunk was a full-sized bed, and it could fit both Natalie and Nancy.

We went to bed, and sure enough, Leonard was up and crawling around on the floor again.

This time, he was in the girls' closet. I got up and ran into the girls' room and started to pull at him to get him out of the room before he woke everyone up.

Nancy asked me if everything was okay. I told her yes as I pulled Leonard out of the room. "Now go back to sleep." I closed the door but not all the way, hoping this would stop Leonard from going back in.

The next morning, Nancy asked me why he was in the room. I told her I did not know, but I thought it was the meds the doctors gave him were making him see things that were not there.

She then told me how he had come over to the bed and was pinching her.

I told her she was safe and I would talk to him.

One afternoon, Nancy brought out a book she was reading and some tarot cards. I picked up the book, and I started flipping through the pages, and I started to taste menthol in my mouth. I asked her, "Who does this book belong to?"

But before she could tell me, I told her, "It's your dad's book, and he was reading this before you came here. Was he sick?" The longer I held onto it, the more my mouth tasted like menthol. She just sat there looking at me. I put the book down, and now I saw the tarot cards on the floor. I told her, "No, you are not going to play with those cards here in my house. After what you and your sister did in Mom's house, you are not doing that here. Either both or just Betty played with the Ouija and brought a bad spirit into our mother's house and our mother could not get rid of it and Betty was not going to even try to get rid of it or she just did not care to. The person who brings the evil into this reality is the one who will need to send it back. That is how it works, so I am told."

I told Nancy, "It is bad enough we burned a candle on the mantel. I am not going to allow you to play with those cards."

She asked me why I did not like the candle burning on the mantel; I told her it was because that was a doorway for both good and evil spirits to travel through. This is why every time Leonard lit a candle, I asked God to protect us and this house.

I picked up her cards and I was shuffling them and one card kept falling out of the deck. I would pick it up and place it back in the deck and then start shuffling them again and again. It would just fall out of my hands, and every time it did, I would pick it back up. I looked at her and I asked her, "How do you play with these cards?"

She just looked at me, a little confused.

I looked at Nancy, and I finally said, "Let me tell you how you play with them. You take this princess card and you place it in the center, then you take the other cards and place them around the princess card, and then you make up a false future, right? It doesn't work like that. You can't control them. I don't know how to read them myself, but I do know you don't use them that way."

Nancy did not say anything to me. I told her if I was wrong then to tell me; she did not say anything or move. I got up and I told her I was going to burn the cards; I did not want them in my house. She then grabbed at them, and they flew all over the room. I picked up the princess card and I took it into the kitchen to burn on the stove; the card did not burn no matter how hard I tried to burn it. It just would not burn. I thought to myself, *This is kind of cool, a card that will not burn, but then also how scary—a card that will not burn. Something is wrong with it.*

I was in the kitchen, and I heard a noise in the living room; I turned around to see that Nancy was choking Natalie. I ran to help my daughter, and I body-slammed Nancy to the couch and told her to let go of my daughter.

Nancy let her go. I told her she would have to go back and live with Mom.

I could not take the risk of her hurting one of my daughters. Natalie was only helping Nancy pick up the cards that had gone everywhere in the living room.

Nancy wrote me a note telling me she was sorry and that she just did not know how to act when someone helped her. She did not know how to live in a home where no one yelled at each other and who were nice and willing to help each other out.

I told Nancy I would still do anything to help her, only I couldn't allow her to be around my children. But if she needed anything, she could always call me. I would do my best to help her.

One night, Leonard got up and was walking around the house, moving the blinds. I got up and went into the living room to see what he was doing. I asked him as he was peeking through the blinds, "What are you doing?"

He did not answer me, so I moved closer to him.

I asked again, "What are you doing? Who are you looking for?" He was looking through the blinds over by the small piano we had. (No one knew how to play it. The only tune we knew was

"Chopsticks." Leonard would tell us to stop every time we would sit down and play the piano.)

I walked over to the door and opened it to see who he was looking for. I almost expected to see someone on the front porch, but there was no one there. He walked over to the door when I opened it, and I looked at him and said, "See, no one is outside. Who are you looking for?" He was so out of it that when I opened the door, he walked outside onto the porch in his underwear. I did not know Natalie had gotten out of bed and was watching us till I closed the front door and her dad was outside.

I heard her say to me, "Mommy, you cannot leave him outside like that. He doesn't have any clothes on."

I looked at her and told her, "He walked out the door, and if he does go out, I will lock him out. This was his choice."

She then looked at me and said, "You need to let him in."

I told her I would but give him some time to find what it was he was looking for.

She then said, "Mommy."

I said, "Okay, I will let him in." I opened the door and walked out on to the porch and started to push him back inside.

He did not want to go back into the house, and Natalie was standing at the door.

I told her, "Look, he doesn't want to come back in."

She said to push him harder. "You cannot just leave him out there."

I finally got him inside the house, and then I locked the front door and told Natalie to go back to bed; her dad was safely back inside the house.

I went back to bed, and Leonard just went back to pulling the carpet up around the fireplace.

The next day, I asked him what he was doing last night. He tells me he wasn't doing anything. I told him that he was outside with no clothes on. He told me, "No, I wasn't."

And then Natalie said, "Yes, you were. I saw you."

He did not say anything more to us.

I told him again, "I need you to cut back on the Vicodin the doctor gave you. You are acting weird."

I got the cable bill, and it was over two hundred dollars on just porn. I took it to Leonard, and I told him he could not keep this up; he would need to stop watching his porn.

He did not say anything other than, "What are you talking about?" I showed him the bill, and he said to me, "And so?"

I told him, "We cannot afford this, and you need to stop. You need to just stop all this porn that you are watching."

He told me, "It's not the porn that is making the bill high, it's just the cable bill itself."

I showed him the part of the bill that had the porn amount, and it read The Playboy Channel and about four other porn channels. He told me, "Who do you believe—me or your lying eyes?"

I told him, "It is in black and white on this bill, and you are the only one who watches the TV at 1:00–3:00 a.m., and that is all printed here on the bill."

He walked up to my face and said, "Are you going to believe me or your lying eyes?" I just stood there without saying anything more to him.

This happened three months in a row. He finally stopped, and then he would now get movies from his friends. I started to find porn movies hidden in our room and in the kitchen cabinets, places he thought I would never go. I pulled them out and I took them out of their cases and threw them outside so the dogs could chew on them, then I put the empty cases back where I found them.

He came into the room and woke me up, asking me where the DVDs were.

I asked him, "What DVDs?"

He then said to me, "Don't be cute, tell me what you did with them."

I told him to go ask the dogs.

He then pulled me out of the bed and told me to go get them.

I told him, "No, if you want them, go get them yourself."

He then started to hit me, and now I had to get up and get them for him. I opened the kitchen door and step outside to get the movies. I pushed them along the driveway, hoping to scratch them so he could not sit up all night watching them.

I then came back inside and handed them to him, and he hit me in the back of the head again and then sat down to watch his movies, and I went back to bed.

He would sometimes come to bed without watching his movies, but that was rare. The nights he came to bed, he was high on something and he would then attack me while I was sleeping. He would strangle me, and I would then fight him to get him off me. He would be saying something to me in Vietnamese, every once in a while, some English would come out of his mouth, and he would say, "Old man." I kicked at the blinds, and this would distract him long enough for me to get away. I would then get up and sleep in the girls' room to get away from him.

I asked him in the morning why he kept calling me "old man."

He told me that he saw an old man's spirit hovering over me and then go into my body, so he needed to get it out of me.

That night, I slept in the girls' room, and before I fell asleep, I saw in the doorway a black shadow.

I asked God to watch over us tonight and not allow any dark spirit to hurt us.

That next night, as I slept in the girls' room, I saw this bright white light coming down on me. At first, it was one very large dove. I could hear it (it made the same noise as the doves we had on our front porch, so I knew the sound and I saw the bird in all this light), but as it got closer to me, it became a bunch of doves, and the closer it come to me, more and more doves would appear all white, almost a blinding white—that sparkled as they got closer to me, and the noise got louder and louder. At first, I thought how beautiful this was, but then as soon as I thought that, I thought, *No.* That was when it was on top of me and when I called out to God for help. Every bone in my body tightened up, my jaw, all the little bones in my fingers— everything tightened up at the same moment. I could not move at all. I then said to God, *Please help me.* That is when this thing just let go of me.

I got up and I was afraid at first, but I was in my girls' room, so I told this thing it was not welcome here and that God would protect us from you, so you would need to leave here now. I told it that it needed to leave Leonard alone as well. I believed this was what he had been seeing and that was why he would attack me and hit me all the time.

The girls would see this black shadow in the bathroom touching their hair. I told the girls not to be afraid of it, and I told them this thing was not allowed in their room and that they would be safe in their home.

I was sitting on the couch one morning before I had to head off to work at the school. I turned on the TV, and I happened to see a program about a man who could talk to the dead. *John Edward* was the name of the program, and he was talking about how when he was younger, he would play with the Ouija board. That was why I stopped and watched this show—not all of it but the first ten minutes. As I was listening to him, I started to think, *I wonder if the rumors of my family were true. Did I come from a long line of witches and one warlock?* That was when I saw about twelve witches and one warlock pop up behind me (I was still sitting on the couch), and I thought, *Cool, the rumors are true because now they are here.* I told the spirit in the house, "Do you see what you are up against? Not only do I have God on my side, I also have a lot of witches in my family, and if I were you, I would leave now, because with all this power on my side, you will not survive."

We ended up refinancing the house, and then we took out a second on it that same year.

This time, Leonard bought himself a Mach 1 Mustang, and we now had a Ford Dually truck to pull a boat (that we could not afford). Leonard decided he was too old to be working as hard as he was without doing something more relaxing for himself. Now we spent a lot of time on the lakes and playing in the water. He was in his late thirties, and he told me he was having a midlife crises.

We put the girls in sports. The girls were now playing softball on different teams, so between school and softball and now boating, we were not spending a lot of time at home.

I had many rules I had to follow. I don't remember all of them, but I will give you the main ones:

1.   No talking to my family.
2.   No talking to other parents.
3.   Answer the cell phone each and every time he calls.
4.   Don't use the cell phone for any reason but to call him.
5.   Don't waste the gas in any of the vehicles.
6.   Don't spend any of his money.

Also, I was not allowed to go to the doctors for any kind of checkup, and if I did have to see a doctor about anything, he needed to be with me. I could not lose weight without him hitting me and challenging me to a fight. I did not get a haircut, so I wore it in a bun (he did not like that). I had to make sure the girls passed all their exams and make sure they knew all the Catholic prayers. I had to have dinner on the table for him every day even if he did not eat it. I could not save any of it for the next day because he did not like leftovers. I was to walk the kids to school and then be back at home in the thirty minutes it took to walk them to school and for me to walk home by myself (he would call me to see if I was home on the house phone). If I did not follow the rules or if he felt I had broken them, he would leave work early to come home and beat me. I was not to question him on anything.

I walked over to the bank per his request, and I stood in a long line to pull out some money. He was trying to call me (so he said), and I was not picking up the cell phone. By the time I got up to the counter to pull out the money, he called, and I answered the cell phone. He started to yell at me, "What the f—— are you doing? I have been trying to call you. Where are you, b——?"

I told him I was at the counter withdrawing the monies he had told me to do. He was very upset with me and told me that he was on his way home to beat the s—— out of me. I was not sure if the young lady behind the counter could hear him or not, so I just said, "Yes, and thank you. I will call you when I am done," then I hung up the phone. I looked at the young lady and told her, "Never get married, it's not worth it."

Once I walked outside the bank, I then answered the phone because he had been calling me while I was still in the bank getting the money he had asked me to withdraw. I did not answer the phone because I knew it was him, so once I got outside, I answered the phone. He was very upset with me because I had hung up on him earlier. He asked me where I was. I told him I had just walked out of the bank, and now I was about to walk home. I would be home in about forty-five minutes, then we could talk.

He told me, "No, stay where you are. I am in Burbank and I will pick you up."

I asked him why he felt he had to leave work. But now he hung up on me.

I saw him come around the corner, and I waited for him to stop so I could get in. I asked him why he needed to come home. "Do you not trust me?"

He told me that he was trying to call me and that I was not picking up the phone. I showed him the phone, and I did not have any missed calls from him.

I asked him, "Did you call the house?"

I then got hit across my face, and he told me he was not that stupid.

We get home, and sure enough, he had called the house. I played the messages for him and I asked him, "Are you sure you did not call the house because this is saying that you are on your way home to beat the s—— out of me."

He jumped in the shower, and then he was gone.

That night, he came home. I did not feel him get into bed this time. I was having a nightmare about him cheating on me, and I was walking out of some house yelling, "You're cheating on me, you're cheating on me, I can't believe you're cheating on me." Only I was not me; I was a young man.

I was feeling the hate within him, and I myself was getting upset with Leonard.

I rolled over toward his side of the bed, and I just barely touched him, and as I did, I started to think, *Oh no, I touched him*, and I started to move away from him.

That was when he rolled over and hit me with his fist in my face.

I started to yell "What the—" as I was pulling on my nose.

I was seeing little white lights flying around my head, and I then heard him say, "What, you want to fight?"

I then said to him, "Thank you. Thank you for fixing my nose." Ever since I had broken it back when I was a kid, my nose had always had this small crack in it, too small to even notice it, and it never bothered me, but after he punched me, the crack was gone, so I just thanked him for hitting me in the face, and I rolled over toward the wall and kept my back to him. I kept pulling on my nose, hoping it did not move up into my head and kill me because I kept seeing all the little white lights and I started praying to God, "Please don't let me die now." Everybody calls them stars but they were not shaped as stars; they were just little white specks of light.

The next night, I had that same dream, only this time I got into the Mustang and I was driving the street and the speedometer read 109 on it.

I was still mad over the fact that someone had cheated on me.

The next thing I remember from the dream was rolling off the road, and the car itself was in pieces everywhere.

I woke up Leonard, and I was very upset with him. At the time, I was yelling at him that he was cheating on me and that he was going to kill himself because he found out that the girl he was sleeping with was now cheating on him. He jumped into the car and raced off down some long stretch of highway or road and killed himself.

He told me that he was not cheating on me and that it was all in my head.

I told him, "No, this is the second night in a row I have had this dream, and I think it has something to do with that car."

We went over to visit Tammy and her husband. Leonard told Tammy's husband in a joking manner that I was having bad dreams about this car.

Tammy's husband is an appraiser for an insurance company and can tell if a car has been in an accident or not. So we all headed over to the car and popped open the hood, and sure enough, the car had been pieced back together. It had about four different ID numbers on it, and you could see all the welding on the underbody of the car. When we opened the hood to look at the engine, anyone could clearly see that the right side of the car was different from the left side of the car.

Tammy's husband asked Leonard if he had even opened up the hood to look at the engine. (Of course, he didn't because the car looked too pretty on the outside so there was no need to open it up and take a closer look at it.)

Leonard looked at me and told me to make a list of things that were wrong with this car and take it back to the dealers who sold him the car.

The next day, after I took the girls to school, I took the car back to the lot and told the men who had sold Leonard the car we needed to return it, and I told them why. We had only had the car three days now. We walked out to the car, and I opened it up and started to show him all the different numbers, and he then told me that he was sorry I had such a bad experience and that they would refund us the money. Had they had known the history of this car, they would never had bought it and sold it to anyone. He then told me how his own wife would not buy their dream house they had been looking at because she had felt something in the house, so she made him walk away from it.

I then had to walk home. They did offer to drive me home, but I told them, "No thanks." I was just walking over to the park (that was down the street from them) to meet up with Leonard because he was working, but the truth was if I had gotten a ride from them, Leonard would have beaten me when he found out.

Leonard then bought a car he saw on his route, and he no longer did business with his friends, the ones who had sold him the haunted car.

Leonard, the girls, and I went out on the lake one day with our pink boat (Leonard's friends did not come with us). I told him that it was too windy to be out on the lake, but he did not listen to anything I said.

We had to pull up next to the floating bathroom because one of the girls needed to pee and she would not pee in the water.

As he was trying to keep the boat up next to the floating bathroom, a big surge of water came up under the boat and rammed it into the side of the floating dock; it took out the left top side of the boat. Luckily for him, that was all it did. It may have looked bad, but it did not take out the bottom of the boat, so we could still drive it without any water getting inside of the boat.

He was very upset and told the girls to next time just pee in the lake because this was their fault.

I told the girls this was not their fault; it was just an accident and things like this happened because now the girls were upset and crying because he was yelling at them and me.

Leonard told me that it was the girls' fault and not to lie to them.

I told him, "Did they cause the boat to hit the dock or was it you because you could not control the boat all by yourself?"

He started to call me some (bad) names and told me that I would get a beating later. I told him, "Then who is going to help you dock the boat? You need to calm down. The boat can be repaired."

He did get the boat repaired and bring it home. The next week, we have an even bigger boat in our driveway.

I asked him, "Where did this come from?"

He told me to mind my own business.

So now we had two boats and we were refinancing the house again.

Annie had discovered she now had colon cancer, so she told everyone to get to their doctors and get our annual checkup. I was thinking to myself, *That will never happen with me. I am not allowed to go see a doctor for any reason. Even Leonard doesn't go see a doctor annually.* With his sister having cancer, I told him he should have himself checked out. "After all, you are bleeding." Leonard had to go in and have a polyp removed. Leonard scheduled his surgery right around the annual camping trip to the Kern River. This was why he felt he could relax and chill, get drunk and not have to go to work for a whole week.

We were all sitting around having lunch, and Leonard was his normal self with me (nasty). I told him he should slow down with all the alcohol he was drinking. "After all, you are taking meds to help you heal after your surgery."

He yelled some colorful words at me, and so I yelled back, "I was just trying to help you."

His sister Tammy looked at me and said something like "Can't you just leave him alone?"

I looked at her and said, "Okay, so do you want him to die? He is taking some sort of anti-inflammatory pills and drinking alcohol."

Tammy told him that he should slow down with the drinking and maybe I did have a point.

After I got the girls their food, I was walking over to the table to make me something for to eat when I heard Leonard scream. I heard him say something about how he had just eaten a hornet. I had the camera around my neck already because we had been in the water playing and I was taking pictures of all of us, so I ran back to where he was sitting and I started to take pictures of his swollen face.

Tammy looked at me as I was taking pictures and said, "You must think this is funny."

I told her, "Next year you will too."

Every time we went camping, I was the one left alone to set up the tent and then all the inflatable beds and then I had to take everything down with no help from Leonard. So to see him do something as dumb as this, yes, I had to admit it was funny to me.

He knew the hornet was there. He was trying to swat it away. He did not know it had landed on his sandwich, so when he took a bite, he had eaten the hornet, and then he bit the hornet in half, and it stung him three times on the inside of his cheek. It swelled up like nothing I had seen ever before. I told him he was lucky because he was already on an anti-inflammatory drug and that should help him with his face.

We packed up and headed home. We headed over to Leonard's dad's house because we found out he was in the hospital. His dad had complete liver failure. The doctor was telling us (the sisters were there with Leonard and I at the hospital) that we needed to start preparing their dad's funeral.

The family just fell apart at that moment.

Their dad stayed in the hospital for two weeks before they let him come home. They told the family again to prepare his funeral and make sure we get everything in order as we left the hospital.

Leonard was upset, and he took it out on me. I understand how when people are faced with death, they get angry. I, for some reason, knew his dad was not about to die. Leonard would hit me on the back of my head and ask me how I knew this for sure when the doctors said he would. Then he would followed it with how stupid I was.

I told him, "Because your mom said it was not his time to die. He is a fighter after all." His dad would make himself some aloe tea with the aloe plants he had in the yard. Every day he would drink it; this would smell up the house. It smelled as if something had died in the kitchen—that is how bad it smelled—and he drank it all the time.

By the time he went in for his annual checkup, his liver was now working. They took him back to the hospital, and they ran scans to see if this was really a miracle. They did say he had a lot of scarring on his liver, but it looked as if it was fully functional again.

The people at their church were telling the family how blessed they were, that God was looking out for this family.

I looked at Leonard and said, "See, have a little faith." This is when things between us got worse. It was about who was more spiritual and believed more than the other. We fought over everything in this world; now we were fighting over who had more faith and whose faith (church upbringing) was stronger, money, sex, and him not being around his own family.

He got rid of the suburban and brought home a Ford Expedition. The girls loved this truck because it had a TV in it, and I loved it because it handled like a car.

We would load it up and drive it to Kern Valley. The girls could watch movies and not be fighting with each other or playing the bunch buggy game and "I spy with my little eye." It was nice and quiet for a change.

Leonard bought himself an old Dotson; he would drive that to Long Beach and back home now.

He did not spend a lot of time around the girls and me. I would be the one who had to take them to all their softball games, and I had to teach them both how to catch and throw a softball. Luckily, both Leonard and I are very athletic, so both girls picked it up without any problems.

I would tell him he was missing out on their childhood, and as he got older, he would regret it because the girls would be gone, and he would be left with me, and you don't even like me.

He would take the monies I put into our credit union account. I told him that every penny that was in that account belonged to me and he could not just take whatever he wanted. I used that money for the girls, and I had to pay their coaches. He did give me back the money he took.

Leonard always got sick in the winter. One night, when we were sleeping, Leonard was coughing and coughing, and as he was coughing, I opened my eyes (to make sure I was not close to him), and the moment I did, he coughed right into my face, and now I got a virus in my left eye.

I had to see an eye doctor because my eye became swollen and red. Leonard then called into work and told them that he could not come in because he needed to drive me to the eye doctor's and that I could not drive myself because I could not see. I heard him laugh about something, he did not get to hear ever; he didn't laugh or smile with me. I asked him why he was flirting with the person on the phone (Leonard thought that any time you smile and/or laugh, you are flirting), so I used his own medicine on him. He told me he was not flirting and that they (the person on the phone) said the only reason I married him was that I was blind, and if I could see, I would never have married him. I looked at him and said, "You find that funny?"

We get to the eye doctor, and he gave me some eye drops and then told me I needed to see a specialist.

I made an appointment with the specialist, and Leonard was right by my side. The doctor was cracking jokes with me and told me that if I had not put the eyedrops in my eye (the one the other doctor gave me), my eye would have healed faster. Leonard got up and walked out of the room. The doctor finished, and then we walked out of the room together. He had to give me another prescription for my eye. Leonard and I got into the car, and I asked him why he walked out. He told me it was because he did not want to sit there and watch me flirt with my lover.

I looked at him and shook my head. "I have never seen that man before, and you were with us the entire time, so I do not understand why you think he is my lover."

He told me it was the way he keeps getting up in my face. "He had to sit right on top of you."

I told him, "You know he is an eye doctor and my eyes are on my face, and in order to examine them, you would have to be up in my face."

He did not say anything more to me, other than the next time, I would not be seeing any doctor for anything or any reason. "Do you hear me?"

One day, when we were out on Pyramid Lake with the pink boat, I jumped off the back end of the boat and swam back toward the boat. A small wave hit me as I was trying to help Natalie into the water, so I grabbed onto the step and my big toe hit the propeller. I helped Natalie into the water and then onto the shore. That was when I noticed my big toe was bleeding, so I walked back out into the water, and when I placed my foot into the water, my toe started to hurt. I jumped into the boat from the side. Leonard had always told us not to jump in from the side of the boat but always enter the boat from the back end, and yes, I heard him yell at me. I told him I needed the first-aid kit because my toe was bleeding. He then yelled at me, "If you get any blood on the boat, I will kill you." I thought to myself, *Then you will have a lot more blood on this boat than just what is coming out of my toe.*

We finished off the day on the lake, and we all had to get on the boat to leave. I walked into the water, and that was when my toe really started to hurt.

I spent two days with pain in my foot before I made an appointment to see the doctor. I walked the girls to school and I drove myself to the doctor's office because now I could barely walk. It was bad enough having to walking fast enough to make sure the girls got to school on time; once I got to the doctor's office, I could not climb the stairs and walk down the hallway to her office. I got inside, and my doctor looked at me and asked me what happened, and I told her that we were out at Pyramid Lake. She looked at me and said, "I want to see you walk." I got up and did my best to not just drag my left leg it too much. She then said to me, "You can hardly walk. What took you so long to get in here?"

I thought to myself, *My husband.* I told her I thought it would heal (I did not know I had gotten an infection).

She then told me that lake water is the most contaminated water because it just sits. She then gave me a prescription and told me I needed to be back in three days, so then I took it over to the pharmacy, and they told me that it would be ready by 4:00 p.m. because they did not carry this medicine and they had to order it. It was only 10:00 a.m. now.

I lay on the couch with my leg up because now it was starting to really hurt and not just my toe—the pain had spread up into my calf muscle.

I watched *John Edward*, and as I sat there, I thought to myself, *I do that already, I talk to my mother-in-law all the time. She even shows me things to help heal me when I am sick.* Like Eagle Balm (only the one I still use to this day is much stronger), I would have my girls rub the ointment on my back when I had a lung infection. So as I sat there watching him, I started to think, *Maybe everyone can do this—they just don't listen and this is not such a big deal.* Then I noticed the reaction of the audience to him and what he was saying to them, that maybe not everyone can hear the other side. I then said to God, "That is kind of sad, not everyone can hear you or their loved ones." I think if they just slowed down in life, they may be able to learn how to hear.

I drove to the school and picked up all the kids. I then stopped by the pharmacy to see if they had my prescription. I knew it was early, but it was close to 4:00 p.m., and they did have most of the day to find it.

I was lucky. They did have it, and after the nieces and nephew went home, I took the pill. I was a little stunned to see that it was only one pill.

I took the pill, and I started to get dinner ready. About five minutes after taking this pill, I had to sit down. The pill was now attacking whatever it was in my leg; it was the most horrific pain I had ever felt before, and it felt as if this pill was eating away at my bone. It felt like my bone was being dissolved and I would no longer have a leg. I rolled off the couch and crawled over to the table where the girls were doing their homework. I pulled myself up, and once I was standing, I slowly walked to the kitchen to call my doctor's office. My girls asked me if I was all right. I told them I was fine; I was just in a lot of pain right now and not to worry. "Now finish your homework."

I dial the doctor's office, and I got their answering machine. I leave a message. I asked them if it was all right for me to take some Tylenol with this pill.

I hung up the phone and waited about two minutes, and I thought to myself, *I have always heard that you can mix Tylenol with meds because they will not interfere with each other.* I slowly moved to the cabinet in the hallway that held all our medicines. I took two Tylenol, and I then lay back down on the couch in pain.

Leonard got home at around 5:45 p.m., and he saw me resting on the couch. He started in with how lazy I was and that he had finally caught me. I told him I was in pain and I don't normally just sit around the house and do nothing. The girls told him that I was in pain; he told them to be quiet and to stop lying to him.

I got up and I was in less pain now. I ran my hand along the lower part of my leg to make sure I still had a bone, and then I stand up. I could stand without any pain, so I then took a step and I felt so much better now.

I went into the kitchen and started to cook dinner. Leonard took a shower and changed his clothes—he was getting ready go to his second job—and as he walked out the door, I heard him say, "You can't even have dinner ready for me."

I was in the kitchen cooking, and I did not care that he had not eaten. He hardly ever ate with us. The only time he would eat with us is when I had to get him fast food and bring it to him at his job, and then he would eat with the girls and me for about three minutes and then he'd be gone.

Natalie was outside with Leonard one day after school, and she was playing. I had Samantha and the cousins inside the house with me. I went into the bathroom, and the next thing I heard was Leonard yelling, "Where is your mom?" I came out of the bathroom after washing my hands, and I walked into the kitchen. I saw Natalie standing in the kitchen, and she was bleeding from her forehead. I took a paper towel and got it wet and put it on her head, and Leonard then came back toward the kitchen, and I told him to meet me in the car because now I was carrying Natalie in my arms and telling the children to get up; we were headed over to emergency care.

As I walked out the door with no shoes on, that was when Renee drove up, and I asked her to take all the kids with her because we were heading over to the emergency care office to have Natalie looked at. She could see all the blood on me, and she then asked me if I needed her to drive me. I told her, "No, Leonard is here and he will be taking us."

I then get in the car, and Leonard finally come out of the house and he stopped to talk to his sister, and he then got into the car and off we went.

We did not talk about anything, but I was thinking to myself, Now how is he going to make this my fault? He was the one outside with Natalie, and I was nowhere near them. Then I thought, That is how he will blame me, by saying I was not watching her like I should have been.

Leonard dropped us off out front of the office, and I walked in with Natalie still in my arms, and the nurse took one look at us and she moved from behind the counter to the door and told me to come in. As I walked by her, I told her, "My husband will be in soon."

She told me she would have him check us in and then she would bring him to the room.

I was sitting in the room with Natalie, and I still had her in my arms, and I had the wet paper towel on her head. The paper towel was no longer white; it was full of her blood and the whole front of my shirt was bloody. I sat there thinking, *No wonder she took us in without checking in. We were a bloody mess.*

Leonard showed up in the room, and he told me to place her on the bed in the room. He took the paper towel off her head and started to look at her forehead. He told me that he could see her skull. I told him to leave her alone and stop playing with her head. He said, "No, look, I can see her skull." I told him it was because it was her forehead and we didn't have much of anything but skin on our foreheads.

The doctor came in and looked at her, then Leonard told the doctor how Natalie was walking along the bricks and how she fell and hit her head. The doctor then told us he would have to stitch her up. Leonard asked him if this will leave a scar. The doctor told us, "She is young and there is really no telling, but I will do my best to make it unnoticeable."

He (the doctor) left to prep the room. He came back, and in we all went.

They took the bed Natalie was lying on from the room we were in and wheeled it into the room where they were going to stitch her up.

I was right next to her because she had a hold of my hair and was not letting go. My hair was longer now; I had not had it cut since Samantha was born. Natalie was not going to let it go.

We got into the room, and the doctor said, "I hope neither of you are squeamish when it comes to needles." I was now thinking, *We are going to stay in here, this is my child, and I hate needles, but I will do this for her. I just don't have to watch.* The doctor placed a cover on Natalie's face, and she started to scream and kick. Up until that moment, she was good—she just lay on the bed—but now she was kicking and screaming and trying to get away. She looked right into her daddy's eyes, and he just stood there doing nothing. I was lying across her hands because she still had my hair in her hands and she was pulling at my hair. She managed to get the cover off her face by moving her head violently back and forth, so the doctor asked if we could help hold her still. I was already on top of her, and I was not looking around the room to see what her dad was doing, I did see him step over to the bed and he tried to hold down one of her legs. They got another nurse to help us out, and he came to the side I was on and held down her other leg. The nurse at Natalie's head was trying to keep it still, but every time the doctor came close to her with the needle, she would move and then try to start kicking. The doctor could not stitch her up if she kept moving like this, and because it was only going to be three stitches, he did not want to give her anything to put her to sleep.

I heard him tell one of the nurses to grab the kangaroo bag, I had no idea what that was. The nurse that was next to me told me I needed to let go of Natalie so they could place her in the bag. I turned my head to look at him and asked him, "How?" He could now see that Natalie had my hair and was not letting it go. So they lifted her up, and I stood up enough to place the bag under her, and then they zipped it up and over her legs. They got to her chest where I was, and I did my best to get off Natalie enough for them to zip it up, and we finally got her hands out of my hair, and they placed her arms in the bag. Natalie was not liking this at all, and before they could encase her in this bag, she managed to pull out her one arm and grabbed my hair again. I now lay back across her chest, and I could feel she is trying to get the other arm out. The nurse who was next to me was now holding Natalie's head with the other nurse, and the doctor managed to stitch her up.

I stood up, and then they removed her from the bag, and Natalie jumped into my arms. I told her, "It is all over, and we can go home now."

The doctor told us that the stitches would dissolve, so there was no need to come back to have them removed. He placed a big bandaid on top of the stitches and off we went.

Leonard then took Natalie from me, and I looked at myself for the first time and saw all the blood on my shirt.

We walked out into the lobby, and the people were just looking at me. I thought, *Yes, it is because of us you are all still waiting, but we are done now. They will be taking you in soon.*

Leonard drove over to his sister's house to get Samantha, and the next thing you knew, we were sitting down to eat. I told him I wanted to go home because I looked like I had gotten shot with all the dried blood on me.

He told me to eat then we would go home.

After we got home and I could shower, I headed off for bed and he was lying in the bed. He told me that was the worst thing he had ever had to do. I asked him what he was talking about. He said, "I saw her eyes looking at me, and she was calling to me to help her, and I could not even move."

I told him it was over and that she was going to be fine.

He said, "You don't understand—she was looking at me and I could not help her."

I reminded him that she had a hold of my hair and I was lying on her chest trying to hold her down without squashing her, and I could feel every time she moved. I did understand how hard it was; I was in the room.

He rolled over and went to sleep, thinking I did not understand him. I was thinking, *Okay, that is how I felt when Samantha fell and hurt herself, but he made me feel like it was my fault, and I never once said this was his fault, only I was happy to know that it happened on his watch and not mine.*

Once Natalie's forehead healed and everything was back to normal, she and her sister were outside playing in the yard. Leonard was out there with them.

Leonard had gone outside to get a lemon off our lemon tree.

We had a lemon tree, a fig tree; we had just planted an apple tree next to the lemon tree.

Samantha got the lemon from the tree and threw it to her sister, only Natalie was not looking at her sister when she was about to throw the lemon to her. As Natalie moved her head (after hearing her sister call to her) she got hit hard in the face, right under her eye.

Now she had to go to school with a black eye. I went in and told the school what happened (this way, they would not write it up as child abuse).

The other kids at school were making fun of her, and even one of the teachers came up to me and asked me if the rumor was true, that Samantha had thrown a softball at Natalie. I told him no, it was a lemon, and that the girls were outside getting a lemon off the tree with their dad when Samantha had thrown it at her sister so she could then give it to her dad, only Natalie decided to catch it with her face and not her hands. He laughed. I said, "You know kids—Samantha thought Natalie was looking and she wasn't, so the lemon hit her in the face." They both played softball and we always told them never to take their eyes off the ball, but Natalie was not paying any attention to her sister when Samantha threw it.

Renee told me to place a hot egg on her face; this would help with the swelling of her eye. I boiled up some egg and I allowed it to cool a little, and then I placed it on Natalie's face, and about one half second later, Natalie moved back and said, "No, Mommy, that hurts." I placed it on her face a second time, and she moved away. I said, "Okay then, let's try some ice." That didn't work.

About a month later, as we were walking to school, Natalie was complaining that her face hurt her. I looked at it, and the small blister-like bubble on her face was turning green. I stopped and I took Natalie by the face, and then I pushed out the green pus. As I was doing this, Natalie started to kick me and yelling at me to stop; it hurt her. I told her I had gotten it out and now the bubble would go away. She told me, "No, it won't," and that she was not going to school today because everybody was making fun of her face. I told her to trust me, the bubble was gone, and she would be going to school today. She then told me she was going to run away. I walked her to where she had to line up, and I waited with her till the teacher got there. I told the teacher to watch her today because she was planning on leaving school. I then turned to Natalie and told her, "Good luck with that now."

One evening, while the family was all gathered at Leonard's oldest sister's house (Cindy), the kids were off playing in one of the bedrooms.

Natalie was the youngest of the girls (by three years) and did everything the older ones did.

They had been jumping off a pull-up bar to see who could land the farthest. When it was Natalie's turn, she had to be the one who landed the farthest out, so she got a lot of air and landed on her right arm.

She came out to the living room only because she could not handle the pain in her arm anymore. You could tell just by looking at it she had fractured her arm.

We had her hold onto the end of a spoon, and then we wrap it with a Medline Sure-Wrap, and the next day, Monday, we took her into the doctor's office.

They place her arm in a cast, and she was not allowed to go out on the playground at recess time. Lucky for her, it was the last week of school. Unlucky for her because Samantha was going to a summer camp that year and Natalie would have been old enough to go, only because of her arm, she could not go camping.

Samantha took lots of pictures of her with many different kinds of snakes at the camp; none of them were poisonous.

When Samantha came home, the two of them would play outside in the inflatable pool we had. I told Natalie she could not go swimming, but as all young kids are, they did not listen, and as I was watching them from my bedroom window, Natalie jumped in, and I called out to her, "Natalie, are you in the pool?"

She told me, "No, Mommy, I am not in the water."

I asked her again, "Are you sure you did not just jump into the pool?"

She got out and told me, "No, I am not in the water."

I then said, "Thank you for getting out of the pool."

Natalie was now looking around trying to see where I was and how I knew she had gotten in and out of the water.

We gave up on trying to keep the cast dry, but we had done our best.

It was the day before we were to go back to the doctor's to have them remove her cast, when Leonard decided to save some money and remove it at home. I told him, "No, we do not know for sure if it is healed, and you can't just cut it off."

He sat Natalie down and cut the cast off her arm.

That summer, my left knee was hurting me. It got to the point where I could no longer bend it and straighten it anymore. When I would bend it, it would get stuck, and then as I tried to straighten it out, it would pop.

I went to the doctors to have them look at it; they took some x-rays and could find nothing wrong with it. Then they gave me some pain medication and told me to take it easy. I told the doctor, "No, I would like for you to run an MRI because I could feel my knee getting stuck when I bent it." Leonard and the doctor were talking about his (Leonard's) knee surgery and acting as if I was not even in the room. I went home with the pain medication (it was called Vicodin); I took only one.

One pill had me out flat on the couch; I could not move any part of my body. I lay there on the couch not moving and not caring about anything that was going on in the room; my girls could have killed one another and I would not have cared at that moment. My head kept telling me to get up and stop them from fighting, but my body would not move an inch.

Finally, after some time (about one hour later), I was able to move my hand, so I tried moving other parts of my body. I slowly rolled off the couch and stood up; that was when I felt every muscle in my body aching. I thought to myself, This is how people become addicted to this stuff. *You hurt more coming off this pain medication then you did before you take it. You can't move, and everything hurts.*

We (Leonard and I) went back to the doctors to get the results of my MRI, and I told him, "Why did you give me such a strong pain medication? I am a mother and I need to be able to function around my children."

He looked at Leonard and said, "I guess she must not be in that much pain."

The two of them started to laugh, and Leonard told him, "You know women, they can't handle any pain."

The doctor looked at me, and he told me he would have me go to physical therapy and then they would schedule a date for exploratory surgery.

I told him, "Fine, and when you find the problem, I would like an apology from you."

I went to my first therapy section, and they told me I needed to go and get a cane and use it. I looked at the doctor and asked him why. He told me he would like for me to not use the leg as much as

I was, and he told me when I walked, he could tell I was not using it now and the cane would act as my second leg.

I told him, "I am young and don't need it."

He told me he did not want to see me next week without the cane, and no one was too young to use a cane when they needed one. I was now almost thirty-four years old.

School started up, and now I had to use a cane walking the girls to school, and the moms were asking me what happened. I told them, "It's nothing, the doctor wants me to stay off my knee until I have surgery."

About two months later, I went in to have my surgery. Leonard dropped the girls off at school and then took me to the hospital in Glendale. I asked Leonard if he was going to stay with me (like I did for him). He told me no, and then he left.

I was upset, but what can you do? The nurse came to get me, and off to my room I went. As I was lying in the bed waiting to have my knee surgery, all I could think about was how much time I had given up for him and how I spent all day and night helping him, and he could not stay just for a little while with me? I was starting to get upset. I had heartburn and then that turned into acid reflux, and I did not want that to happen right now before surgery. The TV was on, and the *John Edwards* show came on, and he was reading someone, when this calm came over me, and from that moment on, I was no longer upset with Leonard. They took me down to the prepping room, and I looked at the clock. The nurse was telling me how the operation would take no longer than one hour and that they would have a tube down my throat, and if I smoked, it would irritate me. I told her, "I don't smoke," and then she said I should be fine. They took me into the operation room, and they had me move on to another bed, and then they asked me to count back from one hundred.

I started at one hundred, ninety-nine, ninety-eight, and then I was out like a light.

I started to chew on this thing in my mouth, and the next thing I heard was the nurse telling me to wake up; my surgery was over, and I was fine. She walked away from me after I opened my eyes. I looked at the clock, and it had been just an hour. I closed my eyes and started chewing on the thing in my mouth again.

The nurse came back over to me and told me to wake up. I opened my eyes again, and she told me she was going to take the tube out of my mouth now.

They took me back up to my room, and then I waited for them to discharge me.

A nurse walked into the room and then went out. I heard her tell the other nurse that they had lost me.

Two nurses came running into the room, and one of them asked me for my name, and I told her. She then said to me, "We were looking for an Asian woman."

I told her, "I am sorry to disappoint you, but as you can see, I am white."

She started to laugh and said, "No, no, that is not what I meant."

I tell her, "It's okay, I get it all the time." I asked her if I could get out of the bed and use the restroom.

She said, "First, I need you to tell me how much pain you are in." She showed me a chart on the wall behind her and said, "From one to ten, with ten being the worst, how much pain are you in?"

I told her, "Three." She then left, and Leonard walked in with different clothes for me to wear than what I had on that day. He told me I would want to wear something that was looser fitting around my knee and not the jeans I had on earlier. I take the clothes he had in his hands, and then I went into the bathroom to change. I had to use the wall to help me get into the bathroom because my knee was all wrapped up and I could not bend it; I was like a walking zombie.

I sat on the toilet and tried to put on the sweatpants Leonard had brought in for me. I could almost not get them to go over my knee, but I got them on. I came out of the bathroom, and Leonard looked at me and said, "See, I told you, you would not fit in the ones you had on today. Aren't you lucky I thought of you?"

I asked him where the girls were, and he told me, "They are in the waiting room." I rang for the nurse and asked her if my children could come in the room with us. She said yes, so I sent Leonard back out to get them.

By the time they all got back, the nurse was in the room with my paperwork, and then she gave me the pain pill. I told her I did not need it, and she then told me because I did have some pain, they had to give it to me before I could go home. I took the pill, and now they would discharge me.

They wheeled me out to our truck and I got in. The nurse handed me a set of crutches, and Leonard told me he didn't need crutches after his knee surgery and mine was nowhere near as bad as his. The girls were in the back seat, and now I was starting to feel queasy. Leonard rolled down all the windows, and that only made it worse for me. I asked him if he could roll up the windows because I was feeling sick. He told me he could smell the anesthesia on me, and it was making him sleepy. So I let him have the windows open.

He took me straight to his father's house, and I told him I would like to go home. I needed to rest, I had just gotten out of surgery, and I did not want to sit around here at his dad's house.

He parked the car and told me to get out. He then went inside and cooked dinner for his family; it was something he wanted the whole family to try.

I was sitting on the couch, and now I was having heartburn, so I asked him for some water. He told me I should not be drinking any water. I tell him my mouth felt like it was full of cotton balls and I needed it, so one of my daughters brought me out some water, and I drank the whole thing without stopping. I asked her to bring me another glass, so she did. I was drinking this one slower, but my mouth was still dry. I was not feeling well, and now I was up and moving around, trying to walk things off, because while sitting, my heartburn was getting to me.

Leonard's younger brother (Richard) looked at me as I was about to throw up. He ran to get me something that I could throw up in and yelled to Leonard, "Your wife is sick. You should take her home."

Leonard came out of the dining room and into the living room and looked at me and said, "I told you not to drink all that water, look at yourself now." I was too busy throwing up all the anesthesia to care about how upset he was at me. I looked at his brother as he took the bucket away, and I thanked him for helping me.

Leonard's dad was now calling me to come into the dining room to eat, I yelled out "BA." I am not hungry, thank you.

Then Leonard came out and told me that I needed to eat something. I told him, "I can smell what you cooked, and it is (a) too spicy for me, and (b) it is shrimp, no thank you."

He then said, "Fine, just sit here."

I told him, "I want to go home."

He said, "In a little while." He wanted to make sure he had made enough food for his family.

I sat down and waited. I started to fall asleep when he said, "Okay, let's go."

Leonard's dad came out to the living room and sat next to me. This is the first time he had seen me today, so he asked me what happened. I told him, "I had surgery today." I don't think he understood, so as Renee was walking into the house (lucky for me at that moment), I asked her to translate to her dad how I had just gotten out of surgery and Leonard would not take me home.

Leonard walked back in the room, and things got heated between him and his dad. Leonard then told me we were leaving and to get the girls. I called to the girls, and out to the truck we go.

I got in, and Leonard was very upset with me. He started in on how I had told his dad that he would not take me home and that I just got out of surgery. I said, "And what part of that is not true?"

He said I would get it when I get home.

I was like, "Okay, whatever, what more could you do to me now? I am already on a pain medication, and I just threw up, and your brother had to help me, and where were you?"

We got home, and I told him I would be sleeping on the couch now. He told me no; I needed to sleep in the room and he would take the couch. I told him I could not get in and out of the bed with my leg like this. I would be sleeping on the couch; that way, I could get up and use the bathroom without waking him up.

The next morning, I got up and walked into the bedroom to wake up Leonard. He had taken the week off to help me with the kids; he was going to take them to school and then pick them up so I could rest.

I walked in using the crutches, and I told him it was time to get up and start to get the girls ready for school. He did not move; he just lay there once again, breathing fast and sweating. He stopped breathing while I was standing by him, so I waited to see what was going to happen to him. I was thinking, *Okay, did he just die on me?* I waited and still no breath. I was like, "Okay, now will you breathe?" but nothing, so I shook him with my right foot. I did not want him grabbing at me and trying to hurt me more then I already was because I had just gotten out of surgery and my left leg was swollen. He finally took a breath, and I asked him if he was getting up.

He did not move at all.

I went into the girls' room to wake them up, and then I went into the kitchen to make their breakfast.

I was smart enough to make their lunches before I had surgery so that way Leonard would just have to place the lunches I made into their lunch boxes. All he would have to do was wait for them to get ready for school after the girls ate breakfast and got dressed; I made it easy for him.

Now I had to put their lunch into their lunchboxes and wait for them to get ready for school.

I went into the room to see if he was going to get up and drive them, but he was still in his comatose state, so I grabbed the keys, and I headed for the door with the girls and the movie we had watched the night before my surgery.

I dropped off the girls at school, and then I drove over to Blockbusters and drop off the movie. Then I drove home. I got into the house, and I was now dripping with sweat. I called my doctor to see if I could take a shower. The lady who answered the phone asked me, "When did you have your surgery?"

I said, "Yesterday."

She told me to hold on; she would ask the doctor. She came back on the line and told me not to get my knee wet.

I hung up and headed off for the bathroom. Leonard was still sleeping, but this time, I did not check on him. I just grabbed some clean clothes and left the room, all while I was using the crutches.

I wrapped my knee with a plastic bag and headed into the shower. Luckily for us, the shower and bathtub were separate.

I had to decide if I was going to step in with my left leg or with the right leg first. If I stepped in with my left leg and I moved the right leg in, I could slip, but if I went in with my right leg first, then I would not be able to hold myself up with my hurt knee. I decide to walk into the shower left leg first and then hold onto the side of the shower door to help my move the rest of my body into the shower (I know I should have just used the crutches, but I did not want to get them wet). As I was about to move my right leg, my left leg slipped out from under me and now I was in pain, so I showered off all the brown stuff (that looked like blood) off my leg and cleaned myself up and got out of the shower as fast as I could.

I grabbed the crutches after getting dressed in the bathroom, and I took the Tylenol with codeine to help with the pain.

I got back to the couch, and I lay there, and I started to think, *I can't go to sleep. What if I go to sleep and three o'clock rolls around and I miss picking up my girls from school? I would be the worst mother ever.*

Then I told myself to relax; it was early enough in the day that I could sleep and then pick them up later, so I tried to sleep. About one hour went by and I was awake again. I got up and I walked over to the cupboard where we kept our medicine, and I grabbed the Vicodin pills and the Tylenol with codeine and took them in the kitchen, and I put water in the pill tubes and let them sit after shaking them to make sure I destroyed all the pills. They did not do much for me because I was a nervous wreck thinking about how I would not be able to take care of my kids.

Leonard finally got up, and the first thing he asked me was, "Where are the pills?" I told him I had destroyed them. I was not going to be taking them anymore. He then said, "I could have sold them, you b——."

I told him, "You can't sell other people's prescription, it is wrong." He was very upset with me; I reminded him that he was home to help out and not to be strung out on pills or whatever he was taking. He went into the bathroom and took a shower, and then he left.

I then got up to use the restroom sometime later. I found white powder on the sink. I thought nothing of it at the time, and I just cleaned it up.

I picked up the kids from school, and as I was headed into the house, our neighbor was out and he saw me and asked me what happened. I told him that I had knee surgery. He told me that I was doing very well for someone who had just had knee surgery. "It is not something most people recover from as quietly as you have, what is it that you are doing? My friend had knee surgery about a month ago, and she is not moving half as well as you are."

I told him that I bent it a lot and I tried to put some weight on it. I told him it was not easy because it felt like I was up against a wall every time I tried to bend it, but I had to push through all the pain and just keep pulling on my leg to bend it.

I then asked him if he knew the owners of the house before the one we bought it from. He told me Yes, and then he told me how the man had gotten a divorce and the wife had taken the kids and he had never seen them again, and this made the man very sad and lonely. As he got older, he became very sick, and his son had to move in with him and take care of him till he passed away.

I asked him if he thought the man was tall. He said yes, he was tall. I then asked if he had died in the house. He told me no, he did not pass away in the house.

I was thinking, *This must be the black shadow figure we all see.*

Now I knew how to talk to him.

Some time had gone by, and I was now walking the girls to school. I asked the supervisor of the yard duty staff if they needed me back; I was feeling better now. She told me no. I thanked her, and back home I went.

It was almost Thanksgiving when I walked my kids to school, and as I was walking, I heard this woman (in my head) tell me that I had to talk to one of Samantha's friend's mothers. She showed me her granddaughter in my mind as we were walking toward the school, and I knew whom she was talking about. I told the grandmother that I was not going to just go up to her daughter-in-law and give her a message if she was not willing to hear it. I told the woman that

I would need to have a sign from her daughter-in-law that would let me know she was open to hearing from her.

As I said goodbye to my girls, she (the woman I had to give the message to) was saying goodbye to her daughter, and the lady then looked at me and said, "Tiffany is having a hard time with the passing of her grandmother."

That was when this lady (the grandmother) said, "Tell her."

I stood there next to Tiffany's mom and I said, "You know that the grandmother has a present for Tiffany and it is up in her room? She did not have time to wrap it."

Then Tiffany's mom says, "Yes, we gave Tiffany the brooch her grandmother always wore to help her feel closer to her grandmother."

I told her, "No, this is something she has in her room still. She has not wrapped it, and she wanted to give it to Tiffany for Christmas. It is in a box on her dresser."

I then headed home.

The grandmother thanked me. I told her, "I hope she will find it."

This was the first time I had someone who was not related to me talk to me and have me send a message to their loved ones. I was like, "Now I am like Whoopi Goldberg in the movie *Ghost*." This did not scare me, for I had always been talking to God and listened to his/her advice (because sometimes God comes to me as both male and female; when God needed me to be strong, he would be a male force, and when I needed to be loved, she would come to me as a feminine force), and Leonard's mom would talk to me by showing me pictures of things, and I would have to ask Renee what she was saying to me.

I started to watch more of the TV show called *Crossing Over*. I was listening to how some of his signs from the other side could help me with the things I was being shown. I keep seeing how we were going to be living in a two-story house and that would be after living in a small apartment. It did not make sense to me at the time, and I keep telling God I loved the two-story house, but with Leonard always taking the money after we refinanced the house, this dream would never come true. You know how he just takes the money and spends it on himself. One good thing, when you refinance, they do pay off your debt before you get any of the monies.

After some time, I started to sleep in the bedroom again. Leonard came home upset about something; he grabbed my ankle and pulled me out of bed. At first, I did not know who it was grabbing my ankle, so I did fight him. I started to kick at him, and then he grabbed my other ankle and pulled me out of the bed and then across the bedroom floor to the hallway, and that is when he let go of me and said, "This house is filthy. All you ever do is sit here all day, not working and not cleaning this place." I slowly got up, and I walked out into the living room to find him with a white towel running it through the blinds to find some dirt—nothing. Then he ran it over the window sill—nothing. By now, he was very upset because he could not find any dirt to beat me up over. He then walked over to the fireplace mantel and still no dirt. Now he was just standing in the middle of the room with nothing more to yell at me about.

I looked at him and said, "You found nothing, right? So why are you surprised? I clean, I cook, I take care of the yard, the dogs, and the kids. You do nothing around here but run off to work and come home to dinner waiting for you. Just because you choose not to eat it, that is not my problem. So what brought all this on? Your sister?"

He then told me I needed to find another job.

I told him, "I have been a housewife now for ten years. I would need to go back to school and learn a trade or something. In order for me to make the monies you need to live on, I would need to go back to school and get an education."

He then told me, "You said you would always take care of me and that I would not have to work."

I reminded him, "That was only if I got into modeling, remember? I would then take care of you, but you were beyond jealous. You did not like to see me just stand next to a man. You do not like me out and about in the world just talking to other parents, male or female. You do not like it when I watch what you call *love stories* because they put ideas in my head. The love that you give me is the only kind of love that I deserve." I then asked him, "So your sister did complain about something again? You agreed with me years ago and before we had our first child that when we did have children, I was going to stay home and raise them. You did not have a problem with that then, so why do you have one now?"

He came at me to hit me again, and that is when I ran into the girls' room, got them up, and the three of us left again.

I drove over to his dad's house, but his dad was in Vietnam for two weeks. I asked his sisters if I could stay there and then I would figure things out in the morning.

I called the police and asked them to escort me back into the house so I could get some of the girls' clothes.

I left the girls at his dad's house and then drove over to my house and waited for the police to arrive. They asked me what was going on, and I told them that we had gotten into a fight and that I just needed someone to protect me as I entered the house to get some clothes. I told the officer I would feel better if you had a male officer here as well, not that she could not take him on, but I believed he was on something and he was very powerful when he was on whatever it was. The officer said that she would call for backup, but she did have training, then she asked me what he was taking. I told her I did not know, but whatever it was, it made him see demons and he thought they were going into me.

We entered the house, and Leonard started up on me and how he would leave and the girls and I could come back and stay. I heard the officer tell me to just go ahead and grab what I need for the day and then make arrangements to get the rest of it.

He told the officer in a louder tone, "I will leave. They can stay here."

The officer told him to calm down and that his wife was going to leave and he needed to stay calm.

Once the officer and I got outside, I asked her, "Why did I need to leave if he was willing to leave the house and not return?" She told me it was because I had already vacated the premises.

The family did everything they could to push me back home with Leonard. They told me I had to go back because their dad was coming home soon and he would not want the kids and I there at his house; this only brought shame on the family.

Leonard and I talked, and he agreed to let us come home.

It was now Christmas Eve, and we were all at church when one by one, Leonard's brothers and sisters got up and left church.

The children were not seated with us; they were all up front with the other children because they had put on a Christmas play and they had them all sit up front, so as the family members left, they told me to stay behind and get the kids and take them to their grandfather's house; this way, Christmas would not be ruined for them.

I asked what was going on, and all I got was that Lilly was over at Saint Joseph's Hospital because she had collapsed at home; they did not know anything more.

I told Renee, "I will make sure all the kids get to your dad's house safely."

As the mass continued, the people around us asked Leonard and I what was going on; all Leonard and I could say was we were not sure, but we believed Lilly (one of Leonard's younger sisters) was in the hospital. Our kids (and the younger nieces and nephews) kept turning around and asking us what was going on. I would put my finger on my mouth and say, "Hush, turn back around and listen."

After church, we all headed over to Leonard's dad's house and we sat the children down and told them that their aunt Lilly was in the hospital.

The older brother's wife told the children that we were going to stay here and open the presents. I told Leonard I wanted to go and see Lilly; I had this aching need in me to see her.

We got to the hospital, and Leonard's family was sitting in the waiting room. Lilly and her husband were in a room, and they were allowing one visitor at a time in to visit her.

I waited, and then finally, the family lets me in to see her. I walked into this small room, and the only light in this room was coming from a small lamp above her bed. I placed my hand on her leg, and I could feel her jump a little, and then I asked God to fix her, and I saw her mom and others in this tight space, so I knew right then and there she (Lilly) was going to be fine; the room was now full of a bright light. As I got done talking to God, one of the older nephews came in and told me I had to leave now because the

Catholic father had arrived and they wanted him to come in and pray over Lilly.

I went back out into the waiting room, and the father passed me. I sat down and everyone was crying and Leonard looked at me because I was not crying and said, "How can you be so cold right now?"

I told him, "I was just in there with her, and I asked God to fix her. Your mother is right by her side, so I know everything will be fine."

He then said to me, "You don't know anything."

I thought to myself, *OK.*

The father then came out and stopped to talk to us. He told the family the moment he walked into Lilly's room, he could feel the presence of God with her and God always hears our prayers. I just looked at Leonard, and in my head, I was saying, "See, told you." I would never dream of saying that to him out loud.

Leonard and I headed back over to his father's house, and we did our best to make this a happy Christmas for all the kids.

The next day, Lilly was moved from St. Joseph's Hospital in Burbank to one over in Mission Hills. Now we had to drive over there to visit her. The kids stayed with one of the family members as we headed over to visit with Lilly.

Leonard and I walked into the waiting room where the other family members were already waiting, and we sat down.

Lilly's husband came in, and he was very upset. He was going off on how he knew this was the time of year that miracles happened, but right now, he did not feel that way and he did not understand why this had to happen.

He was crying out in pain, "Why, why, why?" His mother and father were there, and they were trying to comfort him. I got up and walked out of the room and headed toward Lilly's room. Two of her sisters were in the room, and they told me to stay out; they were going to give Lilly a sponge bath. That was when Lilly's husband started to walk back to her room, and as he was approaching Lilly's room, the doctors stopped him and told him that they would have to transport her by helicopter. I did not understand at that moment what was going on.

I walked back to the waiting room, and everyone was crying again. Leonard decided we were going to go home, and so he told his dad to come with us. Leonard was not in a good mood at all, and he was very upset with the doctors here. He kept telling me this was like the time when the doctors told them that if their mom had the operation she would not die, and then after the operation, she died.

I looked at him and said, "That is not true. She had the operation so she would be in less pain. They never told her she was not going to die (she had cancer)." He almost hit me out in the parking lot.

The ride home was not a pleasant one. He was putting me down for believing in the doctors.

Lilly was transferred to a hospital in Anaheim. Now we carpooled with the other members of the family over to Anaheim. I was hoping with the other members of the family in the car with us he would stay calm. He did on the way down to the hospital, but once we got there, he exploded on me. The other family members went up to the floor Lilly was on, and Leonard and I stayed in the waiting room on the first floor. He was passing back and forth, yelling at me. I did not say anything; I know he was in pain and the only way for him to express it was to yell and scream at me. I was lucky we were out in public because he did not hit me while we were out, only at home, so the yelling was something I learned to ignore.

I got up and started to walk over to the restroom.

He yelled out to me, "Where are you going?"

I told him, "The restroom. Would you like to follow me in there?"

I come out of the restroom and know Leonard's family was in the lobby with him. I slowly walked back to where they were, and I heard them say, "Lilly will be moved to San Diego." The first thing in my mind was, *Great, here we go again. Please God, keep watching over her. I know you will heal her.*

Then I heard a voice say, "And what about you?"

I told God, "I will be fine, you know me. I know you will be with her and you will heal her, and I thank you for that."

As I got back to where everyone was standing, I heard that this doctor here did not want to take the risk of performing surgery on Lilly because of where the aneurysm was. This was the first time I heard that she had an aneurysm and that it was far within her brain. the doctor did not trust himself with this risky of a surgery, but he did know of someone in San Diego that could perform this kind of surgery.

Annie's fiancé's dad had been the head surgeon of this hospital before he retired (the one in San Diego), so Annie's fiancé called his dad, and then Lilly was transported to San Diego.

The car trip home from Anaheim was worse than the one home from Mission Hills. Leonard was yelling at me and telling me, "How could you still have faith that she will be fine? She has been moved three times now and the doctors are saying she may not recover. None of them will perform the surgery she needs to live."

I did not say much, as he was yelling at me the whole time, and yes, we had his dad in the car and some other family members with us. I would say to him once he calmed down a little or if he asked me to answer him, "Did you hear what the doctor said? He could not perform the surgery because he did not trust himself but he knew of someone who could. That is God working for Lilly, because if God was not on her side any one of these doctors would have performed surgery on her and they would or could have killed her." Lucky for me that Leonard's dad did not understand too much English because that would have made him cry or very upset with me at that moment like Leonard was.

He could not find anything more to yell at me about, and for the last twenty minutes of the ride, it was quiet in the car.

The family told Leonard and I not to travel down to San Diego until it was time for Lilly to have her surgery. Leonard then went off on his family. "You can't keep me from seeing her, I have every right to be there." They told him they would tell us when she would be going in for surgery and then we could come down and see her.

She went into surgery sometime around the New Year. I don't remember if it was before or after the New Year because we did not celebrate it that year.

Leonard and the girls and I drove down to San Diego for Lilly's surgery. Leonard had taken time off (about two weeks) from both his jobs to be by his sister's side (that's what he told his jobs), only he was spending time somewhere else and not at home with us. As we made our trip down to San Diego, it was just the four of us; no one dared to ride along with us. We get to the hospital and he had to find a nurse willing to sign a note for him, so he can give it to his boss letting them know his sister was really having an operation (he found one). Now the waiting game started. I did not bother looking at the clock, so I did not know when she went in and when she came out of surgery. The entire family was there, and even Annie's fiancés parents were with us. He was telling us about the surgeon and how he was the best in the world. He knew this to be true because he was the head surgeon here at this hospital once, and he knew all the doctors here because he keeps in touch with them all.

The surgeon (that was going to operate on Lilly) had to cut his vacation short and fly back to the states to perform this operation.

So we were very thankful to Annie's fiancé's father for making this happen or at least being part of the team that made this happen.

After surgery, the surgeon came out and told us to follow him into a conference room. The family could not keep from crying; I think they were bracing themselves for the worst. We all piled into this room, and we stood around the table, and the first thing he said to us was that she was fine and that he was not a religious man, but he knew the minute he walked into that operating room and started to work on her that he was no longer in charge of his hands and that he could feel God moving his hands, doing all the work. Now even I was in tears. He then said we all needed to pray right now and so now we all bowed our heads, and the surgeon then said a nice prayer and Leonard's dad took it and finished it for him.

As we walked out of the conference room, Lilly's husband asked the surgeon if he thought she could ever become pregnant. He said, "I know we can always adopt children, but can she have one?" They had been trying to have a baby for some time now. I walked over to Lilly's husband and told him she was now fixed; you only had to believe in it.

One day as Leonard was driving home from Long Beach, he spotted a red Ducati motorcycle on the back of a truck. He followed it to a dealership, and then he came home and told me to come with him.

We got to the dealership, and he was looking at this motorcycle. Leonard and the salesman were talking and trying to make this deal happen. When I asked the salesman about the pink slip, he said he did not have it right now but he would be getting it soon. I then turned to Leonard and told him, "You will not be buying this. This man doesn't have the pink slip." Leonard stood there while this man and I argued about the pink slip. He told me he was a credible salesman and he was not running some scam here.

I told him, "Then when you get the pink slip, we will be back."

He then looked at Leonard and told him that this Ducati may not be here when he returned because he would not hold onto it for him.

Leonard told me to shut my mouth and go get in the truck and wait for him. I told him, "Do you understand this man can be crooked and sell you something that he has no rights to sell to you, and if you take that motorcycle off this lot with no pink slip, you can be arrested for stealing the thing?"

Leonard just looked at me and told me to mind my own business and go get into the car. "I will buy whatever I want."

So now I was following him home; he was on his new motorcycle and I was driving the truck. I watched him slip and then spin out in front of me because he was driving too fast on the freeway and he did not slow down enough make the turn onto the off ramp. He was lucky I was behind him because I turned on the emergency blinkers and slowed down so he could get up and continue on his way.

We took the new (green) boat out on the lake; Leonard's family did not come with us this time, so he brought two friends with him and their boys. Leonard dropped us off on the beach and took off with his friends. I was left behind to not only take care of my two girls but the two boys as well.

We spent the day playing in the water, and then when the boys got hungry, I would have to make them something to eat. I was very upset with Leonard by the time they all got back. He told me that his friends were having wife troubles and they just needed to get away for a while and have fun. I told him I was not a baby sitter and that this was not far to the girls and I. You just go off for most of the day and leave us here to play on land.

He then told his friends, "See, I told you she would not understand. Look, I too am having problems with my wife. I heard one of them say, "No, you're not, she is not cheating on you and you need to start treating her better or you will lose her."

I just looked at him, and I did not say a word. I was too tired and hot from being in the sun most of the day.

We headed over to one of his friends' houses, and they (the men) went into the backyard to talk, drink, and do drugs.

I sat on the couch, and the one friend who owned the house turned on the TV for me. So I sat there watching *Cheaters* (a TV show on MTV). The kids were upstairs watching Nickelodeon.

I was falling asleep, but every time they came in to use the bathroom, I would watch them. Leonard would always go with his friend into the bathroom. I would hear his friend say, "Look, she is watching us. She knows, she knows."

And Leonard would tell him, "She knows nothing," and then push him into the bathroom. I would sit there and wait for the two of them to come out. It took them a good fifteen minutes before they both came out of the bathroom together.

I would ask Leonard, "Are you ready to go home now?"

He told me, "Soon."

I went upstairs to check on the kids, and they were tired as well. My girls asked me, "When will we be going home?" I told them that their dad had said soon.

We finished watching the program that was on, and then I told the girls, "Let's go get your dad. I am done."

We head back downstairs, and he was just coming inside from the backyard. It was now 3:00 a.m., and I was extra tired now. We jumped into the truck and we headed home. Luckily for us, we did not live far from his friend's house. I told Leonard I did not appreciate him having us sit there in his friend's house alone while he was outside getting high and drinking.

Leonard's family rented a house out by Lake Havasu. We decided to go up for the day and play on the lake.

We got out there, and we docked the boat, then Leonard took it over to where the family was staying, and I pulled the dully around to a parking spot and then walked over to the house.

By the time I reached the house, Leonard and some of the family members were off playing on the lake.

They were out for a very long time, when I finally saw two boats heading back toward the house (he was lucky that someone had stopped to help them). They had to tow the green boat back to the house. Now I heard Leonard yelling to me, "Call your dad."

I asked why.

He told me because the boat's engine had just died on them and he wanted my dad to fix it.

I told him, "My dad is an auto mechanic and he doesn't work on boats."

Leonard then started calling me a f—— c——. I stopped and stood there on the shore while he was still on the boat, and he yelled at me again, "Call your dad, you f—— b——!"

I then told him, "I am rubber, you are glue. It bounces off of me and sticks on to you."

He was now yelling, "Do you see how she speaks to me? No respect."

I then said, "Can you hear me? I said my dad is an automobile mechanic and he doesn't fix boats. Boats do not have wheels on them, do they?"

He just kept yelling at me and told me he was going to beat the s—— out of me once he got on shore.

I told him, "My balls are bigger and hairier than yours. Let's show your family how you love to hit a girl because that is the only way you can feel like a man."

One of the nephews grabbed me and started to move me away from the edge of the water and asked me not to say anything more to him.

Leonard was upset right now, and he didn't mean what he was saying. I told the nephew as he was pushing me back, "You don't understand when he gets drunk like he is now. That is when his true feeling for me comes out, and you do not know him like I do."

He asked me for the keys to the truck.

I told him, "I hope you can catch them." Then I was about to throw them at him.

He yelled at me, "Bring them to me, b...." His nephew then took them from me and walked out into the water to hand them to Leonard.

Before they started pulling the boat back down to the landing, Leonard told me, "Just wait till I get back."

I yelled, "Can't wait!"

His nephew was like, "You don't have to say anything to him."

I told the nephew, "You don't understand. I will finally have witnesses to him beating me."

He came to pick me up and the girls, and I got everyone into the car.

I asked him, "Did you call my dad?"

He told me, "No."

He did not hit me at that moment. I think one of the family members told him not to start anything out here in Arizona; he could go to jail.

The drive home was very quiet, but like always, once we made it home, he would hit me, and again, always when I had my back to him.

Leonard had refinanced the house and had somehow managed to do it without me having to sign any of the paperwork, so now I was no longer on the deed to our house.

He had also taken the green boat in to get repaired, but somehow they had talked him into buying a new boat, one that was still being put together in the shop.

He took the girls and I along with him to drop off the pink boat at the boat shop. As I was listening to them talk, I looked at Leonard and I told him, "We can't do this. We don't have that kind of money, and with you trading in the two boats for the one, you are getting the short end of the stick. They are using you, can't you see that?"

He looked at me and asked me to follow him outside so we could talk in private (and not in front of the salesman).

He told me to mind my own business and not to open my mouth; he then told me that if I said anything more, I would get it once I got home.

I told him he was making a big mistake and not to do it, just get the boat fixed. He shot me an evil look and told me to stay here as he walked away from me and back inside.

It took us most of the day to transfer the two boats over to the boat shop and then get all the paperwork for his new boat (about the same time it took to get a new car, three to five hours). We got into the truck (Expedition), and off we all headed to the shop where they manufactured boats. He had to see what he had just bought before we headed home that day.

We went inside, and they showed us which one we had just bought, and we walked over to it, and he was smiling from ear to ear, and I was just upset to no end. Here he had taken me off the deed to our house and now this new boat—what next?

We went home and we now had the Expedition, the Dully, and his Datsun.

One Saturday morning, he decided to take the Dully to his job in Long Beach. I thought it was odd at the time. Why would he take the Dully when he could take his Datsun to work?

Natalie had a softball game that day, and we were headed off to the park. I get a phone call from him telling me that he had just put regular gas into the tank of the Dully (the Dully was a diesel truck, so it ran off diesel fuel and not regular gas). He told me to meet him at a car dealership in Long Beach; he was having the Dully towed over there now. I asked him, "When did you do all this? You are at work."

He then said to me, "Meet me here now."

I asked one of the moms on the team if she could take Natalie home with her after the game; I would then pick her up after I get back from Long Beach.

Samantha and I jumped into the Expedition, and off to Long Beach we went.

I met him at the dealership, and I asked him about the Dully. I reminded him that we still had our stuff in it that we would have to get out if he was going to just dump the truck and not have it looked at and/or repaired.

He told me to go over to where they had the Dully and clean it out. So Samantha and I walked over to where they had the Dully and we started to open the doors when this man walked up to me and asked if he could help us.

I told him, "This is my truck, and I am just making sure my husband got everything out of it before you all take it off his hands."

He said okay, and as he walked away, I asked him about the engine and how much damage was done to it. This man told me that he did not know if any damage was done to the engine because my husband had just put gas in it and then driven it here to them; he did not go far enough to destroy the engine. They had told him all he had to do was siphon out the regular gas and the put the diesel fuel in it.

Leonard then walked over to me after the man left, and I looked at him and asked him, "How far is it from the gas station to this shop?"

He asked me why I wanted to know that.

I asked him, "How do you know you destroyed the engine?"

He told me, "I was not thinking at the time I put gas into the tank, and as I drove out of the gas station, the truck started to act funny and it was not running normal and it was making a noise, so I knew that it was damaged."

I looked at him and I told him, "From what I understand, you can drive a diesel trunk on regular gas for a short time without damaging the engine, you just have to take the regular gas out and fill the tank with the diesel fuel, no big deal, so why do you have to have a new truck?"

He looked at me and then walked closer to me and told me the truck was no good anymore and that was that.

I looked at him and said, "You know, you have that nice new stereo system in there. You will need to leave it with the truck."

He turned around and went straight to his truck to pull out the system. One of the mechanics came over as he was removing everything and told him that he could not take anything that was screwed down. That now belonged to them because he had just sold it to them and that was now their property, and had he taken it out before dropping it here, then he would still have ownership of it.

He put what he had in his hands down (on the seat) and walked way. As we were walking back into the showroom, he looked at me and asked, "Why did you not take out the stereo system when I was going to throw the truck?"

I told him, "It is because I am a girl and I did not know if you wanted it or not. You did not tell me to take it."

After some time, about three to five hours of sitting at the Ford Dealership in Long Beach, he finally got his truck.

We now had a new Ford F-250 Lariat (white), and I followed him home. I stopped to pick up Natalie from her friend's house, and the mom was nice enough to have already fed Natalie dinner. Samantha and I had not eaten, and we were hungry. We got home and there were no signs of Leonard anywhere, so I cooked something for us to eat, and we all got ready for bed.

On Monday, I walked the girls to school and then I walked home. Leonard was still sleeping. I asked him why he did not go to work, and he just grabbed me and forced me to have sex. As we were in the middle of sex, he started to yell at me, "Give it to me, give it to me!"

I asked him, "What? Give you what?"

He said to me, "The herpes, give it to me."

I told him, "You gave it to me, so how am I going to give it to you?"

He got done and rolled off me. I got up and I heard him say to me, "You are so cold-hearted. When I make love to you, it is like sleeping with a hooker."

I stopped for a moment and looked at him, then as I walked past him, I told him, "How would you know? Do you sleep with hookers? And if it makes you feel better, just leave some money on my pillow," then I walked out of the room. I took one step out of the room and into the hallway (I don't remember if I was headed to the bathroom), when the next thing I remember was being surrounded by white light and hearing voices tell me, "You can breathe." (That was because Leonard had just hit me and knocked all the air out of my lungs.) I could hear that there were many voices talking to me, but they all talked as one voice. They just kept telling me, "You can breathe." I was looking around, and I could tell I was lying on my right side and I was curled up in the fetal position, and when I looked down toward my feet, I could see the shadow of Leonard moving in and out of the light. I keep telling myself to keep my eyes on him; I did not know what he was going to do and if he would hurt me again. I knew if I kept my eyes on him, he would not touch me. As I was watching him, I could fill the energy with in this white light, and all I heard were the voices telling me to breathe, but the only thing I was concerned with was the shadow at my feet fading in and out of the light. Some time had passed, and I started to listen more to the voices telling me that I could breathe. I started to think to myself, *I know I can breathe. Why are they saying this to me?* Then this very strong and forceful voice told me to breathe. This was when I realized I was not breathing, and I took in some air, and as I did, I must have let out some sort of screaming noise, and my body went from the fetal position to being straight as a board, and that was when I realized I was on the floor in my house. I looked at my feet to see where Leonard was, and I saw him head back to the bed. I was lying on my right side, and now I was looking at the cabinet where we kept the meds and the extra towels. I slowly moved toward the wall and then to the doorway that led into the living room. I used the wall frame to help me get up, and then I walked into the kitchen. I felt this pain in my back right below the right shoulder blade.

The nephews borrowed the Expedition one weekend to go camping. Natalie and I were sitting in the truck watching her sister's softball practice when one of the nephews called me and asked if I could find something he believed he left in the truck. Natalie and I started looking. I looked under the driver's seat, and I pulled out a DVD. Not any DVD but a porn one, and it had naked women on it. Natalie asked me why that movie had naked women on the cover like that. I told her, "Because it is a grown-up movie."

I told Natalie to go and sit outside on the felid where her sister was, and I got inside the truck to yell at my nephew. I told him I had found a porn DVD in my truck and pipe for marijuana in the glove compartment and I did not want them driving the truck while they were high and that he was to never again use the truck. He told me he was sorry for the pipe and they would never drive high, but the movie was not his. I said, "What, the movie is not yours?"

He then told me again, "No, that was already in the truck when we borrowed it."

I hung up, and I called Leonard. I yelled at his phone because it went straight to voice message, and I told him I had found a DVD in the truck and I would be throwing it out with the rest of the trash. "Don't even think about looking for it or asking for it back because I will not have it." I took the DVD out of the case and threw it away. With the case, I was too embarrassed to take it out of the truck and throw it away in front of all the young girls and the other parents, so I just left it in the truck under the driver's seat, and when Samantha had finished with her softball practice, we all then went home, and that is when I handed Leonard an empty case.

We took the new boat and truck out to Lake Mead. Leonard loved to drive fast, and as we headed out to the lake—just the four of us were in the truck—he opened up the gas and the speedometer read 105. I asked him to slow down. "You do not drive at this speed pulling a twenty-two-foot boat behind you, and any wind or rock in the road will flip the boat and we could all die out here, so please can you slow it down?"

He sped up and told me, "Then we all die together." Now the truck was vibrating, and he had to slow down. I looked at him and said, "Thank you."

We got to Lake Mead, and we were just cursing around the lake at a nice speed for once. Not many, if any, people were out on the lake that day. Samantha was up front; Natalie and I were down in the cabin. I could see Samantha from where I was.

As we got further out on to the lake, the water became very deep and choppy. It was like sailing in the ocean during a light storm. The signs on the dock had warned us that the water would be choppy, so I asked Leonard to slow it down, because now as he hit the waves, I could see Samantha fly up in the air and then land on the bench (she never let go of the rail). The one thing I had taught them was that if you sit up front, you will need to hold on at all time because the wind can take you right off the boat, and even if you had the life jacket on, you could still drown. So he did, and now it was a nicer, calmer ride on the lake. Natalie and I went up front to sit with Samantha. Leonard then sped up, and Natalie then got off the bench and stood in the doorway back by the cabin. I sat with my back toward the driver, and I then put my legs up on the bench; that way, I was looking forward. I could see the waves hitting the boat, and we were getting a lot of air. Leonard now wanted to see what this boat was made of, and he opened it up. We hit a wave, and it came up and over the boat. I stuck out my arm to hold onto Natalie as the wave hit us. I could feel her in my arm, so I was thinking once the water disappeared, I would then have to see if Samantha was okay. The minute I could open my eyes and see again, I noticed Samantha was missing. I started to yell for her and looked over the edge of the boat. I could still feel Natalie in my arm, and I was yelling out for Samantha. I heard her say, "I am right here." I saw that I had Samantha in my arm and not Natalie at all. Now I started yelling for Natalie, and she finally said, "I am here!" Samantha moved out of the doorway, and we saw Natalie sitting on top of the anchor. This anchor was not like normal anchors you would see on big boats; it looked more like a mini centipede on its back. It had three spikes on each side, and her leg was in the middle of it, and she had hit her hip on one of the spikes. I moved to pick up Natalie, and Leonard was now just laughing, Natalie was not happy, and she walked over to her dad and started to hit him.

I told him, "Could you please now slow it down? You could have killed one of us."

We headed in to go home (slowly).

Leonard decided to take the girls out of softball. He did this without me knowing anything, so when I was sitting at one of Natalie's games, I had a mom come over to me and tell me she was going to miss us. She said it would be a shame to lose such a good player. I did not understand what she meant by that, but I just looked at her and said, "Oh yeah."

The mom then said, "It must be nice spending all your free time out on the lakes?"

That is when the light in my head went on. I said, "Yes, it is nice to spend time together as a family. Leonard doesn't see much of us because I am always at two different parks and he is off working at a third one, and so he is missing a lot of their games."

She then said to me, "That is what he said. He doesn't have time to spend with you and the girls and he has already missed out on a lot." I smiled at her.

Leonard showed up just as the game was ending, and now I could feel the mom's eyes on me. They thought I did not know anything about pulling the girls out of softball, and they would be right, but I didn't want to go into it right in front of all of them, and I was not going to make a scene. I was going to wait, and when we got home, I let him have it. I asked him, "What right do you have to take the girls off their team?" Neither of the girls knew this, and they were both upset over it now. "You do not pay for any of their fees or their uniforms. I did all that for them. You have no right to just decide for all of us what is best and more convenient for you. All you ever want to do is be out on the lakes. Maybe the girls and I don't want that, but you do need to ask us, and we could all make a decision together as a family."

Leonard just laughed and walked away.

We were now spending a lot of time on the different lakes here in southern California, but when his friends couldn't make it and it was just the four of us, he decided that we would no longer be playing on the lakes. We were now spending our time at a casino in Laughlin, Nevada.

We would hit up the casino their once a month. Leonard would always complain to me because I would either just be starting my period or I would be on it every month. I told him if he changed the week that we did this, maybe I would not be on my period every time, and I didn't understand why he was so angry about that. "You spend all your time on the casino floor with your friend while I am up in the room with three kids. You know the kids can't be on the casino floor, and you and your friend are downstairs gambling all night and drinking and maybe doing some flirting?"

The friend (who happened to be with us on this trip) looked at me and said, "At least he comes home to you at night."

I looked at the friend and told him, "I'd rather he not."

Then the friend told me that they had just been talking to the girls. The girls (strangers to all of us) were out in Laughlin for their grandfather's funeral, and after they had lost all their money, Leonard would give them some of his to keep them in their spots, and he was buying them drinks. I looked at the friend and said, "Let me see if I have this right. Leonard pays two girls to sit in their seats to gamble Leonard's money, and he buys them drinks?"

The friend did not say anything more to me.

After we dropped off his friend and his son, Leonard told me on the ride home that his wife didn't come home after work anymore. Once he had bought her the breast enhancements, she started to cheat on him, and he had given up everything to be with her. "You know, he was a lawyer at one time. He gave that up and started to work with her family to keep her happy, but now she never comes home, not even to spend time with her own son anymore."

I told, Leonard "Aren't you the lucky one? You treat me like dirt between your toes and I am still with you."

One day, when we were all out driving to find something for the boat, I asked Leonard to stop by a store. He asked me why. I told him it was because I had started my period and I needed to pick up some pads. I was looking at him as I was talking to him, and the next thing I knew, he slapped me in front of the girls and then told me not to f—ing bleed all over his truck.

I could not believe he had hit me in front of the girls like he did; he had never hit me in front of them or out in public like this before. He then told the girls that it was okay to have a period but that you should always be prepared for it and not have to run out to the store to get pads when it starts. I always carried extra pads in the vehicle he allowed me to drive, and he hated that. He did not want to see them in his truck. I did not have time or even think about hiding them in this new truck of his.

So we got to the place he wanted to go, and I went into the bathroom with Natalie, and she asked me if I was all right. I told her, "Yes, I will be fine."

I was hoping with it being the first day, it would be a slow flow, but no, I was bleeding heavily. I took a lot of toilet paper and folded it up and placed it in my underwear. He never stopped to get me pads, and he took his sweet time going home. We had to stop and eat, so whenever I could change the toilet paper, I did. I did not want to bleed all over his baby.

It had been some time now, and Lilly was getting better. When she had first come out of surgery, she could not see. She had a hard time walking (she could not keep her balance), and she had trouble remembering things. She took tennis lessons with her sisters to get back her hand-and-eye coordination (once she could see again). Annie had an operation to remove half of her colon to help slow down the cancer.

I decided to make an appointment with the Catholic Father to talk to him about how the church was not helping their followers become closer to God.

After everything I had gone through with Leonard's sisters and the way Leonard was treating me, I felt I needed to understand the Catholic faith more.

Cindy, Leonard's oldest sister, bought a new house, and she was having a house blessing party one Saturday. She asked the Catholic Father to come over and bless her new house. As they were going from room to room, I was doing my best to stay away from them all because I had not told Leonard that I was going to be going in and talking to the Father later that week. I was hoping the Father would not say anything to me, but after he got done with blessing the house and as he turned to leave the house, he walked right up to me and placed his hand on me and said, "I will see you Thursday," and then he walked out of the house.

Leonard's sister came up to me and told me how proud of me she was; I was finally going to try to become a Catholic. She had no idea what I was going to do, and I just stood there and smiled at her. Leonard then came storming into the kitchen where I was with his sisters, and he walked up to me and got up into my face and spit on me. He told me, "You had better not say anything to him about anything, do you understand me? The last time you did, they told you to leave me, remember?"

I did not open my mouth. I just stood there looking at him; he finally walked away. Leonard's sister (the one who was so happy about me talking to the Father) came up to me, and she patted me on the back and said, "Good job at keeping your mouth shut, but still go in and see the Father."

I looked at her as I was starting to walk out of the kitchen. I told all of them, "You have no right to tell me anything. You do nothing to help me, and now you're patting me on the back. Back off me. None of you understand anything."

On Thursday, I went in to talk to the Father, and I told him that he needs to change the way they practiced their religion. I told him, "You are so close to finding God, but you allow all these saints to mislead you. I have been attending this church now for seventeen years, and you don't welcome anyone but Catholics to the Lord's table. Whom did Jesus turn away? Nobody. All are welcome, and you stand up there telling everyone only the Catholics are welcome at the Lord's table. You have the people bowing down to statues of saints. God told us to never bow down to anyone but him. You have them pray to saints when God wants us to pray to him."

The Father looked at me and said, "I see you are strong in the faith and that you do love God very much. It is our politics you don't like. So for you, you may come up and take part in communion."

I looked at him and said, "You want me to lie. You want me to pretend I follow all your rules and politics and put God second just to have communion within a church I do not believe in. I will not lie to God."

He understood I was here only because my husband made me come here and he had me baptize my children in this Catholic church I did not believe in. "God and I are very close, and he knows my heart. I can have communion with him every day. I don't need that outward show of drinking the wine and eating the bread to let him know how much he is a part of me." I started to get up to leave, and then the Father asked me about my marriage and how it was going. I was not the kind of person that lied, and I didn't hide my feelings about anything, so when the Father asked me about Leonard, I was now holding back tears (Leonard told me that if I said anything, I would get a beating and Leonard knew I couldn't lie, not even if it were to save my own life). I told the Father how it was going. (If any of you who are married, you know that sometimes you find yourself going from day to day not being happy but not sad either. You just do the best you can day to day. You try not to rock the boat. That was what I was doing, just trying to get through the day without upsetting him.) The father then told me if my husband was hitting the children, he would call Child Welfare and they would take the children from us. I told him, "He only comes after me, and if he ever hits one of them, he will be in jail. I will put him there myself." I then walked out the door.

I got home, and Leonard was there. He asked me what happened and what I had said to the Father. I told him, "I went to the Father to tell them they needed to teach y'all how to pray to God and not your statue of Mary—that's it. Oh, and he understands my relationship with God and said that I can take communion now."

Leonard got up in my face and pretended he was going to hit me; I just stood there. Leonard then said to me, "Oh, someone thinks she's tough now?" because I did not move away from him. I stood my ground. He loved to challenge me like that all the time.

One day out of the blue when we had Leonard's friends over for a BBQ, one of them told me that Leonard had a nice singing voice. I looked at his friend and told him, "Leonard doesn't sing. I am the only one signing in the car when we travel."

His friend then went on to tell me, "Leonard stutters when he speaks Vietnamese, so to help him get over it, he gets up at the coffee shop and sings the Vietnamese songs."

I looked over at Leonard, and he didn't say anything to me. So I said, "Those girls must really love to hear you sing for them. Is that why you're out all night? You are singing to all your admirers? I have been with you for over twenty years now. You think maybe once you could have sung to me?" He did not say anything to me, so I got up and walked way.

Annie had to go back in to the hospital to have the rest of her colon removed due to the cancer spreading.

One Mother's Day, we picked up some flowers and drove them out to the cemetery to give them to Leonard's mother. As we were driving them over to her, Leonard was now arguing with me about how I was flirting with the people outside the car and that I was wishing he would get some flowers for me. I told him it was hard to flirt with someone in a different car or even walking on the street when I was sitting in this car with him. So I got a nice little hit on the side of the head (because I was not looking at him—it would have been my face). I just sat there now, looking at the flowers in my lap. I was now thinking, *Great, a new rule—no looking out of the car window.*

We got to the gravesite, and I placed the flowers in the ground for Leonard's mother and I told her, "This is from one mother to another."

We went over to Cindy's house for a Mother's Day celebration. I headed straight into the kitchen to help out and to just get away from Leonard when Lilly's husband came up to me and asked me how things were going. I told him I was hanging in there (as I was fighting back tears). On the ride over to Cindy's house, Leonard just kept putting me down about everything—the way I looked, how I wore my hair, how fat I had gotten, you name it. I was no good, and this was not a day for me but a day for mothers who deserved to be remember on this day. He looked at me and told me, "It doesn't look like you are hanging in."

I started to walk away from him, and as I did, I told him, "I am doing the best that I can," and I shot him a half-smile and headed into the bathroom so I could cry.

I went outside to get some air, and that's when Tammy's husband walked by me and told me if I were to ever leave the girls alone with Leonard, he would call Child Warfare on me. I looked at him and I asked why.

He just walked away from me.

I said "Why?" again and nothing, so as he got further away from me, I yelled out to him, "You know I can do the same to you if Tammy ever left the kids at home alone with you." He never once said anything more to me. I knew Tammy knew Leonard was taking drugs and drinking. I believed he had told her and her husband exactly what he was doing; he denied everything when I asked him. Tammy had even told him not to tell me, but when Leonard got drunk, he would always spill his guts (because he was always saying to me that he always told the truth and he never forgot anything when he was drunk and I was taking care of him and cleaning up his mess), and then he would tell me that he was doing drugs but he still wouldn't tell me which ones. I always told him, "I know you are. I just need you to tell me what you are taking." The white powder I kept finding in the bathroom, I started to collect. I also hit the jackpot one day when I found a rolled-up dollar bill with white powder on it. I collected it all and put it in a sandwich bag and hid it from him, so that way, when he did something stupid enough, I would have the evidence. The bag ended up missing, and I confronted him on it, and I also told him that Tammy's husband told me if I ever left the girls with him alone, he would call the police on me; because of the drugs he was taking.

He told me, "No, he didn't," and then Leonard made me call his sister and ask her to get her husband on the phone so he could repeat what it was he had said to me.

He (Tammy's husband) told Tammy to tell me he had never said anything to me.

I told Tammy, "Yes, he did. I would like to know what you and your husband know about the drugs your brother is taking."

Tammy told me that I was a liar and that Leonard was not taking drugs. I was now standing in the hallway and the girls were in their beds. When Leonard walked away from me, I was still trying to get Tammy to tell me what Leonard was taking and why her husband would say such a thing. She just kept telling me that I was lying and that I needed some help. Leonard walked back over to me with a knife in his hand. I told Tammy as she was still going off on me over the phone about how much of a liar I was. I said, "Tammy, I need you to be quiet right now. Your brother has a knife in his hand, and I need to focus on him right now. If you hear anything, like me falling to the ground, I need you to call 911 so that way, the girls will have someone helping them because I will be dead." I was now looking into Leonard's eyes and talking to his sister at the same time. I then focused on Leonard's eyes, and I told him, "If you are going to do this, then you better do it now. This is the only time you will have this opportunity, If you don't do it now, then you can never try this again."

I heard Tammy yelling at me that I was lying, and I told her to be quiet and just listen. "I just need you to listen."

Leonard did not move; he just stood there with the knife up in the air, ready to jam it into me. I told him, "Remember, the girls will go and live with my mother because you are the one killing me, and they don't allow the family of the killer to have the children. They give the children to the family of the one who has died, and your family will never see the girls again. Do you really want your children to be raised by my mother, someone you do not like?"

Still nothing. I heard Tammy yelling at me on the phone, "I don't believe you. I don't believe you!"

I told Tammy, "I don't need you to believe me. I just need you to listen." At that moment, Leonard came at me, and I said to him, "Don't miss."

He then jammed the knife into the wall next to me and whispered in my ear, "Next time, it will go right into your heart." He then walked into the bedroom. I said good night to Tammy and hung up the phone; I then put the knife away and head off to bed.

I was dreaming about a two-story house and a one bedroom apartment, but this time I had a new dream. I was in an outdoor arena, like the scene in the movie *The Seventh Sign* with Demi Moore. I was walking around, looking at everyone, when I heard someone saying, "Who will die for this man?" I could not see who it was that they were all talking about, and I was too far away from where he was. I was trying to make my way through the crowd and over to him.

The next morning, I got up and I took Natalie to school because now Samantha was in middle school, and I carpooled with one of the other mothers who lived near us, and this was her week to take the older kids to school. As Natalie and I headed off for school, Natalie looked at me and asked me if she should have called the police last night. I told her "No," then I heard my mother's voice in my head as I told Natalie, "Your daddy was tired, and he did not know what he was doing. We need to learn how to be quieter and listen to him. We don't want to make him mad at us." I dropped her off, and as I was walking back home alone, I called Annie (who was now at home dying from cancer).

She got on the phone and whispered to me (because she had to hide from her family and fiancée that she was up and talking to me because she should have been resting), "You need to stop saving him and start saving yourself."

I thanked her, and then I hung up, and now I was mentally kicking myself in the butt all the way home. I thought to myself, *I am now just like my mom. I can't live without a man, and I am willing to die for him. Why?*

That night I had that same dream again, only now I was able to get closer to where the men were standing and I saw one of them on his knees; the one on his knees was covered with blood. As I moved closer, I looked at the man who was over him and yelling, "Who will die for this man?"

The man standing looked at me and said, "You, will you die for this man?"

I got scared at first because now everyone had turned to look at me, and I moved closer to the one on his knees, and without ever seeing his face, I looked at the man standing and said, "Yes, yes, I will die for him."

I heard everyone in the crowd take in a deep breath, and I then said again, "I will die for this man." I did not know him, but I was thinking it was my husband and I would die for him, then the next thing I knew, I was standing in front of an altar. I was placing my ashes on the altar, and as I did this, God would blow them off, so I would pick them up and place them on the altar again, and then sure enough, God would blow them off. I would then pick them up, and as I did this, I noticed they were getting smaller and smaller as I placed them on the altar, and God would blow them off every time I did this. This went on for some time. I was now telling God, "I said I will die for that man, and here are my burnt ashes. Why are you blowing me off?" as I placed my ashes on the altar again. Then again, God blew then off, and now they were too small for me to grab; they were like little flecks of light in the air. I was now grabbing at the air, trying to catch them but with no hope because as I touched them, they just disappeared in my hands.

I stopped and I looked at God (I didn't see him—I just saw a bright light, but I knew that he was there because I could feel him within this light), and I heard, "I need you whole. I can't have you like this. Do you trust me?"

As I was still trying to grab at my burnt ashes, I said without thinking and in one heartbeat, "Yes, you know I do. That is a silly question." The next thing I knew, I was standing on the edge of a very high cliff. I almost fell over the edge because I had just been in front of the altar grabbing at my ashes when God changed everything on me. I looked over the side, and I backed up. I was afraid of heights, and I was looking down at an endless drop (the one like in the movie *Indiana Jones: The Last Crusade*). I was standing at the edge, thinking of that movie and how this was the same place.

I then heard God say, "If you trust me, then jump." So I jumped, and like in the movie, I did not fall. I was floating in the air, and now I could see the invisible beam like in the movie, so I got smart and I decided to run to my right and off this beam when I stopped and noticed that I was still floating in the air and there was no beam under me holding me up because I had run off it. So I ran back to the beam, and this time, I ran off to the left, and the same thing—I was floating in the air—so I slowly walked back to the beam, and I heard God tell me if I trusted him like I said I did, he would give me wings to fly and he would provide for me. I needed not fear anything, just believe.

I told him, "I do believe in you. You already know this to be true."

We tried one last time to save the house because now we couldn't afford to make payments on the house, boat, and new truck.

We did not get the loan, and now we were forced to sell our house. Leonard told me if I loved him, I would follow him to the streets.

I told him, "I will follow you anywhere, even to the streets if I had to, but you will need to sell the boat. I am not going to pull a boat around the streets and be homeless."

He just looked at me and walked away.

We were now selling our house and looking for a place to live with the dogs. We couldn't find a place that would allow us to keep the dogs. I was the one who had to drop the dogs off at the pound; Natalie was with me at the time. We handed over our dogs with their food and leashes to the officer at the pond, then Natalie broke down crying. I had to pick her up while holding back my own tears as we walked out to the truck.

We got home, and we started packing up everything, not sure where we were going because we had not found anywhere to live. One day, when I was out driving around with the girls in the truck with me, we saw a house for rent, and I stopped. We went in, and I filled out the paperwork with the young man that was showing the house. He told me they would have to look up my info and run a credit check and they would let me know if we could move in or not. They would let me know in about three days. Leonard was not with me at the time; he was at work. We got the phone call saying that we got the house, and now Leonard had his family come over and help us pack. Leonard was at work. He did get home around 5:00 p.m., so once he came home, we could move the boxes from our house into the rental house.

Annie was now bedridden and had a home care nurse taking care of her. The family was trying to keep me away from her, but Samantha and I managed to get in and say our last goodbyes to her. She told me she was afraid. I told her not to be. "Your mom and the rest of your family are waiting for you in heaven. Think of all the time you get to be with your mom without your brothers and sisters."

Annie then pulled my head down onto her chest, and she whispered in my ear, "I love you."

I kept my head on her chest, and I could hear her heart beating, and I told her, "I love you, and thank you." That was the last time I saw her. She died later that same year.

Once we got everything out of our house and into the rental house, Leonard told me that he wanted to take the boat out to Lake Havasu for a week.

It was the start of summer, and the girls were out of school; I was not working at the time. I told Leonard he and the girls could go, but I wanted to stay behind and get the house in order; we had boxes everywhere. He then told me the reason I wanted to stay at home was because I needed time alone with my boyfriend. I looked at him and then said to him, "Do you see all the boxes here? I would like to unpack them and not leave them for a week just to have to come home after doing everything for you and your friend out at the lake to come home to this mess that I would have to clean up by myself."

Leonard called his friend and told him I was not going with them, so the next day, Leonard and the girls packed up the boat and the camping gear and off they went.

I got the house in order, and then I had time to spend with myself.

After they came home, Leonard looked at me and said he was surprised to see that everything was in order and the house looked nice. We had sex that night, and the next morning, I heard Leonard on the phone to his friend telling his friend that I had had sex with him.

I tell Leonard that he needed to sell his boat because we could not store it at his sister's (Renee's) house forever. I told him I was going to put an ad in the penny saver. He did not say anything to me, so that next Saturday, I got up early and I reminded him that I would be placing the ad in the penny saver to sell his boat.

He just walked out the door. The girls were asleep, and they were now nine and twelve years old, so to leave them for a short time by themselves alone in the house was not a crime.

I placed the ad, and then I drove back to the house.

The girls were now up and telling me that someone had been calling the house. They did not know who it was because they did not pick up the phone.

I checked my cell phone, and Leonard had left me several messages. He was telling me that if I did not pick up this phone right now, he would come home and f—ing kill me. I then got to the one where he said he is on his way home and that Tammy was trying to get a hold of me. I called Tammy to find out what she needed, and she told me that the family was going to a business BBQ and they wanted to take the girls with them. I told her yes, she could take them for the day, and I asked her if she wanted me to drop them off at her father's house. She told me that she was going to send someone over to pick them up and to have them ready in about fifteen minutes.

The girls were just leaving as Leonard was driving into the driveway. After the girls left with his brother, he started asking me questions like where I was, what was I doing, and whom was I with. I was walking away from him as he was talking to me. He was following me as I was walking away from him. I would stop and answer his question. That was when he would slap me in the face, so I would start walking away from him again. I told him I had gone out and placed the ad in the penny saver to sell the boat like I had told him early that day. I got back home to find out that you and Tammy had been calling I did not take the cell phone with me because I was not going to be out long.

He got in front of me and hit me in the face again. I then turned around and walked away from him. He then came from around the opposite direction and cornered me in the kitchen. He then hit me again, but this time, when he hit me, his thumb went into my eye, and I yelled out, then I bent down and walked over to where the landline phone was and I called 911. I told the operator that I needed help and to send the police because my husband was hitting me. The operator told me to stay on the line. She could hear Leonard in the background telling someone on the phone he was going to jail for hitting me, and then he would look at me and tell me that I had just ruined our lives. I was thinking to myself as I was waiting for the police to show up this was never going to end. He kept telling me he wanted me dead, and now, after losing everything, he still blamed everything on me. I had to do something. He would every once and a while walk into the bedroom where I was and tell me that I was ruining everything and that I should rethink this; this was all my fault.

The operator would then ask me if I was in a safe place, and she kept asking me where he was. I told her he was walking in and out of the bedroom just talking to me and telling me I had ruined everything and talking to someone on the phone. I asked her what was taking so long with the police. She told me they were outside and they were waiting for more backup to arrive. She asked me where he was again. I told her, "He is out in the living room talking to someone on the phone." The police finally came in, and they started talking to him. Then I hung up the phone with the 911 operator after one of the police officers came into the bedroom to talk to me.

He asked me where I had gotten hit and how my husband had hit me—for example, with an open hand or a fist.

I told the officer that my husband had hit me about four times with an open hand across my face. The officer asked me again, "How did he hit you?"

I told him, "With an open hand. I could feel the palm of his hand hit my cheek.".

He asked me, "Are you sure it was with an open hand?"

I told him, "Yes, why?"

The officer then told me that my husband had told them that he had hit me with a closed fist.

As the officer in the room was talking to me, I heard one in the living room talking to Leonard. The officer asked him about the monies in his pocket. I heard Leonard tell the officer he was on his way home to pay the rent. I started to tear up because I knew that was not true. I told the officer that he was lying and that he had driven home to kill me. He was at work, and something had upset him, and he had driven home from Long Beach just to kill me. He kept telling me this and that the money in his pocket was not for rent; we had already paid that.

The officer then asked me where the children were. I told him, "they are with the family at a family picnic."

He then told me that they would have to take both of us in. I got off the bed, and I put my wrists together and told him to take me in. I just need to get away from him and to somewhere safe.

The officer told me to calm down, and because I was the one with the marks on my face, they were going to take him in. They handcuffed him, and out the door they went.

I waited for the family to get home, and then I drove over to Renee's house to pick up the girls. I walked up to the door, and I knocked. One of the sisters came to the door and told me that the girls did not want to go home right now; they were scared. I asked her, "Scared of what?"

She told me that they had told the girls that I had just put their father in jail.

I told her, "You had no right telling my children anything. You do not know what happened. You need to go and get them so I can take them home."

They told me no, they were not going to be going home with me right now. I told them if they did not hand over my children to me, I would call the police on them for kidnapping and I would tell their father I had just put his son in jail and that they were kidnapping my children.

It took me about one hour to get my children away from his family.

I got them in the car, and they told me that the aunts would not let them leave and come home with me. They told me that they did not want to stay with them, that they just wanted to go home with me and the aunts would not let them leave.

I told them that everything was going to be okay and we would need to work together. I told them that we would need to stick together and work as a team. "I need the two of you to be strong."

Samantha told me that I did not raise them to be strong.

I told her, "You are right, but from here on out, I will teach you how to be strong and independent women, and I was sorry for not showing them both how to be strong women. I put myself in Domestic Abuse counseling class and the girls into counseling.

I was now working part-time at a fire protection company, so now I had to find something that would be full-time and would allow me to work around the girls' school hours.

I found a job, and I then gave my boss my two weeks' notice. My boss then offered to pay me ten dollars an hour and I could work full-time and take off at three to pick up the kids from school and then come back and finish off the day. I called the job I was going to take and told them that my boss did not want me to quit. My boss had offered me more money, and so I would not be taking this new job with them.

I went to sleep that night, and I went into heaven. I had to put myself back together; I had to make me whole again. I went up to the shelf where I had left that small piece of myself years ago and placed it back in me. I forgot how young I was. I told myself not to be scared. "I am going to take care of you now."

Now I had a youthful spirit in an adult body.

I got up one morning and I ran to the bathroom because I was feeling sick. I started to throw up this black tar into the sink, I did not know at that time my eyes closed because I could see everything so clearly (in my mind)—all this black tar-like substance coming out of me. When I felt like I was done, I turned on the water to rinse it away, and that was when I opened my eyes to find nothing in the sink. It was clean, and the water was running down the drain. I then closed my eyes again and I could see the black tar everywhere—I even touched it and it stuck to me—so I ran my hand under the water to get it off. I opened my eyes again and nothing. I even put my hands in the sink to make sure I was not seeing things or going insane. I closed my eyes again and there it was, the black tar, so I pushed it all down the drain, and I opened my eyes and dried off my hands on the towel. I then sat down on the toilet. I could feel myself get lighter. I no longer had this darkness within me. I prayed to God, "Please don't let this emptiness within me fill up with the darkness again. Please help me be a better person and please help me stay the person that I am. I don't want this empty feeling in me to fill up with darkness ever again, and I don't want to become someone I am not".

Leonard stopped paying the rent on the house, so the girls and I had to move out. I could not find us a place to live, so I started to look into shelters for us. The one I found was a halfway house. You slept there at night, and then you had to be out all day. We would be sleeping in one large room with other people. The lady asked me how I felt about that. I told her I had no choice. I had just gotten out of an abusive relationship, and as long as the men kept to themselves, we would not have any problems.

The woman who interviewed me had to leave and go to Louisiana because she needed to help her mother due to the flooding from the hurricane.

I was now looking at three days before I had to be out of the house, and there was nowhere for the girls and I to live. I had been selling everything on the weekends to help me get some money together to help with a deposit on an apartment. I had the money in a box in a drawer when someone must have seen where I put it, and yes, it was gone—everything I had made that morning plus the monies I had in it to make change. Lucky for me it was just the money I had made that morning and it was just on that first day (I kept everything on me from that weekend on).

I told my boss I needed to take off because I could not find a place to live and that I did not make enough money to afford an apartment, so I needed to go over to the shelter to talk to someone. She looked at me and asked me how much I needed. I told her I had to make three times the rent, and the rent was one thousand dollars a month for a one-bedroom. My boss then gave me a raise, and I called the management office, and they faxed me over the paperwork, and now I had a place to live, and the girls and I were moving in at night when I got off work. We only had that one night to move out of the house and into our one-room apartment.

As I was trying to divorce Leonard, we decided to try counseling to see if we could save our marriage. Our first visit to the marriage counselor, Leonard would tell me that I needed to teach him. The counselor looked at me and asked me what I needed to teach him. I told the counselor that sometimes I felt like I am his mother and not his wife; he needed someone that would pay him attention twenty-four seven. If I was not praising him in some way, he would get angry with me and beat me, and he would call me by a different name and not the one I was born with just to upset me. I would, for once, have liked it if he could use my name and not this Chris person he kept calling me. Leonard then stood up and started to yell that I was just like my mother and that he did love me and that I did not know what real love was and that this was the only kind of love I deserved. I did not deserve anything more, and I did not understand that this was real love. I told Leonard that real love didn't hurt. It was not jealous; it didn't put you down all the time.

Leonard walked out the door, and the counselor got up and told me that I needed to make a decision. "That will never change." (He was now pointing to the door where Leonard had just walked through.)

I told myself, *Thank goodness someone else can see this*. I thought this was something that I had made up in my head. I did not want to see Leonard for the monster he really was; I loved him after all.

Once my divorce was final (four years later), I was out on a run. I had started exercising to lose weight, I would run by homes that were for sale, and my heart would ache. I would talk to God and ask him to make this pain go away. The girls and I were happy, and we were doing well. I knew the place we had was small, but we were making it work. "I just need you to take this pain away from me." I did not want to have this pain in my heart every time I saw a house for sale.

I received a letter in the mail inviting me to a meeting over at one of the elementary schools to see if I would be interested in owning my own house. It was from Habitat for Humanity. I walked in and sat down just to listen to them; I found that I made all their requirements. I was now thinking to myself, *I am going to have a house for the girls and myself*. I got back to the apartment, and I closed the door behind me and I told the girls, "We are getting a house."

They told me, "You're dreaming, Mom."

I told them, "No, I met all the requirements for a Habitat for Humanity house."

About two years later, we were building our house with Habitat for Humanity, and then one year and four months after, we were moving into a three-bedroom, two-bathroom house (two stories). As I was standing in my new house, I remembered the dream God has been showing me, and I thought, *God, you were right. I did move onto a one-bedroom apartment, and now you have given me this two-story house. Thank you. I love you more than I can express. You have always looked out for me and now my girl. Please, please never leave our sides.* I felt my soul being held tight, as if God herself was hugging me (remember when I need softness, God comes to me as a female, and when I need strength, God is a man).

In conclusion, I would like to take this time and say to you, if anyone who is in a relationship where your partner is treating you with disrespect, is not appreciating you, is treating you as if they own you, is always putting you down calling you names, and is telling you that you are nothing without them and the only reason you have anything is because of them, I want you to get out.

If this person is not allowing you to talk to your friends and family and they keep you away from everyone and tells you you are not worthy of love and respect and will not treat you with kindness, get out.

Go to your local police station, and tell them you need help. You will need to be strong. You will need to want this. You will need to want to get out and stay away from the person you love and start over alone. It will be hard; it will be lonely. You will want to go back. Please do find strength within yourself and get out for good. Don't let them back in.

About the Author

The author lives with her two daughters in their three-bedroom, two-bathroom house (that they helped build) with their adopted cat (from the fiancé of Annie) named Annie. Annie the cat is an American Bobtail.

CPSIA information can be obtained
at www.ICGtesting.com
Printed in the USA
BVHW051155230523
664717BV00016B/882

9 781642 146486